Louise Nicholas
My Story

Louise Nicholas
My Story

Louise Nicholas & Philip Kitchin

Margaret,

Thank you for your support.

Kind Regards

Louise Nicholas

RANDOM HOUSE
NEW ZEALAND

Note: Some names in this book have been changed because of court suppression orders.

A catalogue record for this book is available from the National Library of New Zealand

A RANDOM HOUSE BOOK

published by
Random House New Zealand
18 Poland Road, Glenfield, Auckland, New Zealand
www.randomhouse.co.nz

Random House International
Random House
20 Vauxhall Bridge Road
London, SW1V 2SA
United Kingdom

Random House Australia (Pty) Ltd
20 Alfred Street, Milsons Point, Sydney,
New South Wales 2061, Australia

Random House South Africa Pty Ltd
Isle of Houghton
Corner Boundary Road and Carse O'Gowrie
Houghton 2198, South Africa

Random House Publishers India Private Ltd
301 World Trade Tower, Hotel Intercontinental Grand Complex,
Barakhamba Lane, New Delhi 110 001, India

First published 2007

© 2007 Louise Nicholas and Philip Kitchin

The moral rights of the authors have been asserted

ISBN 978 1 86941 873 1

This book is copyright. Except for the purposes of fair reviewing no part of this publication may be reproduced or transmitted in any form or by any means, electronic or mechanical, including photocopying, recording or any information storage and retrieval system, without permission in writing from the publisher.

Design: Anna Seabrook
Cover illustration: Brian Budgeon
Cover design: Katy Yiakmis
Printed in New Zealand by Geon

This book is dedicated to the memory of my little brother
Kevin Michael Crawford (Bucky) —
a beautiful son, a beautiful brother, a beautiful man.

Louise Nicholas

I'd like to pay tribute to my anonymous police sources. They know who they are, and without them my work would have been impossible. They are brave and honourable men and women who saw injustice and wanted it righted. I also salute the courage of those women who came forward to tell me their stories.

Philip Kitchin

Introduction

IN MARCH 2006, I WAS the complainant in a trial that involved one serving and two former members of the police. I had accused these men of raping me on numerous occasions when I was 18. The media dubbed these men 'pack-rapists'. Those accusations made huge headlines as soon as it became known that the serving member of the police was Assistant Commissioner Clint Rickards. Although the public didn't know it at the time of the trial, the two ex-policemen, Bob Schollum and Brad Shipton, were already serving sentences for the rape of another woman at Mount Maunganui back in the 1980s.

During the 2006 trial I was in the witness box for about three days, having to relive in front of 12 strangers the evil those men had inflicted on me. I was then subjected to watching their lawyers dissecting my whole life and shoving it back in my face. I was slammed around that courtroom like a tennis ball, repeatedly being told that I was nothing but an uneducated, vindictive, sex-crazed liar. The three men were acquitted of all 20 charges against them.

That was the day I knew that somehow, in some way, I needed the New Zealand public to know the truth. I needed the New Zealand public to stop taking as gospel what they were reading in the newspapers or hearing on TV. I needed the New Zealand public to know who I was, not who the defence had made me out to be, and to understand the reasons why I came forward after 23 years of being a silent survivor of rape.

That was when *Louise Nicholas — My Story* was born.

There is so much about the story that the public does not know. One of the most important issues for me is to get across that the bad things that happened to me didn't start with these three men when I was 18. They started when I was 13 years old. In this book I explain how I tried to do something about what was happening to me, by telling people I thought I could trust. I also recount how, after 10 years and two aborted trials, the cop who did these bad things was

Introduction

acquitted in a third.

My aim is not only to tell my side of the story as it unfolded over the years, but also to send out a message to people who have not experienced the horrors of rape or sexual abuse. That message is: 'Don't pass judgement or venture an opinion until you have heard both sides of the story.' I hope to help these people understand what it is like to go through the physical, mental and especially the emotional torment of being raped or abused. For most survivors it is a life sentence. It is also very important to get across to victims of rape and sexual abuse that they should not put any blame on themselves for what has happened: the onus falls directly on the person or people who have hurt them. Never accept or carry blame. Never take ownership of what has happened to you.

There are passages in this book that are explicit. Basically, I tell it how it was, and in order to do this I had to go back to those horrific days when bad things happened and relive them all over again. I leave nothing to the imagination: after all, why try to gloss over the real horrors of rape when the intention is to make people feel some of the emotions that I had to endure on those awful days? I want them to feel some of the same fear as I did. I want them to feel humiliated, as I did. I want them to feel powerlessness, as I did. Most important, I want them to get just as angry as I did. Then perhaps they can understand, even if it is only in some small way, why I didn't scream, why I didn't fight back, why I didn't run away when the opportunity arose, and why, when finally I did tell someone about what was happening, nothing was done about it.

Throughout the last three years, so many interesting things have happened to cause the public to get fired up. There was the second trial, involving another woman, in February 2007, in which the same three men were involved — that was an amazing time for me. Being in that courtroom and hearing the words 'Not guilty' again was sickening, but look at the public outrage that followed. Now people will be able to read about what really happened behind the scenes during the time spent playing a waiting game. We had the Commission of Inquiry into Police Conduct, the findings of which could not be released to the public until the trials were over and done with. When that time eventually came at the end of March 2007 it was one of the most incredible weeks I have ever experienced. The best thing of all is that I can now allow others to read about these experiences, allow them into my life for a while and hopefully, as I have said earlier, help them to understand.

When I decided to go public with my story back in 2004, I had to take into account how it could affect my daughters. I was putting myself out there publicly:

I could handle it, but consideration had to be given to the girls. My husband Ross and I took our time with this, and explained to them in as much detail as we needed to what had happened to me, and my reasons for going public. I have never been more proud of my daughters than when they turned to me and said: 'Mum, you have to do what is best for you, and we will support you right the way through.' Together with their father, Ross, the girls have been my inspiration for this book. They have taught me that I don't need to wrap them in cotton wool and keep them safe from the evils of the world. They have learned so much in the last three years about life and humanity that they are more than capable of stepping out on their own and taking whatever the world throws at them, knowing that they will learn from it.

As for Ross, he has saved my life more times than he can ever know. Ross and I celebrated 19 years of marriage in the week that I wrote this. He has stuck with me for 19 years, even though he knew the truth about my past. That's the sign of a true man. And when I look back on the past, the best bits are the bits that involved him. He has stood by me, he's never doubted me, and he has continued to support me through thick and thin, especially over the last three turbulent years. As a family, we have endured so much, but we have all learned many valuable lessons about life and about people. I have most certainly learned that I have absolutely nothing to be ashamed about — no survivor has. I am proud to finally be able to stand tall, with my head held high, and show them that in the end, as much as they tried to take away my self-worth, all they did was fuel a fire within.

Louise Nicholas

Rotorua
August 2007

Louise

IT WAS JUST BEFORE THREE in the afternoon on Friday 30 March 2006 when Lynne Adamson from Operation Austin walked into Room 615 of Auckland's Copthorne Hotel and announced that the jury had reached their verdicts and were ready to come back into the courtroom.

Room 615 had been my home for the past three weeks, and today it was full of the family and friends who had been waiting with me, my husband Ross and our three daughters for the three days the jury had deliberated. Even so, an eerie silence fell over the room as Lynne made her announcement. We had all been eagerly awaiting this moment, but now that it was here none of us was sure that we were really ready for it.

It took me a few minutes to get myself together, and it was then that I realised this was what the last three years had been leading up to. That morning, while I had been rummaging through the wardrobe to find something appropriate to wear, I had tried not to assume I knew the jurors' decision. But after three weeks of waiting, going through all that had gone on in Courtroom 12 of the Auckland High Court, I knew we had to have the defendants on at least half of the 20 charges. That would be good enough for me.

Lynne was hurrying us up, and finally she pushed me out the door. I kept looking back for Ross, but he was nowhere to be seen. We hit the hotel elevator and still no Ross. I started to panic, telling Lynne we needed to wait for him. She was adamant that we had to keep going, and she was sure Ross would catch up. We crossed the busy main road and headed across the little park towards the side entrance of the courthouse. As we rounded the corner the small contingent of media photographers lifted their cameras. A few shots were taken as we walked in, but what nearly stopped me in my tracks was when one of the photographers said, 'Good luck, Louise.' As I turned to look at him, my immediate thought was that this was just a ploy to get the money shot, but to my amazement he had lowered his camera, and he met my eye and smiled.

Ross was nowhere to be seen, and as we approached the doors of Courtroom 12 I really did begin to panic. I couldn't walk into that room without him. Lynne kept me going, and as Mark, the courtroom policeman, opened the doors for us, the smile he gave me was so warm and caring that I calmed down enough to be able to enter the room with my head held high. As we entered, all the faces turned to look, and as I gave the room a quick scan I saw for the first time the families of the accused, who stared back. I quickly looked away and allowed Lynne to usher me to a seat beside other members of Operation Austin. I kept turning to look at the doors, hoping to see Ross, but all I saw were these strange faces looking at me. I wondered for a moment whose 'side' they were on. Then Ross was sitting beside me. Oh, my gosh, what a huge relief as he took my hand and gave it a squeeze.

'I was in the bathroom getting dressed,' he said. 'When I walked out, everyone had gone.'

I told him I had been panicking because he wasn't with me. Ross just grinned, squeezed my hand again, and said, 'Well, I'm here now.'

That was all I needed to hear. I knew then that whatever the outcome, I had done the right thing, and I was damn proud of it.

I never saw the faces of Brad Shipton, Bob Schollum and Clint Rickards. Apparently they were seated around the corner to my right, where a wall obscured them from my view. I was pleased about that, as I really didn't want to see them, or for them to see me, especially if it all turned to custard for us.

I hadn't been settled for long when the Clerk of the Court entered.

'All rise for the Honourable Justice Randerson.'

We stood as the judge came in, glanced around the courtroom and sat down. After we had all resumed our seats, he explained to everyone in the courtroom that they must keep their emotions in check until Madam Forewoman had finished reading out all the verdicts. I had promised myself very early on that I was going to do my best not to show any emotion over the verdicts, and I hoped the families of the men would do the same. A pretty forlorn hope, I know, but I really wanted everyone to show respect towards one another, regardless of the outcome. It was going to be a very difficult time for all concerned.

The jury of seven women and five men entered the courtroom and took their seats. The forewoman stood up. She was a fairly young woman, maybe in her early to mid-twenties. She was quite small in stature, but appeared to be confident enough in her role. There was a hush in the room as she was asked to give the verdict on each charge as it was read out by the court registrar. She clasped her hands together in front of her, looked straight ahead, and waited for the registrar to read each charge.

I knew that the first half of the verdicts were likely to be 'Not guilty', and the police had explained why they thought this would happen. Sure enough, the first charge was read and the forewoman responded with 'Not guilty'. The second charge was read, and once again she responded 'Not guilty'. As each charge was read, the forewoman seemed to gain confidence, and her responses became a lot louder. It reached a point where I wanted to get up, slap her down and tell her to cut it out. It was like she was taking my whole life and shoving it back in my face.

It was then that I decided I needed to focus on something else until the 'Guilty' verdicts started coming. I looked around the room and noticed a small rip in the carpet in front of me. By this stage I had lost count of the charges that had been read out, and as I focused on the ripped carpet I found myself thinking back to the reason why I was sitting in this courtroom. It wasn't long before I was back in Murupara remembering the happy-go-lucky kid who, at the age of 13, became a very frightened little girl.

Phil

IT BEGAN WITH A PHONE call in the winter of 1998. The man on the other end was a police officer, so paranoid about talking to a reporter that he was ringing from a public phone. I could hear rain hammering on a corrugated-iron roof.

We spoke for about 20 minutes and agreed to talk again. What I heard triggered flashbacks to a story I'd briefly looked at four years earlier. Back then, in 1994, my sources were only able to give me fragments of the story. They spoke of their unease about a decorated and high-ranking police officer and the way he had handled a teenager's complaint of rape by another policeman.

In 1993 Sam Brown (not his real name — we cannot reveal the true identity of this man because of a suppression order) had been charged with repeatedly raping a 13-year-old girl while he was a police officer stationed in Murupara and Rotorua in the 1980s. The case went to trial three times. I was told the first two trials were aborted because the investigating officer, Rotorua CIB chief Detective Inspector John Dewar, gave hearsay evidence at both trials. My sources insisted this was an unbelievable error for a senior and experienced policeman to make — giving hearsay evidence at one trial was odd enough, let alone at two. They likened it to a maths teacher telling students that two plus two equalled five. My sources were left wondering whether Dewar had deliberately sabotaged the prosecution to set Brown free and silence the rape complaint — that is, even though he had led the investigation. There were further questions over Brown's third trial, in which he had been acquitted.

In those days, I was Wellington-based *The Dominion* newspaper's regional reporter working from Hastings, three hours' drive from Rotorua. Too far, I thought, to chase a rumour. How often I've regretted that decision since: had I jumped in my car, I would have got the story far earlier. Instead, I relied on the phone and got nowhere. Those I spoke to were vague or outright dismissive. With nothing concrete to show for letting my fingers do the walking, I was directed by my bosses to move on to another story.

But now here I was in 1998 taking phone calls from a new source, who was able to provide more detail and made fresh allegations. Some of these were nothing less than explosive: three other policemen had also raped the girl who said she'd been raped by Brown, the nervous whistle-blower told me. He didn't know the name of the girl, but he gave me the names of three Rotorua cops. He wouldn't say how he knew they were involved, but he told me that the hapless complainant had been passed on by Brown to this trio like a piece of meat. She was a teenager who had learned not to complain about misbehaviour by police officers, and there were stories going around that they'd raped her with a police baton, he said. My source said a policewoman by the name of Caroline had lost her baton and it was rumoured it had been used on a teenager.

I objected. Surely a girl would complain if she were repeatedly raped?

My informant gave me a crash course in the psychology of young sex-abuse victims, male or female. More often than not, children who are sexually abused are too frightened or ashamed to complain. Sometimes, even if they do speak up, they're not believed, so they shut up, feeling even more shame. Sometimes it takes years before they complain. In this case, my source said, the girl had complained, but maybe it wasn't in the interests of the police to act. A policeman's notebook recording the teenager's allegations was missing, and it appeared there was a high-level police plot to protect the reputation of the New Zealand Police force.

This was the first time I heard the names of Clint Rickards, Bob Schollum and Brad Shipton, but it wasn't to be the last. I was back in business.

Clint Rickards was by now a powerful man, and police were wary of talking about him, on or off the record. First, he had been made District Commander of the Gisborne Police by (then) Assistant Commissioner Rob Robinson. Then, just a year later, he was made Waikato District Commander. Facing blanket suppression orders on the three Brown trials, and with silence prevailing in Rotorua police circles about Rickards, Shipton and Schollum, any progress on the story was a slow crawl. Occasionally, bits and pieces crossed my radar, but the story remained patchy at best.

Then, in 2000, a story about another policeman surfaced. I began an investigation into allegations that Sergeant Stephen Tressider had deliberately lied on the witness stand to protect a mate. *The Dominion* eventually published two major stories naming Tressider and outlining the evidence I had obtained. The police launched an inquiry based on our allegations, and in April 2002 Sergeant Tressider became the first New Zealand police officer to be charged with perjury. He was subsequently found guilty and jailed.

While I was working on the Tressider story and others I received solid advice from *The Dominion*'s chief reporter, Barrie Swift. I told Barrie about my frustrations over the Rotorua cop rape story. He urged me not to give up on it.

'This is a small country,' he said. 'Secrets surface, no matter how long it takes.'

Over the next few months we thrashed ideas around on how to advance the investigation, but it wasn't until 9 October 2001 that we decided I should try a different tack. I wrote to the Rotorua District Court asking for permission to look at the suppressed transcripts of the three Brown trials. I wanted more names, and I hoped I'd find them in those documents.

Months passed. By this time I had made repeated requests to Sandie Jackson, a senior official at the Rotorua District Court, to see the files. To view the transcripts of court trials requires the approval of a judge, and I was staggered at how long it was taking for a judge to consider the request — something that would normally have happened in weeks. Finally, six months after I had made my first request, I got a call from my editor's personal assistant saying Judge Michael Lance had approved the request.

At this time there was major upheaval afoot in New Zealand's newspaper industry, and in June 2002 the two Wellington daily newspapers, *The Dominion* and its sister, *The Evening Post*, were merged into a single paper, *The Dominion Post*. Management called for 100 redundancies. Barrie Swift was one who took his redundancy cheque and got out. Before Barrie left his desk for the last time, he sent me his file notes on the Rotorua rape allegations, with a covering note saying: 'Enjoyed working with you and you might want to get stuck into this again, young man.'

My new bosses wanted to know what story prospects I was chasing. As I briefed Bernadette Courtney, the new paper's chief reporter, on the Rotorua allegations, I could sense her journalistic excitement growing, 300 kilometres away in Wellington. Trouble was, although I'd been told I could see the suppressed Brown files, repeated calls to Sandie Jackson asking when I could inspect them were met with noncommittal replies. Eventually she claimed there was no paperwork from Judge Lance confirming that he had granted permission. I would have to resubmit the request. And, sure enough, while she promised to address the request urgently, she didn't.

The story went on the backburner yet again when *The Dominion Post* received anonymous information alleging that ACT MP and education spokeswoman Donna Awatere Huata had stolen money from a charitable trust teaching disadvantaged children to read. My next year was largely devoted to that investigation. It was December 2002 when we published details of the scandal. We broke story after story. Donna denied it all, but a month after we ran the first story the Serious Fraud Office was called in. Eleven months later, Donna

Awatere Huata and her husband Wi Huata were charged with multiple counts of fraud and attempting to pervert the course of justice. Two years later they were tried and convicted, and they lost subsequent appeals.

By now it was 2003, nine years since I had heard the first rumours of the Rotorua rape allegations. My bosses were keen for me to chase the story, but others kept cropping up — one about wide-scale misuse of taxpayer money in a health trust employing a bogus nurse; another exposing an illegal immigrant who had been deported after covering up the savage genital mutilation of his baby granddaughter then crept back into the country. He was jailed, and the bogus nurse was eventually convicted. Finally, Tim Pankhurst, *The Dominion Post*'s editor, directed me to work only on the Rotorua rape case.

I'd been talking all this time to Sandie Jackson, who had again been making excuses about why it was taking so long to get a decision on the resubmitted application to see the Brown files. I kept my cool on the phone with her, as I sensed that to do otherwise risked having her make things even more difficult. But I had begun secretly taping her, and in September I decided enough was enough. I told her I felt she had been stonewalling and that I would complain to the Chief District Court Judge if it continued. Jackson now began shifting the blame to Judge Lance, claiming the file had been before him for some time.

Looking back, it's amazing the range of things that could have derailed the whole investigation. In July 2003, I was introduced to TVNZ news and current affairs boss Bill Ralston at a charity function in Havelock North. I immediately liked Ralston — and I liked him even more when he offered me a job. I had been with the same newspaper — give or take name changes — for 16 years, and I had great respect and loyalty for Tim Pankhurst because of the courage he'd shown in publishing some of my more difficult stories. But I'd lately begun to think that if I was ever to make a career change, it was now or never. After some to-ing and fro-ing, I accepted the TVNZ offer and it was agreed that I would start at the end of November.

It was now October, and each month, it seemed, brought news of another step in Clint Rickards's ascent of the police hierarchy. He was now Assistant Commissioner, in charge of the Auckland police, and eyeing the summit, the Commissioner's job itself. The string of empty promises continued to emanate from the Rotorua District Court. I began to wonder if there could be a cover-up at the court. I hinted as much in my next communication to Sandie Jackson, saying that if what I had been told about the Brown case was true, there were serious issues of open justice at stake. If, on the other hand, my information was wrong, the files would end the matter. Either way, I needed access to the files to determine the matter, and I asked for an answer within 24 hours.

No answer came. When I contacted the court, I learned Jackson had been 'moved on'. The court manager took over my request, and a mere three weeks later I was told that Judge Lance had approved it again. I also learned that Jackson hadn't even sent my second request to view the file to the judge.

Judge Lance confirmed he'd approved my request 18 months earlier, and he fired a memo off to the court staff: 'It seems the instructions I gave then have been misplaced.' He apologised for the delay, and I had no difficulty accepting his apology, as it wasn't his fault. The judge then revealed that the transcript of the third trial, at which Brown was acquitted, had gone missing. I was intrigued and suspicious that court files containing such serious allegations were missing. I wondered who had them.

Still, they hadn't lost everything, and I now had officially approved access to what remained. In November 2003, I received word that the files had been sent to the Hastings District Court for me to inspect. I walked to the courthouse one morning and told them why I was there. The court manager appeared with a stack of folders in his hands.

'Gidday, Phil,' he said. 'This is all a bit old hat, isn't it? It's done and dusted.'

'Dunno about that,' I replied. 'I'll have a look and see what's there, eh?'

It turned out there was plenty. Photocopying the material was forbidden, so I handwrote 45 foolscap pages of notes. At the top of the very first page was the name of the rape complainant: Louise Frances Crawford. And there were the names Rickards, Shipton and Schollum. Reading them took me right back to the phone call I had received years earlier. As I recorded the graphic details from Sam Brown's first two rape trials — the transcript of the third was still missing — I felt I was finally getting somewhere. And it became obvious that the third trial transcript wasn't the only missing file: absent, too, were details of the $20,800 award for court costs that Brown had won against the police.

I told the court there were other important documents missing. They tried to find them, while together with the hard-working staff of *The Dominion Post*'s research library I tried to track down Louise Crawford. We discovered her parents were Jim and Barbara Crawford, and that she'd married Ross Nicholas. At last we had the name I'd been seeking for so long: Louise Nicholas. Soon, I had an address for her, in the tiny rural village of Ngakuru, and I had a Rotorua address for her parents.

The Rotorua District Court emailed late in November, sheepishly admitting they still couldn't find the missing files. I phoned a friend of mine — a police contact I could trust — because I wanted advice about questioning sexual-abuse complainants. I outlined what I'd been told and seen. He was amazed.

'Be very careful,' he warned. 'If your information is right, influential people will fight hard to keep it under wraps.' It was to be a prophetic warning.

He advised me to talk to Louise Nicholas's parents first.

'Tell them what you are investigating, how you will go about it and why it is important you speak to their daughter. Talk to the complainant first and she'll probably slam the door and you'll probably never get another shot.'

The next day, 25 November 2003, I drove to Rotorua. No one was home at the little Rotorua house in which the Crawfords lived. I hung around for a few hours before my impetuosity got the better of me and I decided to risk an approach to Louise herself. I drove to the quaint little village of Ngakuru, about 15 kilometres south of Rotorua in the direction of Taupo. I drove past the little school and the picture-perfect church to the Nicholas driveway. I was nervous. I knocked and waited, and after a while it became obvious no one was home. Half gutted, half relieved, I asked a neighbour if Louise Nicholas still lived there. She did, the neighbour replied, but was working — like everyone else at that hour. She eyed me suspiciously, so I tried to chill her out by making out I knew Louise. Then I jumped in my car and drove back to the Crawford home.

This time, as I opened the gate, I saw a man come out of the garage: a tough-looking customer wearing baggy woollen pants and an upmarket brand of bush shirt.

'Gidday, Jim,' I called out. 'Jim Crawford?'

Jim looked me over, and didn't seem too impressed by what he saw.

'What d'ya want?' he asked.

I told him I was a reporter, and I'd heard stories and seen documents suggesting his daughter might have been badly treated by the cops. There was a bit of a pause.

'You'd better come in,' he said, and ushered me into a spotless garage. He lit a cigarette while I introduced myself, and he smoked pensively, flicking the ash into an old silver Wattie's tin. I rolled myself a cigarette and got down to business.

For openers, I carefully tested him on Detective Inspector Dewar. My sources had told me all those years ago that both Louise and her parents believed Dewar was on their side, so I figured Jim might still think he was one of the good guys. I was right to be cautious — it became pretty clear that Jim reckoned Dewar had done a good job.

Dewar was railroaded out of the Rotorua police, Jim told me. 'Top bloke, that Dewar,' he said.

'So Louise was happy with how Dewar treated her complaint?' I asked casually.

'Yep,' Jim replied. 'She thinks the world of him.'

I brought up the names of Rickards, Shipton and Schollum. Jim's face hardened, and he said it still rankled that they had got away with what they did to his daughter. Dewar just hadn't been able to get the evidence to pin it on them, he said.

I took a breath and told Jim I wasn't so sure about Dewar.

'Oh, yeah?' he said.

I pressed on, telling him I'd seen documents and had spoken to people who agreed there were serious discrepancies in Dewar's investigation.

'Who told you that?' Jim wanted to know.

I wouldn't say, and I don't think he liked that.

I asked Jim if he knew Rickards was almost certainly going to be the next Police Commissioner — the top job in the New Zealand Police. He didn't. 'What was the name of that newspaper you work for again?' he asked. I told him. He'd never heard of *The Dominion Post*, but when I said it was the most politically influential newspaper in the country because all the politicians read it, he seemed a bit more impressed.

Jim said he'd talk to his wife Barbara. Depending on her reaction, they might speak to Louise. I told him I'd already been out to Ngakuru to find Louise and his hackles lifted. He bluntly warned me off trying to speak to her before they'd had a chance to sound her out — if they decided to talk to her at all.

We yarned for a bit, and I detected a thaw. Jim said he had a few documents from the case, and started rummaging around looking for them. He came up with a sheaf of promising-looking papers and began to leaf through them as I waited, itching to get my hands on them. He selected a couple of sheets — I didn't push him for the whole lot, because I sensed he wasn't going to show them all to me, or at least not right away. But when I looked down at the two he gave me, I realised they were like gold nuggets. Two police job sheets — the interviews John Dewar conducted with police officers Bob Schollum and Trevor Clayton. Schollum and Clayton were stationed in the forestry town of Murupara, and it was the Murupara Police Station in which Louise Nicholas said Sam Brown had raped her. Trevor Clayton had since died of cancer. But Jim said Clayton and Schollum were mates of Brown's and all three had been his and Barbara's friends when they all lived in Murupara. Jim didn't know it, but as I glanced at those job sheets big pieces of a jigsaw started falling into place.

I was well satisfied with the meeting, but it was about to get better. I left to drive home to Havelock North and was nearly at Taupo when my mobile phone rang. Turn around, Jim said. Barbara will hear what you've got to say.

I drove back. Jim met me at the door, and showed me into the living room where Barbara rose to greet me. She's a small woman, with a serious, sensible air — the product of her conservative clothing and her short-cropped hair. She was clearly nervous, and it wasn't hard to read deep parental concern in her careworn face. It was perfectly understandable, after all their daughter had been through.

We got talking about it. Jim angrily recalled the three rape trials Louise had already endured.

'For nothing,' he said.

I told them most of what I knew and what I wanted to investigate. They heard me out, and, when I'd finished, Jim got more fired up. Then Barbara said she'd ask Louise if she'd talk to me.

Tired, but pleased with my progress, I drove home and talked for a couple of hours about it all with my wife, Nicky. Over and over, I read the documents I'd obtained and the notes I'd made, looking for clues to — or rebuttal of — the claims my source had made in those anxious phone calls five years earlier: namely that Louise Nicholas had been stitched up by those on whom she had relied to procure justice for her.

Detective Inspector Dewar had written two of the job sheet documents himself, but they still indicated one of two things. Either he was an honest but hopelessly sloppy investigator, or he wasn't the noble cop the Crawfords and Louise believed him to be. Again and again, Nicky and I thrashed through all the information. Then there was nothing we could do but wait.

As it turned out, I didn't have to wait for long. The next day, Jim invited me back to Rotorua to talk to the three of them: him, Barbara and Louise. All the way, I was thinking about what I was going to say, and wondering whether it would be sufficient to take the gloss off their knight in shining armour, Dewar.

Jim met me at the door as before, and showed me into the living room again. There was Barbara, and there, too, was Louise Nicholas. She was nothing like I'd pictured her. She was tiny, to start with. She was what you might call unsophisticated in her dress sense, wearing jeans and a T-shirt. Everything about her, from her speech and her mannerisms to the complete absence of war paint on her face, screamed 'country girl'. She wore an open, if rather guarded expression as she shook my hand. There were lines on her face that spoke of a tough life, with heart-aches and -breaks along the way, but there were laughter lines too.

Airs and graces were absent from the room. There was tension and suspicion, and it wasn't just the Crawfords and Louise who were nervous. Jim nursed a recently opened flagon of beer, while Barbara and Louise perched on their seats with straight backs, waiting.

Trying to keep eye contact with each of them, I said it seemed there were two scenarios from the evidence I'd seen so far. Scenario one was that John Dewar tried his best to investigate what had happened to Louise, but was shafted by the police hierarchy.

Three heads nodded.

I then put several documents on the coffee table and said that, to my mind, there might be an alternative scenario.

I asked Louise if she clearly remembered telling John Dewar she'd been raped and violated with a baton by Schollum, Shipton and Rickards *before* Dewar interviewed Brown. Louise nodded, and said she'd most definitely told Dewar that. She said that even before she told Dewar, she'd also told Ray Sutton, another senior police officer her father knew, about the baton rape. Sutton took notes, she said, but his notebook disappeared from his office.

I showed Louise one of the police job sheets her father had given me.

'So,' I said pedantically, 'before John Dewar records this interview with Bob Schollum, you reckon you'd definitely told him that Schollum, Rickards and Shipton used a police baton on you?'

'That's right,' Louise said.

I asked her to read the job sheet. It said Bob Schollum knew Dewar was investigating Brown before Dewar had even arrived to interview him. Schollum promised Dewar full co-operation because, he said, when he worked with Brown in Murupara, Brown had tried to seduce his former wife. If he had any information that would help, Schollum said, he'd happily provide it. Schollum said he 'was in no doubt that what Louise Crawford claimed did happen'. Brown, Schollum said, was 'ruled by his cock . . . and was into everything, meaning females, whilst at Murupara. He also had a large collection of pornographic videos . . . he imported those videos by having them addressed to the Murupara Police Station. That way they were never challenged by the Post Office or Customs.'

Dewar wrote that Schollum ended the interview, saying 'he had some matters which he could speak off the record about but then declined to do so'. The interview took 30 minutes.

Louise finished reading Dewar's job sheet. I asked if she found anything unusual in it. She'd made an incredibly serious allegation to a senior police officer: she'd alleged that Schollum, Shipton and Rickards had baton-raped her. But a mere three weeks later, when Dewar spoke to Schollum, he didn't ask a single question about the allegation.

Louise's mouth started to tighten.

I picked up the other job sheet Jim Crawford had given me, which was then the most revealing and potentially incriminating document I had. It backed the suspicions rippling through my mind that there had indeed been a high-level police conspiracy, a conspiracy Louise and her parents were blind to.

This job sheet was John Dewar's record of his interview with Trevor Clayton, conducted just a day after he had interviewed Schollum. Like Schollum, Clayton had worked with Brown in Murupara, but when Dewar interviewed him Clayton, like Brown, was no longer a serving police officer.

So what was so significant about this job sheet? In it, Dewar wrote that

Clayton claimed he hadn't known of any sexual allegations made by Louise about Brown until quite recently — two weeks, in fact, before Louise had even spoken to Dewar. This had given me pause for thought when I first read it. Where, I wondered, had Clayton learned of the allegation, if not from Dewar? Did it have anything to do with the missing police notebook? And surely, if the story was being put about before Dewar was even conducting his interviews, it meant that Clayton and Brown had had plenty of time to get their stories straight.

There are other revealing details, too. Clayton told Dewar that when he was stationed at Murupara, Louise complained she'd been raped by a group of Maori on horseback when she was about 13 years old.

Dewar wrote: 'I asked Clayton what he did about it [the claim] and Clayton replied: "Nothing." I asked him why and he said he believed it was all bullshit. I asked him why . . . he said because she'd asked that her parents not be told. I asked if he recorded that conversation and he thought he may have in his diary which he had recently looked for, but was unable to find. I asked him if he took any official action and he said . . . "No, it was just one of those country chats."'

Dewar then criticised Clayton: 'I told him [Clayton] this was an allegation of rape he was receiving, not a country chat and proper police practice would have been to record the complaint and despite the wishes of a 13 or 14 year old girl advise her parents.'

This was pretty rich! Here was Dewar lecturing a former junior policeman on his failure to act on a complaint of rape. But just a few weeks earlier Dewar himself had been told Louise had been baton-raped, and what had *he* done?

The next part of Dewar's interview is absolutely extraordinary. Clayton 'said whilst he was serving in Rotorua at some stage late 1986–1987, Louise complained to him about what some Rotorua police members were doing to her.' Dewar continued: 'I asked Clayton if there were criminal implications and he said there could have been. I asked him what he did about it as a serving member of the police and he said that he took no action. I asked him why and he said: "To protect his mates." I asked him if this was what he was now doing for Brown and he replied: "Yes."'

Dewar asked Clayton if he'd ever had sex, consensual or otherwise, with Louise. Clayton refused to answer, and he told Dewar he would 'tell lies in court' to protect Brown. Dewar ended the interview, saying: 'Well, Trevor, I expected this reaction, particularly from an ex-member of Police. Would it surprise you to learn I have a tape recorder in my jacket?' Clayton replied: 'Oh, shit, thanks very much, John, thanks very much.'

Louise watched me carefully as I summarised the chain of events for her:

1: She told Senior Sergeant Ray Sutton she'd been baton-raped by three policemen — Rickards, Shipton and Schollum. His notebook recording the allegation mysteriously disappeared.

2: Next, she told Dewar about the baton rape. Three weeks later, Dewar interviewed Schollum — a serving police officer — but didn't ask a single question about the baton-rape allegation. Dewar didn't even ask Schollum if he had ever had sex, consensual or not, with Louise.

3: The next day Dewar interviewed Clayton — an ex-policeman. Ironically, he berated Clayton for not acting on Louise's 'allegation of rape'. He asked Clayton if he'd ever had sex with Louise.

4: Critically, Clayton told Dewar that Louise had complained about what Rotorua police officers other than Sam Brown were doing to her in 1986 and 1987, around the time of the baton rape. Clayton even said there could have been criminal implications in what she'd alleged. Yet Dewar didn't ask Clayton for the names of those police officers, nor did he press Clayton for particulars of their behaviour, even though it must have seemed to be the same incident or incidents that Louise had told him about.

5: Then, straight after interviewing Clayton, Dewar drove to interview Clayton's mate, ex-cop Sam Brown. Brown had a different memory to Clayton. He remembered Clayton telling him Louise did in fact make a rape complaint when she was aged 15. Brown reckoned she had made the complaint to Clayton, who then told Brown, his mate. Brown even said he spoke to Louise's mother about the rape allegation. Without attempting to pursue the other allegations of rape that had arisen in the course of his enquiries, Dewar had no hesitation in then arresting Brown and charging him with rape of a minor.

I saw Louise shiver. Her eyes flashed. She was silent for a few seconds. I didn't record her words because I didn't want to pull out a notebook, but there was no need. I have as clear a memory of what she said as though it was yesterday.

'Sweet Jesus, no,' she said quietly. 'The bastards have shafted me again.'

I knew then that we were going to get a story: I just didn't know how big that story would be.

The atmosphere in the Crawfords' living room changed in seconds. I said I might be wrong, but that it seemed to me there was a lot more behind what had happened than met the eye, and I wanted to expose it. I said that if we did bring it to light, the story would probably be the most defamatory story ever published in New Zealand. But, I said, telling the truth was a complete defence against a charge of defamation.

There was going to be an amount of difficulty getting at the truth: we were dealing with powerful people, and if they discovered what I was investigating, more documents might go missing, more people would be told to shut up, more people would jack up their stories. I said it could take a long time, because we had to get it right. I said it was possible that we could spend a long time on it but never run a story if our lawyers were not satisfied with the evidence. I said my bosses would not like me saying it, but if Louise wanted to pull out at any time, I would kill the story. I talked of trust, and how it didn't cut both ways — that I had to be able to trust them to tell me everything and that everything had to be truthful. However, I warned them, it couldn't work perfectly in reverse, because there would be some things I wouldn't tell them, to protect my sources: they would simply have to trust me. I said they must not talk to anyone about what I was doing, but I promised I would keep them briefed on the story's progress. I said if I discovered Louise wasn't telling the truth to me at any time, I would turn my back on her.

There was silence when I finished speaking.

'Do we have a deal?' I asked.

'Damn right, we do,' Louise said. Jim said I'd better have a beer. Barbara chided me for not telling her I hadn't had dinner.

I left Louise, Jim and Barbara, thinking they needed to talk privately, and drove to stay overnight with my in-laws, Des and Nod, in Taupo. I trusted them to keep quiet about details of my work that needed to stay quiet. Like true family, Nod worried about me while Des gave me some wise advice. They were good listeners.

Over the next month, I commuted to Rotorua weekly as my enquiries gathered momentum. I'd briefed Tim Pankhurst and the paper's lawyer, Peter McKnight, on the jigsaw I was gradually assembling. I'd been given a month's extension from Bill Ralston on my starting date with TVNZ, but Tim naturally wanted the story out before I left *The Dominion Post*. He put me under increasing pressure to break the story even if we had to do so without using names. But when I argued that I had more enquiries to make, he too agreed to give me more time. He knew as well as I did that the only story we could have run at that point would have been a bunch of vague insinuations about an apparent police plot to nobble an unnamed woman's rape complaints. The authorities and the rest of the media would have probably ignored it, and the culprits would have been forewarned and that much better prepared to defend themselves if anyone did come calling.

Back in Rotorua, I wanted the whole story on the record. On 27 November 2003, Louise and I sat at Jim and Barbara's dining-room table with a cup of coffee and my file. I placed my tape recorder on the table between us.

'Where do I start?' Louise asked.

'Why not at the beginning?' I replied.

She took a deep breath, and began to talk.

Louise

I WAS BORN AT ROTORUA Hospital, Jim and Barbara's third child. My brothers, Peter and Robert, are two and three years older than me. Three years after I was born, Dad applied for a job as a store man with the Kaingaroa Logging Company, based in a little town called Murupara, about 40 minutes' drive south of Rotorua. Murupara sits quietly on the edge of the Urewera National Park, a huge playground for any avid hunter who enjoys the thrill of tracking, finding and finally taking down a massive stag or large boar for his freezer.

The guardians of this impressive land are the Tuhoe tribe. My father's sister, Aunty Elaine, married Tipene Teka, a descendant of the Tuhoe. Uncle Tip explained to me some of the ancestry of his people. His ancestors are called Children of the Mist, and their ancestry has been traced to Hine Pokohurangi and Te Maunga, as well as to Toi Potiki Hapi Mouri-ori. They were the original inhabitants of this land, with Ngapotiki being the ancient tribe. Later, in the 1300s, the Tuhoe, who are descendants of Captain Toroa, arrived on the Mataatua waka. After a few battles they soon asserted themselves, and with that came peace and intermarriages between the tribes. For these tangata whenua the rugged Ureweras are their special and spiritual homeland.

This area is also known as the Western Gateway, and it lies under Mount Tawhiau where the two mighty rivers Whirinaki and Rangitaiki meet. It is also the home of the Ngati Manawa tribe in Murupara. The Ureweras also became my special place. When bad things were happening to me, I always found that going bush or being able to ride my horse around Murupara enabled me to release my fears, even if it was only for a few hours.

To illustrate what I mean about the spirituality of this land and why it means so much to so many, I recall a Search and Rescue operation that took place on 16 July 1980. Two sisters, Salina and Noti Apirana, from Ruatahuna, were reported missing in the Huiarau ranges. As the days dragged on, the need to find the two girls was heightened by every hour that passed. Because of their staunch faith in the Ringatu religion and the Church of the Holy Spirit, the girls' parents and whanau never gave up hope that they would be found alive. Eventually their prayers were answered. After nearly a week both sisters were found — Salina first, then the next day Noti. The girls were totally exhausted and very hungry, but said that they had been cared for by their spiritual ancestors and their guardian angels.

When my little brother Kevin was born, I found myself really outnumbered by boys. Luckily, Kev didn't join his brothers in tormenting me: I was four years older than him and bigger, too, so I was more his playmate than a guinea pig, as I was for the others.

I attended Murupara Primary School along with my big brothers, and as Murupara was predominantly Maori we, as a family, became pretty familiar with Maori values. The fact that we were Pakeha meant nothing to the Maori community. They always treated us as their whanau, and the respect for one another instilled back then has stayed with me and my family all this time, and throughout all we've been through. An example of the way we were accepted into the local community was how we were treated at Christmastime. As soon as the presents had been opened Mum would have Christmas lunch organised, and after we'd all stuffed ourselves you could pretty well guarantee there'd be a phone call or a knock on the door inviting us all to a mouth-watering Christmas hangi. Of course, bearing in mind that the majority of the community worked in the bush, they were well known as people who not only worked hard, but played hard too. There were some wild times.

My school years were a lot of fun. Some things stand out, looking back. My first school disco, for example. When you paid your entry, you were given a number that could win you a prize — the album *Grease*. The movie was a number-one hit, especially in Murupara, and to have the album in your record collection would make you 'the bomb' with your mates. I could hardly breathe when they made the draw, and when my number came up it was like I'd just won a hundred bucks. I couldn't move my feet to go up and receive this massive prize. I remember everyone clapping and cheering for me, and then someone shoved me forward, so with shaking hands I took the album and ran all the way home to show the family. I guess I was about eight or nine years old. It was the biggest event of my life: I couldn't sleep for days afterwards.

I fell head over heels for a boy in my class. Ronald was his name, and the most distinctive feature I remember about him was his white teeth. He was darker than most Maori I knew, and when he smiled his teeth just shone right out of his mouth. The day he asked me to walk home with him — oh, my God! My heart skipped all its beats and my tummy had butterflies running around inside it. I was so shy that every time he said anything I would make these silly giggling noises. What an embarrassment! I remember thinking that he was the one and only for me and that I would grow up and marry this boy. I was all of eight years old.

Life then had its downs as well. A girl called Rena used to give me the bash most days after school. I would hear her coming and would take off, but she always caught me and a punch to the head inevitably followed. One day, I decided this had to stop. Her punches were really starting to hurt! So, instead of taking off, I just stopped, waited for her to get to me and, in an amazing Matrix-like move, I turned at the right time and my fist landed smack-bang in the middle of her face. She dropped like a swatted fly, then looked up at me with this look of absolute shock, promptly burst into tears and ran home. I was so proud of myself, but my hand hurt like a bitch for days afterwards. The next day I was crapping myself at the thought of facing Rena in class. I figured that, with her mates as back-up, she would probably do me in good and proper. To my amazement, though, she just smiled at me, and from that day on we were the best of mates.

I should thank Rena for all the running she made me do, because I found I'd developed a good turn of speed, especially when it came to school athletics. My biggest competition was Geraldine. Man, that girl could sprint! She had the longest legs ever and she knew how to use them. I decided that, before I left primary school, my goal was to beat Geraldine in the 100-metre sprints. So hard did I try and so often did I fail, but then the day of reckoning came. I got into the finals, and I knew that this was my last chance to achieve my goal. I don't know where I got the strength or the speed from, but I flew down that straight, right past Geraldine, and won the race. It was the most amazing feeling to have all those kids yell and scream and egg me on, and then to cross that finish line first — it was a moment that I have never ever forgotten. What a blast! It was like I had won the gold medal at the Olympics. Geraldine kind of burst my bubble when she came up to me later and said, 'I'll get you back at high school.' She tried, but she never did beat me again, even at high school. That's the power of sheer determination for you.

My first brush with the police came while I was at school, too. Peer pressure was to blame, as I'm sure it is for all school kids at some stage. Who knows how many bad or stupid things get done by kids anxious to 'fit in with the group'. One day, when I was six or seven years old, instead of leaving school to go home at three o'clock, I was asked by 'the group' if I wanted to go with them to the shopping centre, which was right next door to the school. Thinking that this was my opportunity to be in the cool crowd, I followed them over. We ended up outside the stationery shop. 'The group' dared me to go in and take something from the shop. I told them that I didn't have any money, and as they all stood there laughing at me, one of them informed me that I didn't need money. Just take something, she said, and bring it out and show it to us.

I was young, but old enough to know damn well this was wrong. Yet I still felt that, to be accepted into 'the group', I had to do what was asked of me. In I went, nervous as hell, and probably looking as guilty as hell too, but the owner Mr Murray was busy with customers and didn't really take much notice of me. I walked up and down the aisles looking for something small and discreet, something that I could hide up the sleeve of my sweatshirt. Aha! Yes, of course, that small roll of Sellotape is perfect and Mr Murray won't miss it . . . The really scary part of the whole bad situation was how easy it was. I picked the roll up, slipped it up my sleeve as easy as anything, and walked out of the shop, not feeling guilty so much as strangely exhilarated by the whole experience. I guess, looking back now, it was really all that adrenalin pumping away inside me that allowed me to feel that way.

Of course, my so-called mates weren't there when I walked out, and I felt absolutely gutted that they had set me this task but weren't even going to hang around to see my accomplishment. I walked slowly and quietly away from Mr Murray's shop, hoping and praying that his hand wasn't going to land on my shoulder and his voice bellow in my ear: 'What have you got up your sleeve, young lady?' The voice and the hand never arrived, so I quickened my step until I was well and truly away from the shopping centre, whereupon I broke into a sprint and ran all the way home.

It wasn't until I was heading down the alleyway that ran between our house and our neighbours' that it suddenly dawned on me: How do I explain to Mum where I got this Sellotape from? Easy! I'll just tell her I found it. And that's exactly what I did. I can't, even to this day, work out why she didn't believe me. I just walked in and said to her, 'Look what I found.'

'No, you didn't,' she replied. 'Where did you really get it from?'

'I found it down the alleyway.'

'No, you didn't, Louise. Where did you get it from? And don't lie to me!'

I figured this was a good time to throw in the tears and beg for forgiveness. Nah, that didn't work. I told her 'They made me do it'. That didn't work, either, and to the bedroom I was sent. Oh, boy, was I in big trouble. I was sobbing on the top bunk in the bedroom, wondering what kind of punishment was coming, when Mum came in and said that Mr Policeman was here to talk to me about what I had done. Mr Policeman was ginormous! His big, dark eyes met mine, and I was sitting on the top bunk! I got the biggest, meanest ticking-off in the whole wide world. Boy, did he let rip! He told me that what I had done was really bad, and that bad people who do bad things go to jail. All I could do was sit there motionless and so scared, as I was sure he was going to slap those handcuffs on, throw me into the back of the police car and cart me off to jail. He continued to lecture me, but I didn't really hear much of what he was saying. I was too busy envisaging my prison cell, where I would eat nothing but bread and water.

Mr Policeman finally left and I was alone with my imagination. I had myself tarred and feathered, hanging from a tree with a noose around my neck, walking the plank — you name it: whatever I had seen on TV happening to the bad guys was going to happen to me. In the end, all that happened was that Mum made me go back to Mr Murray's stationery shop and return the Sellotape with a 'from-the-heart' apology and a huge plea for forgiveness. I think having to face the person I stole from was the worst punishment anyone could have dreamed up. Many years later, Mum told me Mr Murray was more shocked by the fact that it was me who had stolen from him than the act itself. And my experience with Mr Policeman would have a big part to play in my life later on.

Growing up with my brothers there was a lot of laughter, some tears, and loads of love. I'll never forget the time when my eldest brother Pete got caught smoking. Dad figured that if he made him smoke a whole packet of cigarettes that should be punishment enough. Pete had obviously done this before, and he handled the first cigarette quite well. He also handled the second one like an old pro, but as the third, fourth and fifth ones were lit he started to look quite green. I'm not sure how many he got through but eventually he conceded and promised Dad that he would never smoke again. Pete's now in his forties and still enjoys many a good fag!

We were a regular provincial Kiwi family. We enjoyed the outdoors, especially hunting, fishing and camping, and spent many happy weekends in the bush. Dad owned a rifle that had belonged to my Granddad Pawley. It was a .303 and we all learnt to shoot with it. The hard-case thing with this rifle was that it could shoot around corners! No matter how much Dad and the boys tried to sight this gun in, it had a mind of its own.

Dad's love of hunting rubbed off on the boys and they still spend as much time as they can out in the bush. Dad bought them a slug gun when he felt they were old enough to respect the fact that even though it was considered a low-powered rifle, it was still a rifle, and could inflict serious injury on its target. It was made clear that the slug gun was not to be brought out of the wardrobe without Dad's permission. But Pete and Rob thought otherwise, and decided to cull a few of the neighbour's chooks for Aunty Betty and Uncle Josh Tanirau. Unfortunately they hit one poor chicken, then of all the dumb things to do they tried to bury it. Dad caught them in the act and I don't think those boys could sit down for a week after that.

My older brothers were just downright nasty buggers, not only to helpless chickens but to me and Kevin too. There was the time playing hide and seek when they locked me in a suitcase and hid it in a wardrobe. I now suffer from claustrophobia and the boys still think that was funny. Then there was the Zorro episode. The boys thought that they too could hang someone from a tree. They managed to hang me from our big willow tree by my cardigan. Baby brother Kev saved me by telling Mum, 'Wees in da twee.' Mum got me down and I was fine, but it was a long time before the boys thought it safe to return home.

So it's hurt me when I've heard the likes of talkback callers who I've never met suggesting I must have come from a dysfunctional family. Ours was, and still is, as ordinary a family as you'd find anywhere.

My passion was horses. There was a man by the name of Johnny Motion who lived down the road from us, and he owned hunting horses. These horses had no fear of anything and that included rifles. Johnny had a dark bay mare called Dolly that I had taken a shine to. If she was tied up down the back road, I was allowed to ride her. My friend Donna had taught me to ride on her horse Kim, so when the opportunity arose to take Dolly out, I was in like Flynn. The only drawback was that I was not allowed to ride unless I had done my Saturday jobs. My dad's a fussy old bugger: everything has its place and every place has its thing. I hated the fact that I had to spend a good hour or so in the morning doing these chores, and if they weren't done properly I had to go back and do them all again. All this valuable riding time being wasted!

Eventually, out that door I went, running down the road to Johnny's house, where I grabbed Dolly's bridle and then was off again to get her. When I was riding Dolly I had to keep her at a fast walk, as this was how she would be ridden in the bush. For the first hour of riding, I would have the stitch. I would also ride without a saddle. Bareback was the only way to ride, as quite often in the summer we would head out to the back of Murupara to ride the bush roads and swim with the horses through the river. Even today, when I ride my daughter's horse, I find the saddle very uncomfortable.

Most of the time, Donna and I rode together. We also had a mate, Truby, who had a big horse — easily 17 hands — that only he could ride. That horse was mad, but wow, he was handsome. In those days, my dream job was to be a vet specialising in horses. One day, I told myself, that dream would come true. I knew it meant a few years at university, but I only had to do well at high school and I was halfway there. Dreams are free, and in those days they seemed worth the wait.

Summertime was the best for us, especially when Mum and Dad bought a Para pool one Christmas. We had such a blast. The pool seemed huge, even though the water came to just above my belly button. We swam for hours. Dad was strict about routine though — showers at 4.30pm, dinner at 5.30, watch the news at 6.00, *Coronation Street* after that, then bed at 7.30. The weekends weren't as bad though, as Dad seemed to mellow a bit by Friday.

My family went through a very sad time with the death of my Aunty Joy, Dad's sister. Mavis and Graham Archbold, who lived behind us, and Colleen and Neville Knight, who lived across the road, were a huge help as Dad, Mum and the whole Crawford family were devastated by this sudden and tragic loss. But three months later, great joy fell upon the whole family with the announcement from my parents that we were going to have another baby. I was so happy with this wonderful news, because I just knew it was going to be a girl. It had to be: I needed back-up against my brothers, big time.

How wonderful it was to watch Mum's tummy grow and to be able to feel and see that little life kicking away quite happily. Frances Joy Crawford was born on 13 April 1977, and on 14 April Frances Joy Crawford passed away. She lived for only 12 hours. Other family members arrived to be with us at this tragic time, and I remember my dad asking me to go and get Nana Pawley, Mum's mum, from the other room. When we entered Dad's bedroom and I turned to leave, he stopped me and told me to come and sit on the bed with Nana. I had never seen my father cry before, and the tears he shed were full of deep sorrow and heartache. He spoke so openly to Nana, just letting all that grief go. It was an amazing sight for me, because Dad was like any typical son-in-law who loved to give his mother-in-law as much crap as he could (behind her back of course!). Soon afterwards, Nana Crawford told me that the angels had taken Frances to heaven to be with God. I remember looking at my grandmother and wanting to scream that God was a bastard for doing this to us. But I held back, because Nana Crawford was Catholic and went to church every Sunday. Presumably, she knew what she was talking about.

There was an old Maori lady who lived across the road from us, who we kids knew as Nanny Oakey. I remember sitting in the lounge with the rest of the family and hearing someone ask who was coming up the driveway. I heard Dad say that it was Nanny Oakey. She was invited in and handed Dad a bunch of red roses. She gave him a kiss, and told him how sorry she was for our loss. Then she told him to get her a beer, and they sat at the dining table and shared a couple of beers and a few laughs — it was just what Dad needed, but the look on my grandmothers' faces was worth a photo. Someone explained to them that this was how the people of Murupara helped each other in times like this. And help they did. The house was always buzzing with people coming in and out, bringing food, flowers and offers of help, and just being there for us.

The day of the funeral was the saddest day of my life, not because I was going to my sister's funeral, but because I *wasn't* going to my sister's funeral. It had been decided that Kevin and I were too young to be exposed to such sadness. I was heartbroken, but there was nothing I could do about it. We were packed off to my Aunt Colleen's place. I remember my cousin Sharon, Colleen's daughter, asking me if I would like to listen to some records. She put one on for me and I lay down in front of the speaker with my head on the record sleeve and silently mourned my sister. When Sharon woke me some time later there was a huge puddle of tears on the record cover. But if it was hard for me, it must have been much harder for Mum, as she couldn't go to the funeral either. She was still recovering from the birth.

When the Kelson family moved in across the road from us, Pearl (Dinky) Kelson became my best friend. Dinky wasn't into horses but we did everything else together. Dinky and I moved on to high school together and our competitiveness moved with us, each trying to outdo the other, whether it was in sports or academically. I must admit old Dinky was the better student academically but I could whip her butt in sports . . . well, most of the time.

I remember my first day at Rangitahi College, with my brand-new uniform, brand-new school bag and brand-new shoes. I was thinking, 'Damn, I look good!' Then the Galatea bus stopped and all the rural kids descended on the school. And then the Ruatahuna, Minginui and Te Whaiti buses rolled on in. It had never occurred to me that there were other primary schools in our district, let alone all these kids. I decided that high school was going to take a lot of getting used to, and I wasn't wrong. Unlike primary school, we had a different teacher for different subjects in different classes. We had a timetable for the first time in our lives, and it sure as hell wasn't easy finding where your next class was. But the good part was the new friends you made. There was a huge group of us who hung around together at interval and lunchtimes, and with both my brothers at the school their mates soon became mine. Pete was in the sixth form and Rob was in the fifth, and they had a lot of friends. I also made a lot of neat friends in 3BC1, the class I was put into in my first year — one of the top classes, as it turned out. My favourite subject was typing, and I decided right away that Mrs Radford was a great teacher. She was to become a pretty important person in my life.

It wasn't school or the friends I made there that changed my life forever, though. It was my second brush with the police, which happened that year I started college.

My mum and dad had become very involved with the New Zealand Mountain Safety Search and Rescue organisation. With all the people who came to Urewera National Park for the various outdoor activities it has to offer, accidents were bound to happen. Deer farming had taken off too, and there was an upsurge in the use of helicopters to bring live deer out of the bush. Unfortunately, chopper crashes became an all-too-regular occurrence for the Murupara Search and Rescue squad. There was a year when every time the phone rang it seemed you'd hear those awful words: 'Another one down.'

Dad's role was to phone all available search and rescue members and have them assemble at the Murupara Ranger Station ready for a briefing. Dad also had the bright idea of getting a trailer purpose-built to house all the equipment required for any search, whether it was for a downed chopper or a lost hunter. This trailer and its contents were kept at the Murupara Police Station, and when the call came to go in, the trailer went too. Mum's role in the squad was one of the most important, as she had to keep a log of everything — what time it happened, how it happened, who made it happen, and so on.

Besides those with specialised skills, such as Jill and Dave Messent, who were keen amateur radio operators, the local people also played an integral part in search and rescue activities. The local men knew the area like the backs of their hands, and they brought this knowledge to ground searches. When it became evident that a search was going to take some days, the community banded together to ensure the searchers were well fed, donating food and refreshments, organising hangi for the main feed, and food packs to take back out into the bush. At the end of a successful search, when lost hunters or downed chopper crews were found safe and well, a celebratory beer would follow the debrief, and sometimes this 'beer' would be enjoyed at our house. If the search ended with a body recovery, on the other hand, a debrief would occur after the search was wound up and then everyone would go home to their families and work through the loss in their own way. The Murupara Search and Rescue squad was dubbed the best in New Zealand, and that was a tremendous source of pride for all involved.

With all search and rescue operations, it was the norm for the cops to be involved. It was their job to co-ordinate searches, and they'd be involved in any body recoveries. They would report back to Air Accident Control if a chopper went down, or decide if a fatality in the bush was an accident or perhaps something more sinister. So, given Mum and Dad's involvement with search and rescue, it was inevitable that we got to know the police pretty well.

Two new cops took up postings at the Murupara Police Station. Bob Schollum arrived first, and he soon established a no-nonsense presence within the community. This was generally appreciated, as Murupara had a gang problem at the time. Bob settled into the old police house with his wife Judy and their two preschool children. Then he was joined by Sam Brown, his wife Jane (not her real name) and their children, who moved into the police house behind the station.

It soon became evident that these two coppers were here to stamp out the riff-raff and ensure Murupara became a safer little community. And you have to give credit where it's due — these guys certainly achieved that. It was well-known that their approach to certain incidents was not textbook police procedure, but it worked. Within the first year of these two taking up their posts, according to the local newspaper, the rate of clearing offences jumped from around 35 per cent to 75 per cent, well above the national average of 47.8 per cent. These statistics were brought to the attention of Police Commissioner Robert Walton, who sent letters of commendation to Sam and Bob praising the 'excellent manner in which the two men have carried out their duties in Murupara and the enthusiasm and efficiency each has displayed'. They really made a difference.

At first, it seemed as though their arrival — and our family's involvement with them through search and rescue — would be a good thing for me. They would bring their families around home for a swim and a barbecue, and as I was old enough to babysit, I could earn money for (um, yeah) cigarettes. It was a welcome top-up over and above what I got from my part-time weekend job at the Murupara Hub dairy, where I worked either the morning or the afternoon, about five hours a day. (My friend Donna's mother worked at the dairy, so when Donna and I applied for jobs there, we both got them. I remember receiving my first pay: $27 — a lot of money back then — and, of course, I blew it straight away on my new habit of smoking on the sly.)

The police station was only a two-minute walk from the shopping centre and it also sat straight across the road from the Murupara Hotel. Whenever I was out riding my horse or going to my friend Cliff Turner's house, I would have to go past the station. If Bob or Sam were there, they would either yell out gidday or come out for a yak. That was all fine. I knew them and liked them and had every reason to trust them.

But then it happened: the day that screwed my life forever.

I had left home a bit earlier than usual, because I wanted to go to the Turners' place on my way to work. As I wandered past the police station, Sam opened the window and called out to me. I walked up to him and he asked what I was up to. I told him that I was going to see Mum Turner before I started work. Sam then asked me to come inside for a minute. Thinking nothing of this, I walked to the side entrance of the station and he let me in. I walked through the door ahead of Sam, who closed the door and locked it.

That was the first sign that not all was as it seemed. Why did he lock the door?

I turned around to face him, but he just smiled at me and walked me not into the office area, but into the meal room. At this stage, I was thinking, what is he up to? There were no real alarm bells ringing — I just figured he was going to show me something or tell me something. I wasn't afraid of being there.

And then I was very afraid of being there. He walked up to me and started caressing my shoulders and arms, then started telling me how much he liked me and how pretty I was. I was standing there trying to work out what on earth he was doing and why he was saying these things. Finally it dawned on me that I was in serious trouble. I asked him to stop, but he wouldn't. Then he reached down to the button on my jeans and tried to undo it. I grabbed his hand and said, 'No, Sam,' but he just pushed my hand out of the way and carried on. Sam was a tall man and I was just a little skinny thing. I didn't have a shit-show in hell of stopping him touching me. I felt quite stupid, because all I remember saying was, 'Please don't, Sam. I don't like it.' As if that was going to stop him. And it didn't: he just kept going until he got the button on my jeans undone and the zip down. He then put his hand down my jeans, and that's when I knew I was done for.

Finally he got my jeans off and put me on the meal-room table. I kept telling him that I didn't want him to do this, but he just said it would be all right and that he would be gentle. Then he went down on me, and all I remember was feeling not only sick but really embarrassed — I never knew this was how you had sex. What made it even worse was that when he came up from 'down there', he had 'stuff' all over his moustache. Sam then removed his clothing and I could see everything. This was when he spread my legs and entered me. I was really crying by this time, but all he said to me was, 'Relax, just relax.' How the hell could I relax? All I wanted to do was scream, as the pain was excruciating. I didn't know how to get out of this, and I couldn't think how on earth I could have stopped it happening. I still don't know.

When he'd finally finished and had started to get dressed, I remember saying to him that his wife could walk in. His answer to that was that he had locked the door and she would think he had gone out. The worst part of all was that I was only 13 years old, and while I knew that what was happening was very wrong, there was nothing I could do about it. Here he was, this married man, this father of two little kids, this so-called friend of my family, this respected member of our community . . . and to top it all off, he was a man who you would think would know right from wrong because it was his job to know. This man was our local policeman, our community's upholder of law and order. All I could think about was that I was too young to have to beg someone to stop doing something I didn't like. I desperately didn't want this to have been my 'first time', but Sam had other ideas. I walked out of that police station thinking, if that's what sex is all about, then I most definitely don't want any part of it ever again.

I quietly walked on to the dairy to start my job, but clearly I was not in the right frame of mind to be the happy little shop assistant I was paid to be. I was bleeding and I had this yucky-looking discharge so I had to buy some pads to fix that problem. I hadn't even started my periods, so I didn't have a clue as to what sort of product to buy. All I wanted to do was go home and scrub myself clean, and after that, curl up into a little ball and die. My body felt so gross, so dirty that even a hot bath couldn't take away the ugliness I felt.

I didn't tell anyone about what had happened. Somehow, I just knew there was no point. And the most sickening thing of all was that Sam knew that too. He didn't even have to say: 'Don't tell anyone, or else.' He knew damn well that I wouldn't, that I couldn't, because who on this earth would believe my word against his?

Anyway, I told myself, what had happened was wrong. I should never have gone into that police station, and I should never have let him do that awful thing to me. I was a bad person for letting it happen, and I remembered being told by Mr Policeman when I was little that people who do bad things are punished. I didn't mean to be bad. I didn't want or ask him to do anything to me: he just did it. I thought he was my friend.

Even though I wanted my life to end, I just had to keep things as normal as I could, so I would get up, have breakfast, go to school, come home, do my jobs, have tea, scrub myself raw in the bath, then just go to bed. This routine carried on until the weekend came. This, I thought, is where I'll be able to lose myself on my horse and be as far away from any memory of that day as I can possibly get.

I soon realised that this was easier said than done. That awful day played over and over in my head and I couldn't find a way of making it go away. I couldn't tell anyone. I wished I could, but it was never going to happen. I told myself I just had to learn to live with it, that this was the only solution to my ugly problem. What more could I have done?

It never entered my head that that hideous day could repeat itself, but it did. It was like a mirror image unfolding before me: same scenario, going to work early, walking past the police station and Sam calling out to me. He acted as if nothing had happened. He spoke to me normally, treated me normally, until he said, 'Come inside for a minute.' I quickly told him no, I had to get to work, but he wasn't going to take no for an answer. Things got beyond my control, and I once again found myself inside that police station and back in the meal room.

This time I was determined that nothing was going to happen, and I tried my best to talk him out of doing anything to me. I told him that he could get me pregnant, as I was not on any contraception, but he just said he couldn't get me pregnant as he had had an operation. I didn't know anything about vasectomies then, and I was so sure I'd get pregnant that when I arrived home later that day I spent time in the toilet bashing the hell out of my stomach hoping I would bring on a miscarriage. Not satisfied with doing just that, I took a bottle of antihistamine tablets into the bathroom and decided I was going to end my life. There was no way I was going to bring shame on my family by having that man's baby. Even though I was only young, I still understood that he would be the type of man who would deny everything and I would never be able to prove the kid was his. I figured taking an overdose was the least painful way I had of ending my life, so take them I did.

I was so determined to end it all that I rushed the job, and instead of dying, I ended up choking on the first lot I tried to swallow (too many at once!) and consequently threw up everywhere. I was absolutely gutted at my pathetic attempt at suicide. All I could think about was how dumb I was and how useless — not only could I not stop this man from doing awful things to me, I couldn't even commit suicide properly. I hated myself so much after that. (A little while later I needed those antihistamine tablets, as I got a bad dose of hay fever. Trying to explain to Mum where my full bottle of tablets had gone was hard, but I managed to do it by lying, something I was getting good at doing.)

Bob Schollum turned out to be not as bad as Sam, but not far off either. Bob was the sort of man who could sell ice-cream to Eskimos. He had a way with people, and by that I mean he could smooth-talk anyone. It's probably why he was a good copper, able to defuse any situation by talking whoever out of doing whatever.

One day, I got thrown into our swimming pool, then a few others got thrown in, and then everybody ended up in the pool. As I was swimming to the side to get out of the mayhem, a hand went inside my bikini pants. I spun round and saw Bob smiling at me. I couldn't believe what had just happened, and it took me a minute to gather my thoughts and get the hell out of that pool. I was totally pissed off, as I never thought in a million years that Mr 'Nice' Bob Schollum would do such a thing. I guess it was pretty obvious to me then that Schollum and Brown were two peas in a pod. To cap it off, I was invited by the Schollum family to go to Ohope and holiday with them at a beach house. Despite the incident in the pool, I felt I couldn't say no because then I would have been asked why not. Why don't you want to go to the beach, a place you never get the opportunity to go? I was good at putting up a front when required, and I had to carry on doing that. I went, and I guess I can count my lucky stars that for the week or so that we were there, Bob only tried the hand in the bikini trick once.

Schollum finally left Murupara, as he had been transferred to Rotorua. In his place came a copper by the name of Trevor Clayton, with his wife Mary and their two preschool children. Trevor was a really quiet guy, to the point where I would say he was quite shy. His wife Mary was a neat lady, and the two little kiddies were just gorgeous. Trevor and his family became really good friends of my family, and in later years Trevor was a good mate of my brother Pete. Once Trevor got over his shyness, his personality really shone. There were a lot of laughs and happy times with him around. That man would have you in stitches, especially when he'd been drinking.

Unfortunately Sam Brown was still around at that time, and I was still having to beg him not to do anything to me. I was asked to babysit for the Browns on occasion, and at least twice Sam came home to 'pick something up that he had forgotten'. Once, he put a porn video on.

'Do you like what you see?' he asked me.

'No,' I replied. 'That sort of stuff doesn't interest me.'

Of course, what did and didn't interest me didn't matter to him. Sex took place, and even though I was telling him not to, he just kept on going. The fact that the kids were just down the hall in their beds meant nothing to him either, and that sickened me. What if they got up? I was panicking and trying to make him stop, but that didn't bother him either. This happened a couple of times, yet I could never say no to babysitting because Sam was sly. Rather than ask me direct, he would ring or see Mum and Dad and ask them instead.

Finally things got to the stage where I broke my silence and told Trevor what was happening and asked him to make Sam stop. Trevor just turned around and told me that there was nothing he could do, and that there was no point in trying to tell anyone else about it as they wouldn't believe me. I was crushed. I'd always thought of Trevor as a friend, and a damn good friend at that. I really thought that if anyone could help me, it would be Trevor.

Why Trevor then decided that he too could do what Sam was doing is beyond me. One night when I was babysitting for him and Mary, Trevor came home earlier than Mary, drunk but in good spirits. He started telling me about the party, saying that he and Mary had had an argument and that was why he had come home early. I listened to him for a while, then told him I was off to bed. I got up and was walking out of the lounge when he grabbed me by the hand and pulled me into his bedroom, which was across the hall. I pulled back and asked him what the hell he was doing, but he just grabbed me again and pushed me onto the bed. Once again, I found myself trying to keep bad things from happening, but it didn't matter what I did or said to him. He just did what he wanted, and once again there was nothing I could do. After he'd finished, he fell asleep and I just lay there trying to come to terms with what had just happened. Why did you do this to me, Trevor? What the hell did I ever do to you to make you hurt me like Sam does?

I got out of his bed, went to the spare room and just lay there in stunned silence. It was then that I heard Mary come home. She came into the house ranting and raving about Trevor leaving her at the party on her own. It sounded as though she'd had more than a skinful. She tried to rouse Trevor, but he obviously chose to ignore her. I then heard her go into the kids' room, then she came into mine. I held my breath, hoping and praying she wouldn't work out that I was still awake, because I was terrified that she would realise what had just happened. She pulled my door closed and I quietly sobbed into my pillow until I eventually fell asleep.

The next morning I didn't hang around to bump into Trevor. I just wanted to get the hell out. Unfortunately, Mary was up with the kids, but I told her I'd grab breakfast at home as I wanted to get organised early to ride my horse. I ran. The next time I saw Trevor, he acted as though nothing had happened. Was he that drunk that he didn't remember, or was he just ignoring the fact of what he had done? Whatever it was, he never said a thing about it, not even 'Sorry.' Some friend.

Once again, life for me just carried on. During this time, there were occasions where a relief cop would come when either of the others was away, or when a third cop was required to help out. Two of these policemen also abused me, but it was in the nature of groping. I can't say who they were because they are protected by name suppression. That doesn't particularly concern me, because their behaviour was not in the same league as Brown's. But it really made me start to wonder what was it about me that seemed to attract these animals. I wasn't doing anything around them that would suggest I wanted their attention. I never dressed to try to impress them. In fact, the only dresses I owned were part of my school uniform. For me, jeans and sweatshirts were what I was comfortable in, or shorts and T-shirts in summer. Didn't everyone else dress this way? Neither was I an overly attractive kid. I wasn't ugly, but hell, I wasn't the type of teenager who had the boys running after her either. I just wished over and over again that they would leave me alone and let me live a normal life like everyone else my age. But I knew my life would never be the same again, and I just had to try to keep myself as safe as I could. Mission impossible? Yes, as things stood. But surely, I told myself, it can't last forever. Can it?

Around this time, I heard that Sam Brown and his family were leaving

Murupara to take up a posting in Rotorua. This wasn't quite far enough away for my liking, but hell, it meant I stood a chance of never seeing him again. It was shaping up to be a good year. School Cert was looming, and I told myself that this was where I knuckled down and worked my little butt off so that I got good marks, moved on to the sixth form, got even better marks, then moved on to seventh form, Bursary and on to uni, where I'd study hard to be a vet. Yep, I had it sussed. I was going to put all that bad stuff behind me, even try to pretend it hadn't happened, and move on to a bigger, better, brighter future.

If I had foreseen how things were really going to pan out over the next six months, I would have taken Dad's gun, ridden my horse out to the back of Murupara, let the horse go, lifted the gun to my head and pulled the trigger.

Sam and Jane Brown turned up at our house one day just before they shifted into Rotorua. They sat at our dining-room table and came out with this heart-stopping suggestion to Mum and Dad, not even bothering to look at me as they spoke. I could go and live with them in Rotorua, they said, so that I could attend Rotorua Girls' High. What little self-worth I had left within, whatever remained to help me to heal myself of the scars left by those animals and move on, died as I listened. By the time they'd finished I knew that any chance I had of a better, brighter, normal future had also died.

I couldn't believe my parents were actually going to consider this dumb-arse notion. But consider it they did, and they pretty much told the Browns on the spot that it was a good idea. They told me they thought it was a brilliant opportunity to attend Girls' High, as it was better equipped to help me achieve my goal of becoming a vet. I told them that Rangitahi College was just as good, and besides, I would be leaving behind not only all my mates, but also my horse. They quickly pointed out that I would have the weekends to catch up with friends and to go horse-riding. I knew then that I was screwed. There was no point in fighting the decision any further as they would then start asking for the real reason why I didn't want to go. I wasn't prepared to tell them anything, as I knew that if Dad found out he would just take his gun and shoot Sam. Perhaps I should have told him.

In March 1983, I moved with the Browns into Malfroy Road, Rotorua. I had my own room right next door to the lounge. It didn't have a proper door on it, only a kind of vinyl bi-folding arrangement to screen it off. The rest of the family had their own bedrooms at the other end of the house. The bathroom and toilet were also at the other end, which was a nuisance if I needed to go during the night, as I didn't want to disturb anyone.

Jane became a totally different person from the withdrawn stay-at-home she'd been in Murupara, which was understandable as there was a lot more to do in Rotorua. She joined up with Judy Schollum and they would go off to Jazzercise and badminton together. I would walk to school with the Brown kids, as their primary school was just before the high school, about quarter of an hour's walk away. I would help around the house as much as I could — not that there was a lot to do, but I made the effort. I used to help the kids with their homework sometimes, but most nights I was in my room doing my own homework or just watching TV.

It wasn't long before Sam started up again. Several times when Jane went out for the night and the kids were in bed, he would start. One night he walked out into the lounge with just a short white towelling robe on. My heart just sank.

Even having a shower was a mission. There was no lock on the bathroom door, so Sam would just waltz on in. I remember one night he did this and, as he was fondling me, he kept putting his head out the window to see if Jane was on her way.

How do I get out of this? How do I keep myself safe? How do I get to go home? So many questions with no immediate answers, nobody to tell, no pillow big enough to cry into.

I lived for Fridays when, straight after school, I would head home to Murupara to my safety net. Sometimes Trevor would give me a lift. I bet he knew damn well what was going on, and on the odd occasion he would ask me how it was working out. I guess my silence answered that question for him, if he needed an answer. But mainly it was Dad who would come and get me, and then on Sunday he would take me back again, back to the lion's den!

I did come close to blowing Sam's cover. There was one time when I told Jane that I wasn't well and needed to go to the doctor. There was a doctor's surgery close by, so she booked me in. I don't really recall what I said to this doctor, but years later I was shown the notes he took that day. Apparently I told him that I'd been raped, but I said it had been by an 18 year old. I guess, thinking about it now, I was trying to let him know that bad things were happening to me, but I still felt unable to tell him the whole truth. I really do wish now that I'd had the guts to tell him everything and maybe, just maybe, he could have been the one to put a stop to it.

I only lasted in Rotorua for about two months. I'm not sure whether it was the size of the phone bills they were getting as I made call after collect call to Mum, or whether it was because I spent most of the calls going on about how homesick I was. Either way, it was decided I would return to my own home and back to my proper school, back to Murupara. The best day of my life was walking back through the gates of Rangitahi College with my mates. Everyone gave me stick about not being able to handle it in Rotorua — if only they had known how right they were — but I just played it down, telling them it was a dumb school and that I didn't like the town at all. That seemed to work.

I didn't really settle back into school as well as I'd hoped. My marks were down and my whole attitude had changed (mind you, I thought I had the whole 'act normal' thing down to a fine art). I didn't really put the effort in to helping myself and it was starting to show, so much so that my typing teacher, Mrs Radford, asked me to come and see her after class one day. Unbeknown to me, Mrs Radford was also the stand-in guidance counsellor. She sat me down in her little room, which was just off her classroom, and asked me if there was anything troubling me. She said she was concerned with my performance at school and at the obvious change in my attitude. I asked her what she meant, and she replied that before I went to Rotorua I was quite a bubbly, high-achieving, no-problem kid. Now she thought I had become the total opposite. She told me my grades were down, I didn't seem to want to make the effort any more, and my bubbly personality had disappeared.

I don't know why, but after all that time keeping everything bottled up, I just blurted it all out. I pretty well let her have it with both barrels. I told her everything about what Sam had been doing, and by the time I'd finished I don't know whether I was crying because the biggest burden ever had just been lifted from my shoulders, or whether I was hating myself for telling someone about all the bad things that had been happening to me — all the things that proved I was a bad person for allowing them to happen.

Whichever it was, I was totally shocked when she told me that she was going to help me. She said I should tell my parents, but I explained that this was one thing that simply couldn't happen. My dad would go nuts and do something bad to Sam. Of course, I was thinking more about the trouble my dad could get into than about the risk of Brown getting hurt. So we agreed that she would keep all I had told her between the two of us, but she did say that she needed to talk to someone who had a better understanding of this sort of thing, to help her to help me. I was OK with that. After that we met a number of times, and all I remember is that I felt a hell of a lot better for getting it off my chest.

Despite my wishes, Mrs Radford went ahead and told Mum. I wasn't privy to her decision, but when Mum approached me one night and asked me about it, I had no choice but to tell her. From what I remember, she wasn't angry or anything ugly like that, but I do recall her saying that Dad need not know. She obviously had the same fears as I did.

From there, things looked like they might get back to normal — or at least as normal as they could ever be. But then Mum decided to go and see Trevor and pass on what Heather Radford and I had told her. Like me, she thought of Trevor as a friend and, like me, she thought she could rely on him to help. But, once again, Trevor said there was nothing he could do, as nobody would believe me over Sam. The only course of action he wholeheartedly agreed with was keeping it from Dad.

It was some time after this that Mum received a phone call at work — it was Trevor, who asked her to come to the police station during her lunchtime. Sam was there and wanted to speak to her. Trevor wouldn't tell her what Sam wanted to talk about, but she had a pretty good idea. She hurried straight down. Sam handed Mum a letter that was signed by Jane Brown. Mum says she remembers reading the letter, but not being able to take it all in as Sam wouldn't stop talking while she was trying to concentrate. The only thing she recalls clearly is that Jane wrote that I had made accusations about Sam abusing me, and that Jane was satisfied it was a total lie. She said it was a young girl's imagination running away with her, and that she wanted Mum to know what I'd been up to.

When Mum had finished reading, Sam just leaned over and took the letter from her. That was pretty much it. Mum went back to work, not really comprehending what the hell had just happened, but she realised it was obvious she could do nothing about it. Basically, she was in the same boat as me: faced with Sam and Jane Brown's denials and Trevor Clayton's refusal to help, there was no way she was going to be believed. But we both wondered what it was with Trevor. Why wouldn't he help us? Was he frightened of Sam, or was it because Sam had something over Trevor? We'll never know. The answer got buried with Trevor a few years later.

Once again, I found myself just going through the motions of living a normal life. Nothing major happened for me, especially not my School Cert results. I had just enough marks to get into the sixth form, but definitely not the kind of marks in subjects like science and maths that I would need to go on to university. There was nothing I could do about it except knuckle down and try my hardest to get those subjects up to where they had to be, but I just didn't have the same drive as before. I had totally lost myself. It was as Heather Radford had said; I'd developed this don't-give-a-rat's-arse-about-anything attitude. Even while I still cherished the dream of becoming a vet, a big part of me was asking what was the point in busting a gut?

In 1984, things weren't looking too good for the timber industry. Redundancies were offered to workers at the Kaingaroa Logging Company. Dad decided to accept, and the decision was made to move out of Murupara. Mum and Dad put the house on the market and eventually it sold. Peter and Robert had by this time flown the nest. Robert was an electrician at the Tasman Pulp and Paper Mill in Kawerau, and Pete was working in the bush. Only Kevin and I were left. As I was still only 16, I had no choice but to pack up and go with the family. No worries — Mum and Dad made it sound like we were off on a huge adventure. They had decided we would move to Nelson. This sounded cool, as we got to go over Cook Strait on the ferry. They'd also decided that when we got there, instead of buying a house we would buy and live in a caravan. Oh, that sounded exciting! . . . sort of.

There was nothing left for us in Murupara, but when it was time to go, a lot — and I mean a *lot* — of tears were shed. Even though I was leaving the awful ghosts of my recent past behind, I was also saying goodbye to 13 good years. Goodbye to all my neat friends. Goodbye to my best mate, Dolly the horse. Goodbye — and good riddance — nightmares. For all it broke my heart, I decided it was a good move.

With no furniture and only our most precious keepsakes and the clothes in our suitcases, we set off. The trip over on the boat was cool, not least because this was the first time I was allowed to smoke in front of Dad. It had been OK with Mum for a while, so it was just a matter of the old man giving the nod. He just shrugged and said there wasn't a hell of a lot he could do about it if I was determined to smoke behind his back. It was a nod of sorts: good one, Dad!

At first, the South Island was promising too. After a few days in a motel, we found the caravan — a huge 26-footer — that we would call home. Mum and I went shopping for kitchen stuff, bed linen and pillows, food and a clothes dryer. It was like Christmas as we unpacked it all! We ended up moving the caravan to Motueka, where Dad got a job at a car plant. Mum got work around the campground where we were living. Kevin went to school, but as for me, there was no point in going to school, so I tried to find a job. No luck, so I went on the dole.

For a while life seemed fine except for the bloody weather. We all thought Nelson was meant to be the sunniest part of New Zealand. Not even — it rained all the time. It was an awful time for all of us. We stuck it out for four months, living in a steamy, stinky caravan far away from our family and friends, then everyone agreed it was time to go back to Rotorua to live. Dad organised a company to tow the caravan back for us, and it was pack-up time all over again.

It felt right being back in the Bay of Plenty, even if we were still living in a caravan park. Once I'd caught up with all my friends, I felt settled again. I managed to get a job at a local fruit and vege supermarket belonging to Clive, a bloke we knew from when he had run the café in Murupara. One of my co-workers, Carol Malaquin, was the sister of Tracy, one of my best friends from school.

The only thing I struggled to get used to was getting up early in the mornings. I started work at 6.00, so I had to be up and ready to leave the camp at 5.30. I would work until two in the afternoon. At first, Dad would give me a lift, but after a while I bought myself a 10-speed pushbike for $150 to save him the hassle. It had a light on the front, so there were no worries about biking in the dark.

Kevin went back to school at Rotorua Lakes High. Looking back now, I think Kev was the real casualty of the family shift from Murupara. His performance at school fell away, and he got caught up with a bunch of no-hopers and tended to get into a bit of trouble. Kev grew into a very caring young man — if ever anyone in the family needed help, Kev would be the first there with a shoulder to lean on or just to lend a hand — but the chances of him turning out so well looked pretty dim the morning after he didn't come home one night. Dad found him lying in a field near the caravan park, reeking of whisky.

During my time at K Market I managed to have fun. There were times when I would go out with my co-workers and have an absolute ball. I ended up on the checkouts, which meant no more early mornings, although it did mean getting home slightly later. My friend Tracy Malaquin started at K Market as well, and we decided to go flatting together.

Clive had a couple of flats down Meade Street, which is at the top of Rotorua's main street. Tracy had a little blue Morris car, so getting to work was no problem. The flat was thermally heated, which was so yummy. The only drawback was that it only had one bedroom, but we bunked down OK together. I had to learn to fend for myself for the first time, and I managed — even if I had to ring Mum one night to ask how to make cheese sauce for the cauliflower!

Tracy and I lived happily at Meade Street for about six months, until Tracy decided to move to Hamilton. It was back to living with Mum and Dad, but not in a caravan any more; by now they were renting a proper house. Dad had found a job as a security guard with Armourguard. He did a lot of night work, and decided to buy himself a German Shepherd pup. I'm not sure how serious Dad was about turning the puppy, Lisa, into a tool of his trade; I think he was just glad of the company during those long, lonely nights.

Through one of the ladies at K Market, I landed a job in August 1985 at the Bank of New Zealand. All I had to do was answer the phone and put the calls through to the right department or person. It also involved some typing, which made me really happy as I enjoyed that sort of work. I finally felt very important, and I figured I could climb the ladder with a job like this. The BNZ offered a lot of opportunities for those who wanted to grab them, and I definitely considered myself one of those people.

The past kept nipping at my heels, however. Around this time, I boarded with my brother Pete and his partner, Moana, in Pukehangi Road. Moana had some neat clothes that I would borrow and wear to work, and she could make the most mouth-watering hamburgers. Pete had become good mates with Trevor Clayton, and even though it reminded me of Murupara every time I saw him, I soon learned to deal with it. Trevor never said anything to me about what had happened there, and I sure as hell wasn't going to bring it up; it was as if we had this mutual understanding, a code of silence that we both knew had to stay that way.

Sometimes I would go out in town, either with friends from the bank or with Pete and Moana, and Bob Schollum would turn up with the Team Policing Unit. He and his cronies would swagger into the pub looking for anyone who was causing trouble, or for underage drinkers. Watching those cops walk around the pub as if they owned it was pretty frightening for me; it wasn't so much the guys who wore the uniform as the blue uniform itself. When Sam raped me at the police station in Murupara, he was wearing his uniform. Instead of seeing it as a symbol of protection, for me the police uniform stood for hurt, fear, intimidation — all the emotions you feel when you are in a frightening situation over which you have no control. The horrors of Murupara had happened five years earlier, but every time I saw that uniform the years just fell away.

Still, it was very important to me at that time to keep my emotions in check. I was determined that nobody would ever find out what happened, as I still felt that I was just as much to blame as those animals. So when Trevor Clayton stopped to talk to us I would be polite and talkative, and even have a laugh with him. Man, I was good at pretending these days! Schollum made it easy. He would always ask after Mum and Dad, and he never gave me any cause to want to run and hide. Same old smooth-talking Bob.

At work, I became very good friends with a woman named Tessa, who was the Dictaphone typist for the loans department. When I decided to return home to live at Mum and Dad's, it was Tessa and her husband Trevor who gave me a ride to work each day. Tessa and Trev were renting only 20 minutes' walk from Mum and Dad's, so on weekends I would wander up to see them. This is where I first laid eyes on Ross. Ross was Trevor's nephew, and I didn't actually meet him in person right away. I had to be content with drooling over his image in a family photo! When Tessa told me they were going to Ross's 21st one weekend I so wanted to go with them, but it wasn't going to happen. Come Monday morning, I pestered Tessa for details of the party so much that she finally said she could arrange for me to meet Ross at her place, if I wanted. I couldn't concentrate for the rest of the week!

It's so funny looking back at that day. I just cruised on up Old Quarry Road as if I was out on a mid-afternoon stroll. But when I got close to the house, I saw a white Escort 1600 Sport parked out front with its bonnet up. Leaning over the motor was Ross, wearing just a pair of shorts and with his hair tied back, looking every bit as good — if not better — than he did in the photo. I just went weak at the knees, but I managed to pull myself together enough to speak my first words to him.

'Gidday,' I said. 'Tessa home?'

Ross straightened up and faced me.

'Yep,' he said. 'She's inside.'

Man, I was in seventh heaven. From then on my life just got better with each hour I spent with Ross. I felt at ease, confident, slightly ridiculous, but so happy! The only drawback was that he drove stock trucks, which meant he was always working weekends. He would have to go to the yard on a Saturday if he was unable to get his truck cleaned on the Friday, and then most Sundays he would be carting stock to the works ready for Monday's kill. But once I really got to know him, he would invite me to go with him in the truck on Sundays. I really enjoyed these rides, as he would go all over the place — Napier, Hastings, Gisborne, Feilding — absolutely everywhere. I got to see places in the North Island that I'd only ever seen on a map. It was awesome.

Ross wasn't a pushy male wanting to jump into the sack every five minutes. In fact, what impressed me was that he was quite the opposite. We stayed the night at Tessa and Trev's on several occasions, and even though we slept together in the same bed, nothing would happen. The time came, though, when it finally felt OK for me to go that one step further. But when it came time for this wonderful moment to happen, I blurted out, 'Please be gentle! It's been a while!'

Ross looked at me strangely (as you would) and just said, 'Don't worry. I will. It'll be OK.' It was better than OK. That night was the first time I felt like a woman, a real woman.

While I was working at the bank, I became good friends with a girl who was about the same age as me. Sue Grant (not her real name) was also the girlfriend of Ross's mate, Matt. Sue was flatting on her own at that time, and we decided to look for a flat that we could share. She said that a friend of hers, Scott, was also looking to move into a place. We found a three-bedroom house on Corlett Street, within walking distance of the CBD, which was a real bonus for Sue and me as neither of us had a vehicle. So it was that we all moved in, and in no time we became very comfortable with each other's company. Scott was working at Pizza Hut and his hours included some nights.

I had no furniture to speak of, so Dad helped me to put a bedroom suite and a washing machine on HP. I'm not sure if we all put in to buy the second-hand lounge suite or if one of us bought it outright: either way, it wasn't long before we were comfy as. Not long after we moved in Sue picked up a second-hand car, a little brown Vauxhall Viva. It wasn't much to look at, but hey, it got us from A to B and back again.

Our landlady, Mrs Hodge, lived right next door. She was a very nice lady, but it was always in the back of our minds that she was right there, so we felt we had to be on our best behaviour. Not that we went in for raging parties or trashing the house, but we were always conscious of her presence.

In the summer of 1985/86, Ross and I headed off to Whangamata for a few days. Ross splashed out and bought me a beautiful muslin dress, three-quarter length with a beautiful embroidered bodice. It was scarily see-through, so I had to wear a petticoat with it, but I was so happy with him for buying this dress for me. I was so over the moon with it that I wore it everywhere, even to work. It cost him around $90, a lot of money back then, so I felt very spoilt, especially since it was something he was determined to do for me.

Still the past was snapping at my heels, and it was only a matter of time before it got hold of me and dragged me down again. While I was living at Corlett Street, I had the bad luck to be introduced to Brad Shipton and Clint Rickards. To this day I can't remember why, but a group of us from the bank were invited up to the police bar by Trevor Clayton. Trevor met us at the side entrance of the bank after we finished work and escorted us to the bar. Once we were settled in, he introduced me to a couple of cops — big, hard-bitten-looking men whose sheer physical presence was intimidating. My first impression was: 'Hell! Wouldn't want to meet you in a dark alley and piss you off!' It was the first time I'd heard the names Shipton and Rickards. I was also introduced to one of their wives; I'm pretty sure it was Sharon Shipton. Not much of a conversation developed beyond the usual niceties. That, as far as I was concerned, was more than enough. I just wanted to move away from that table. It wasn't only their size that put me on edge: I think it was more the way the pair looked at me. I put my discomfort down to being surrounded by a heap of those blue uniforms.

Not long after that evening, I was home alone one day when there was a knock at the door. I opened it, and there standing on my porch were Brad Shipton and Clint Rickards. This visit was the first of many. They came around for sex — sex I was not prepared to give them, but it soon became blatantly clear that I had no say in the matter. All the horrors of Murupara came flooding back and once again I was put into a situation over which I had absolutely no control. These men would turn up at my home, uninvited, on days when I wasn't at work. Whether it was because I was on leave or I was having a sick day didn't seem to matter. Somehow, they knew I was home on my own.

They would turn up either in a police car and in uniform or in a mufti car and in mufti clothes, usually suits. I was made to perform indecent acts on them as they performed indecent acts on me. I was by no means helpful — I wouldn't remove any of my clothing; they did that, taking off the bottom half of whatever I was wearing. As for them, well, they just downed their trou. The only thing that I freely offered on any of their visits was my objections. I was forever saying 'No, please don't do this, I don't want you to do this', but I might as well not have bothered. They just carried on doing what they wanted regardless. The only thing I was grateful for was that when they'd finished, they wouldn't hang around. They would quickly fix themselves up and leave.

There was only one time that I know of when they nearly got sprung. Ross had gone to the farm to get us a load of firewood and had done his back in using the chainsaw. He stayed that night at Corlett Street with me, and I took his car to work the following day while he took it easy. As he was resting on the floor of the lounge, he heard a knock on the door. He managed to get up and answer it, but was taken aback slightly when he saw Shipton and Rickards standing there. You'd be hard pressed to say who got the bigger surprise, but those guys composed themselves enough to ask Ross if Trevor Clayton was there. Ross told them no and they left.

In fact, Trevor would come around sometimes, but usually it was at night and most often after he'd been drinking. There was one particular night when he turned up quite late. Ross was staying as I was going to go for a ride in the truck with him the next day. Sue answered the knock at the door, and when I heard Trevor's voice I was up and out of bed and pulling on clothes that bloody fast. Ross stopped me and asked me why I was going out there. I told him I didn't trust Trevor with Sue and I needed to make sure she was all right.

I got out to the lounge and told Sue on the quiet not to get involved with Trevor or any other cop. I stayed up for a while, but it was pretty obvious three was a crowd. I went back to bed and, sure enough, the next morning Trevor's car was still parked out the front of the house. Sue hadn't heeded my warning. I felt sick, as I knew if she got involved with Trevor then those other two would probably start hanging around her too. I don't know if they ever did hurt Sue as well. I pray not.

It was like being back in Murupara all over again. I reached the point where I just couldn't take any more of what these guys were doing to me. Just like in the bad old Brown days, I decided my only hope was to tell Trevor and beg him to make them stop what they were doing. And just like in the bad old Brown days, Trevor came back with the same pathetic answer. 'I'm sorry, Lou,' he said. 'There's nothing I can do. No one will believe you over them.'

All over again, I was gutted that this so-called friend, so-called policeman, so-called human being could stand back and allow this stuff to go on. As far as I was concerned, it made him no better than them. I began thinking about taking my own life again, as that seemed like the only way out of the mess. But the difference this time was Ross. I loved him so much, and it was because I didn't want to hurt him that I put those dark thoughts aside. He didn't know it, but he was keeping me alive. I ached to be able to tell him what was going on, but I was scared that if I did he would decide I was a dirty bitch who was letting this happen and enjoying it — or that he would think I was nuts and wouldn't believe me either. Whichever way it went, I couldn't see how he would stay with me. Ross was the best thing that had ever happened in my life, and I wasn't prepared to kill that off.

So once again I had to put on my 'I'm all good, nothing bad's happening to me' face and act as if everything was normal.

One lovely January afternoon I was walking home from work. It was about 5.30, and as I wandered down Pererika Street, thinking about nothing in particular, I was brought back to reality by a car pulling up beside me. It was a tan Triumph, and sitting in the driver's seat was Bob Schollum. He got out of the car and leaned on the roof. Our conversation went like this:

'Hi, Lou,' he said. 'Where are you off to?'

I walked up to the car.

'Hi, Bob,' I replied. 'Just on my way home.'

This was the first time in a long while that I had actually seen and talked to Schollum, so we spoke for a wee bit and then he told me to get in and he would give me a ride.

'Nah, it's all right,' I said. 'I'm nearly there. It's not far.'

He insisted, and at that stage I couldn't see any reason why not. I got in.

We drove off down Pererika Street, turned left onto Old Taupo Road and drove straight past Corlett Street.

I turned to him.

'Where are we going?' I asked, trying to stay as calm as I could.

'I've just got to go to a mate's place,' he replied.

I felt pretty uneasy about this, but there was really nothing I could do. We turned down Rutland Street and I started to feel slightly better, as I wasn't that far from my own house. Just before we got to the turn-around area at the end of the dead-end street, Bob turned left into a driveway. As we pulled in I looked up at the house. There, standing on the balcony, were Shipton and Rickards. My heart just sank. I felt physically ill. I knew this was not good.

Bob told me to come in, but I said I'd wait in the car. Once again he insisted, telling me that we wouldn't be long. I knew if I got out of that car bad things were going to happen. I was in two minds, thinking, I can't go in, I just can't. But I was also thinking, what if I don't and I just make a run for it? Will they come after me?

All the while, Bob was telling me that everything would be fine and we wouldn't be long. It seemed as though I sat there forever before I finally grabbed the handle of the door, opened it and stepped out. Because Bob had said we wouldn't be long, I left my handbag, which had my cigarettes in it, in the car, as well as my shoes. Bob got out of the car and walked up the concrete stairs to the left of the house. I followed behind him like a lamb to the slaughter, my head hanging low, knowing I was in big trouble. Why don't I run? Why did I get in that car in the first place? Why the hell am I following him into this house, knowing damn well who's in there and what's in store? Because I'm bad, of course. I'm such a bad person. Once again, I'm in a situation I have no control over. Why not? I'm big enough to look after myself — I'm 18 years old, for Christ's sake! I can tell them to bugger off if I want! Well, why don't I?

I do tell them. I tell them I don't want them to do anything to me, but they won't listen. Why not? Because they're policemen, and they know I won't say anything because no one will believe me. That's it. They are cops.

I hate them with a vengeance. I want them dead. I want them to go to hell and let the devil do nasty things to them, and I bet they won't like it. I bet they will scream out for the devil to stop and I bet they'll beg and beg for him to stop just like I have to. Feel the fear, you bastards! Suffer the degradation, you bastards! Die, you bastards!

Someone, please, help me . . .

The kitchen was the first area of the house that I walked into, and it looked like any other normal kitchen. The house looked like any normal house, but I knew different. I knew this house was evil. I walked through the kitchen and into the dining room where someone asked if I wanted a drink. I said no, thank you. I needed my wits about me. Standing in the dining room and out on the balcony were Shipton, Rickards, Schollum and another man. Who's he? Do I know him? God, I can't remember if I've been introduced to him. Why is he here? What does he want? Is he one of them? I'm really screwed now — four against one. The odds aren't looking too good for me.

Oh, hell. Please, someone help me . . .

I go and stand out on the balcony. At least out there I'm not in the house and, hey, jumping over might be an option. Don't be dumb, Louise, you're too chicken for that. Now I'm being led back into the house by Schollum, through the lounge to the right of the dining room. I'm hanging my head again, I don't want to know where I'm going. I don't want to see anything. We enter a bedroom, a bedroom right by the lounge. The curtains are pulled closed. It's slightly dark, but not so dark I can't see a double bed and some drawers, and some stuff on the drawers.

I'm standing at the foot of the bed. Now I'm sitting on the bed. How did that happen?

Good, though, because Schollum is having trouble taking my dress off, my beautiful dress that Ross bought me in Whangamata. He's having problems and I'm feeling quite good about that. Oh, hell, it's off. My petticoat has been removed as well; there go my bra and knickers. Damn him, he's just dropped them on the floor — my beautiful dress that Ross bought me is just lying on that dirty floor getting all crumpled.

Verbal diarrhoea is starting to set in. I'm telling him I don't want this to happen, I'm begging him not to do anything, and then there's Shipton standing there with nothing on. This is so gross I just want to be sick. Go away, you bastards.

It's started, their bodies on top of me, sticky, sweaty, heavy, gross bodies, all taking turns. Bastards! Why is that man looking at me? Who the hell are you? Don't just stand in the doorway, you idiot, fucken help me! You sick bastard, you're enjoying this, aren't you? Who are you? Where the hell are you going? Don't go! Please help me!

Oh, Jesus. Rickards is beside me. What do you want? My head is spinning, I need to get out, but I can't. I feel like I'm suffocating. I need air. I want to scream at them, but the words won't come. I'm screaming at them in my head: you bastards can take my body, but you'll never take my mind, my heart, my soul!

Goddammit, they're not listening. Shit, how did I get up here? I can see everything. I'm looking down on them, and I can see the ugliness.

That man's back again. Why does he just stand there, looking? You're sick, mate. Go get a fucken life. Look at the mongrels, taking turns. They look like a pack of rabid dogs fighting over a chunk of meat. I don't want to pleasure them. I don't want that in my mouth — take it out! Oh, hell, I'm going to be sick.

Oh, my God. It's stopped. Is it over? What the hell's that? What the hell is Shipton going to do with a fucken baton? Oh, hell. No. No, please. I've got to keep telling him — keep screaming at him — there's no fucken way you're using that on me!

He's not listening. I've got to get off this bed. Oh, hell, I've hit the back of the bed. Please, wall, open up and let me out.

He's using it. It hurts, oh my God, it hurts so much. Get it out, fuckya! Get it out!

Don't cry, Lou. That'll probably annoy him. He'll stop in a minute . . .

It's out. It's over.

What are you doing? Why are you turning me over? You're kidding me! Please don't put it in there! You'll rip me open — oh, Jesus, the pain! Oh, dear God, make him stop! I'm going to die. I just know I'm going to die.

I'm crying uncontrollably now and begging Shipton to get it out, telling him I can't take it anymore. Then, out of the blue, Schollum just says, 'That's enough, guys', and that's it. It's all over. I slump onto my stomach and just lie there, sobbing.

'Go have a shower, Lou.' That's all Schollum said to me. I got off the bed, found my clothes still on the floor but more crumpled up. My beautiful dress that Ross bought me has been trampled by those bastards — no respect for my beautiful dress, no respect for me, no respect full stop. I followed Schollum down the hallway to the bathroom. He gave me a towel and then left. I closed the door, walked to the shower and turned it on. There was no hot water. I couldn't make it hot, and that made me angry, setting off a vicious little voice in my head. Dumb-arse taps don't work properly. I need the hot water to burn the ugliness off my body; I need to scrub myself raw so there's no more of them on me. But the hot water won't work. I really do wish I could stop crying. It's not doing me any good, I need to concentrate, I need to walk out of here alive.

I got into the cold shower anyway, because a cold wash was better than no wash at all so that I could feel even slightly human. I washed off what I could, but still it didn't make me feel clean. I turned the taps off, towelled myself dry, put on my underclothes, my petticoat and my beautiful crumpled dress. I just left the towel lying wet and cold on the floor and walked out of the bathroom, straight down the hallway, into the kitchen and outside.

Even the heat from that January sun couldn't warm me up. I was numb, and to this day I don't know how the hell I managed to walk unaided. All I knew was that I had to get the hell out and that I didn't want to set eyes on any of them again. I didn't want to know that these animals still existed. I walked down the concrete steps and to Schollum's car to collect my handbag and shoes. I was slightly taken aback when I found him already sitting in it. I opened the door, got in, and he started it up. He backed out of the driveway and, without even looking up at that evil house, he drove me home. I was so relieved that it was only a short trip. It was a silent trip, too, until he pulled into my driveway and stopped the car. As I gathered my handbag and shoes, he just said: 'Sorry, Lou.' I didn't flinch, I didn't stop what I was doing. I didn't look at him, I didn't answer him. As far as I was concerned, he no longer existed on this earth.

I walked away from that car, heard it back out, and without looking back I heard him drive off. What I did when I reached the door of my house is a blank.

All I know is that I am still here today.

The horrors of that day were still firmly fixed in my head a few days later when I answered a knock at the front door. Standing there, bold as brass as usual, were Shipton and Rickards. I just turned around and walked into the lounge. I politely asked them not to do anything. I must have sounded pathetic, but it was all I could muster, and I knew that anything I could say would be a waste of breath.

They just did what they'd come to do and left. There were several other 'visits' after that, and by that stage I had given up totally. My way of thinking then was the sooner they got in and did what they wanted, then the sooner they would leave. I just didn't have the strength to fight them anymore. I finally succumbed to the fact that they had won.

Phil

LISTENING TO THOSE INTERVIEWS FOUR years later, the line of questioning sounds just as it should have: detached, formal, clinical. For the legal safety of my newspaper, I tried to trick Louise to see if she would lie. I wouldn't have dared if I'd known Louise then as I know her now: she'd spit tacks if I asked her now whether there was any element of 'recovered memory' about her allegations. Personally, I've always thought that theory was pure psychobabble, with little or no basis in reality. No, Louise replied, her eyes blazing, she hadn't 'recovered' her memories at all. There was no need, as they'd never been away, much as she'd have preferred to forget them all through the years she'd bottled everything up.

'You don't want to remember things that have happened in your past,' she told my tape recorder, 'but they're always there.'

She was a strong, confident and credible informant. You could read the pain on her face as she spoke, and there were moments when she had to pause to control her emotions. Jim came into the room and sat quietly, occasionally chipping in with a date or a name. She smoked a lot, and fidgeted with cigarettes and a lighter. But there was no hesitation in her story beyond the occasional muddling of dates, and certainly nothing to suggest she was making it up or telling me what I wanted to hear. I remained vigilant, on the lookout for any discrepancy or telling contradiction. If I detected anything amiss, I was swift to challenge her on it. But Louise was unfazed. Some things — such as her claim to Trevor Clayton that she'd been raped by a group of Maori boys on horseback — were difficult for her to explain. But to me this didn't throw doubt on the substance of her allegations. On the contrary, they were more the kind of thing a frightened little girl would make up than the fabrications of a brazen and malicious liar.

The interviews that followed were sometimes disjointed, which had less to do with Louise's recall than with how tough it was to get to grips with the mess of information in the fat sheaf of documents I'd collected. My questions were peppered with extracts from statements, police job sheets and court transcripts. But the most cogent documents, where the real genesis of the Louise Nicholas story as we later broke it lay, comprised the two statements she made to Detective Inspector John Dewar in 1993.

I was by now taking great precautions with the evidence I was accruing. I locked one copy in my gun safe, and asked my parents to lock another copy in theirs. My parents were keen observers of the story as we pulled the threads together, and as we talked about what I knew of Louise Nicholas's childhood my mind often went back to the dream childhood I'd been given. The first 18 years of my life were split between my home in Malawi, in central Africa, and boarding school in New Zealand. My brothers and sister and I had an upbringing that you'd struggle to match nowadays. We were privileged. We lived the fantastic life of white Malawian children with our white friends. My parents, while cracking the whip during formal occasions, gave us freedom.

We lived alongside another slice of African life, and we also played, schemed and fought with and against black children whose daily existence contrasted starkly with ours. So I had seen the good and the bad in life, and by now I knew that what had happened to Louise was bad.

Louise

DESPITE ALL I HAVE BEEN through, I still find it strange that some victims of rape and sexual abuse go through life hating men, trying to have nothing to do with them — I guess really fearing them. I wasn't afraid of men. I was afraid of the uniform. By now, I feared anything that had any association with the police.

That's why it wasn't a problem for me to move into a two-bedroom flat with Paul, a guy who worked at the bank, after Sue and I moved out of Corlett Street. It was only for a couple of months, as Ross and I had decided we would find our own place and move in together. Another friend from the bank had a unit he was looking at renting out. Ross and I grabbed it and, with the help of our families, we moved in together. It was the first time since my early days in Rotorua that I'd felt settled, and it was the first time since I was 13 that I felt safe. The only problem we had was transport, so Ross went out and bought me a space-age motorised scooter. I would wear Ross's motocross helmet instead of buying one of my own. I thought I looked pretty good, but everyone at work gave me stick because Ross had written 'BEEP BEEP' on the back of the helmet in black marker pen.

I left the bank in August 1987, and managed to get an office job at Moore and Chapman Transport, where Ross drove trucks. It was different from the bank, and even though I still had phones to answer and sometimes radio-telephones — I got quite good at using the truckie lingo — the work was mainly debtors and creditors. Around this time, I took it upon myself to go out and buy an engagement ring. It took me a long time to pluck up the courage to ask Ross to marry me. I beat about the bush a bit, just dropping a few hints to see how the land lay, but after a while when I didn't get much to go on I decided, bugger it, I'll just ask. And ask I did. But I tell you what, it took me all my time to persuade him it was a good idea! I felt really bad pressuring him like that, but I had it stuck in my head that if I didn't marry him I was going to lose him. I couldn't tell him in so many words, but I needed Ross to keep me safe forever.

In the end he agreed, and we set a date for an engagement party. That was the best night ever! All our friends and families gathered together, and what made my night was when Lin, my father-in-law-to-be, got me up for a dance. Not that I could waltz, but hey, I gave it a bloody good go! It was a wonderful time for me, and nothing was going to spoil it. I put my nightmares into a box, locked it with a heavy-duty chain and stashed it out of sight and out of mind. It felt as though I finally had release.

Ross and I were married in St Michael's Catholic Church on 7 May 1988. What a day that was! My dad walked me down the aisle, and he made me feel like the most important person in the world. All our family and friends were there, and the day was made even more special when I took Ross's arm at the altar. When I looked at him, there were tears in his eyes. I knew then that our life together was going to be so special. It just felt right — nothing, and no one, was going to take it away from us. I knew I'd found my soulmate.

In October of that year I discovered a lump in my breast. I thought the worst and immediately made a doctor's appointment, only to be told that I didn't have breast cancer — I was pregnant! My first reaction was, 'How the hell did that happen?' Ross and I hadn't planned to start a family: in fact, we hadn't even got around to talking about that stage of our lives, as we were only just getting used to the idea of being married. Not that it threw a spanner in the works; it just made us think about the future sooner than we would have otherwise. On 30 July 1989 Jessica Frances Nicholas was born. Mum was present at the birth, which was a special time for both of us. Ross took the whole pregnancy and birth thing in his stride — it was as if he had done all this before! He was the proudest dad ever, and let everyone know it too.

At this time we were renting a house belonging to his parents, Lin and Phyllis. Lin had been asked to manage the Ruakura experimental farm, with which their property shared a boundary, and a house came with it. They decided to take it up, and Ross and I moved into their place. So this is where Jess spent her first year. Ross's sister Karen, who had been one of my bridesmaids, ended up moving into a house just down the road from us with her new partner, Stu, so I had a friend to yak to and also to help when things got too much.

Ross was still driving stock trucks. With Phyllis's help, I found a lady who would mind Jess for me, and I went to work with Karen at Barnetts Service Station. Ross and I were saving the best we could so that we could purchase our own home. In 1990, we purchased a lovely three-bedroom home in Martin Street — just down the road from Corlett Street.

How does that song go? Always something there to remind me . . . In May 1990, Mum and Dad told me my brother Rob had finally been accepted into Police College. He'd tried to get in a couple of years before, but he was too short. He was told that the police were soon going to remove the height restriction, and sure enough, as soon as it came off he was there waving his application form. Of course, I was in two minds about his career choice. I wished him all the best in whatever he chose to do, but I couldn't bear to see him in that uniform. Didn't he know it could turn him into an evil person? We were all invited to attend his graduation at the Police College in November. Mum, Dad, Ross and I headed down to Wellington, and I had to sit there surrounded by this sea of blue uniforms. How I kept it together is beyond me, but I managed it. I did it for my brother.

Ross and I had our second child a year later. Kerriann was delivered less than two hours after I awoke with sharp contractions in the wee hours of 14 October 1991. Ross called Karen, and by the time she arrived it was pretty much all on. My doctor arrived soon after, and I heard him doing his balls at the nurses for not getting him there sooner. Ross and Karen left, and all I remember is the nurse walking in and asking me if I was OK. The last thing I remember saying was, 'No, I don't think so.' The birth was hard and fast and I was spent at the end of it. I came around some time later with a whole bunch of nurses doing all sorts of things to me. Apparently I had haemorrhaged and lost a lot of blood.

Kerriann was such a placid baby, but I found I was having trouble coping. Some of it was Jess. I put it down to her age — the terrible twos and all that — and the adjustment I needed to make to get my head around being mum to two little ones as well as keeping house and looking after Ross. Karen came for lunch every day. I thought it was lovely having someone else there during the day, even if it was for only an hour — it never occurred to me that the family was worried about me and had their eye on me. I thought I was getting on fine.

We had other worries too. Ross had left Moore and Chapman to take up a job with Rotorua Forest Haulage, driving a logging truck. One day, after he'd been in this job about a year, I got the usual phone call from Ross to pick him up from work at 4.30pm. I thought something funny was going on when he loaded not only his smoko bag, but all his other gear in the car too. He wouldn't respond to my questions till we were nearly home. Then he told me that at 4.30 that morning he'd rolled his truck, and he'd been sacked. He'd tried to tell his boss that his trailer needed urgent maintenance done on it. Nothing got fixed, but he was still expected to tow it around loaded with logs. So when the springs broke as he drove around a corner, the whole unit rolled down the bank. The truck was a write-off. Thankfully, Ross wasn't injured, but he got the blame and the sack all at once. I was furious, and I was scared. What the hell were we going to do without his income?

Ross's dad Lin came to the rescue by giving him work on the farm. At that time there was an 11-week stand-down period before we were eligible to receive any government assistance to tide us over until Ross could find another job. Ross soon found another driving job with Terry Moore, but if it hadn't been for Lin and Phyllis, I really don't know what we would have done.

I suppose it was all taking its toll, and one day I had a very unusual conversation with Karen. Right out of the blue, she asked me if I was on drugs or hitting the liquor cabinet on the sly. No, I said. Why would she think a thing like that?

Her response came as a complete shock. She told me she thought there was something badly wrong with me and she was concerned for the kids. I dismissed her worries and insisted that I was perfectly normal. Who knows whether she was reassured, but I forgot about the whole thing.

Then, not long after Christmas 1992, Lin and Phyllis rang and asked if I would like to go with Lin on a trip to Feilding. His Auntie Maude, the sole surviving older member of his family since his mum and dad's recent deaths, had been staying with them and he was driving her back home. Phyllis said she would look after the kids for me. I thought it was a lovely idea, so off to Feilding we went. Lin and I stayed the night at Auntie Maude's, then we headed home the next morning. Lin and I yakked away as we drove, and then he just asked me straight out if there was anything on my mind.

So convinced was I that I presented a front of perfect normality to the world that I wasn't sure what it was he was asking.

'No,' I said brightly. 'Everything's fine.'

He took his eyes off the road for a moment and I could see the worry in them. He told me the family was anxious, and that I seemed different somehow. This conversation went on for a bit — him probing, me insisting everything was fine — and then we pulled over for a cup of tea. Perhaps he sensed I was on the brink of opening up. It was then that I told Lin about what had happened to me in Murupara and Rotorua. Just like that. I let it all out. I didn't go into all the gory detail, but I did tell him who it was, where it happened and that a baton had been used. Whatever he was prepared for, I don't think he was expecting what he got.

The trip home seemed a lot quieter after that, with Lin asking only the occasional question, or making the odd comment here and there. It was as if he was trying to come to terms with what I had just told him, and that he was struggling with it all. Perhaps he was wondering whether to believe me. I don't blame him at all. To sit there and listen to all that would have blown anyone's mind. I felt the same as I had felt when I'd opened up to Heather Radford all those years ago: part shame, part terror, part joy at sharing the burden.

Lin must have believed me in the end, because he suggested that we all needed to decide where I should go from here. A family meeting was called, which included Lin, Phyllis, Ross and me. Everyone agreed I needed expert help, even — especially — me, because suddenly I understood what it was Karen had been driving at when she'd mentioned her concerns. It really made me stop and take a long, hard look at what I was really like within and how I was beginning to let the past affect me without realising it.

This was the first time I'd told Ross what had happened to me. I was terrified of how he would react — maybe he'd decide I was a bad person when he learned of all that had gone on, some of it since we'd been together, and leave me. True, Ross was absolutely gutted, but only because I hadn't told him while it was all going on. As I tried to explain to him, there was no way I could have done that, as I was so afraid he would try to do something about it. My fear was that he could get hurt by these guys. I had to explain to him why I did things that even I was having trouble dealing with.

Even though he was angry at me for keeping it all from him, he did say that he now had an understanding of why I was not the same person that he had first met. He said: 'You know, missus, I just thought that you had a bolt that got loose every now and again because of the kids. I guess now I know why it got loose. You need to remember that I'm still here to help tighten it.'

He couldn't have put it better. He was so right. I had felt like I was losing it, and had just put it down to being a mum. It was a huge release to finally be able to tell Ross the whole sordid story and not have him judge me or hate me. That decision to open up to the people who loved me was the beginning of the long road back from a very dark place.

So off to my doctor's I went, and there I was given the name of an ACC counsellor who I hoped would help me deal with the past. I was uncomfortable with the first woman I spoke to. I don't know what it was, but I decided to go back to the doctor and see if he could suggest someone else. He found someone I could talk to properly, and the counselling continued.

I'm not sure who suggested that I should take things further, but after discussing the options with the family, I decided I would talk to someone within the police and tell them what had happened. Dad, who now knew some of what had happened, said he'd contact Ray Sutton. He'd had a fair bit to do with Ray in the Murupara Search and Rescue days, and he trusted him. In January 1993 he arranged for Ray to visit me at my parents' home. Ross was working and couldn't come, but I think that was a good thing, as there was still a lot of stuff I hadn't told him. I didn't want him to hear it that way.

I was sitting in one of the La-Z-Boy chairs and Ray was seated at the dining-room table. Mum and Dad were both present, and as Ray opened up his black police notebook and readied his pen, I started. I told Ray the events in sequence, basically starting with what had happened with Sam Brown in Murupara, then moving on to what he had done in Rotorua while I was boarding with him and his family. I don't recall whether I told Ray about the other policemen who had abused me, the men who are now dubbed the Murupara Four, but I did tell him about Shipton, Rickards and Schollum and what happened in Rotorua, which of course included Rutland Street and the baton.

Even though my parents knew that bad things had happened, I had never until that day gone into any great detail. I must say that I was still not prepared to go right into it with Ray, but I gave him more information than I had ever given anyone else. Mum and Dad were hearing a lot of it for the first time. I couldn't look at them while I was talking to Ray, but every now and again Dad would ask me to repeat what I had just said, and then just stare at me in absolute disbelief. As for Mum, well, on the odd occasion that I glanced her way, I knew she was just dying inside. She was just sitting there with the most awful blank expression on her face. But I had to try damn hard to ignore all that and tell Ray as much as I could. So, for about an hour, as I talked, Ray wrote, stopping only to ask me a question every so often. When I had finished Ray closed his notebook and put away his pen. Then he told me to take a few days to discuss with my husband and family where I wanted to go from here. It was my call, he said, either to continue to deal with my past through counselling, or to take the matter further and, with his help, lay a formal complaint with the police. I told him I would contact him through Dad and let him know my decision. Ray then left, and the silence that followed was unbearable.

Later, after I had talked it over with Mum, Dad, Ross and his parents, I decided I was interested in taking it all further. I hadn't even told Ray all the details of what had been happening over the last 13 years, but he assured me it was enough to go ahead and lay a formal complaint. With his help, an appointment was made to see the head of the Sexual Abuse Squad, Anna Cummings. It was arranged that I would meet Anna at the Rotorua Police Station, and after giving myself a stern talking-to I reached deep down within myself and managed to find the courage to walk into that place.

I asked for Anna at the front desk and, after some time — it seemed to take forever — she appeared. She seemed rather agitated, and promptly told me that she didn't have time to see me as something had come up that she needed to attend to immediately. She then said that she would contact me to arrange another time. I must have looked totally stupid just standing there staring at her. It took a while before I gathered my wits enough to say 'Fine', and to turn around and walk out. Who knows whether I would ever have plucked up enough courage to try again. But as it turned out, it was only a matter of days later that I received a phone call from the head of the Rotorua CIB, Detective Inspector John Dewar.

My first impressions of Dewar, when talking to him over the phone, were that he sounded nice enough and that he appeared to be taking me and my reasons for wanting to lay a complaint seriously. He asked me if I would like to bring someone along for support while I was making my statement. This seemed a good idea, as the thought of going back into that police station, even for this purpose, was making my stomach churn. I told him I would ask my mother, and she was happy to do this with me. We arranged to meet in his office on 28 January 1993.

When I phoned Dad to tell him that this Detective Inspector Dewar had phoned and that we had arranged a time to meet, he was impressed. For me, rank meant nothing, but, as Dad said, it must have been considered serious for such a high-ranking cop to be taking over. We all had a lot to learn about the police back then.

Mum and I went into the station on the appointed day and asked for Dewar. We weren't kept waiting long, but I tell you now, the walk to his office is one that I will never forget. It was like walking through a rabbit warren — upstairs, along corridors, continually walking past uniforms. I felt extremely intimidated, and oh so vulnerable, and I don't think I would have gone through with it if Mum hadn't been there beside me. At no stage did I look ahead — I just kept my head down and watched the back of Dewar's shoes. Every now and then I would hear people we passed acknowledge Dewar. All they would say was 'Sir'.

Eventually we arrived at his office, and the most sickening feeling came over me as we entered the room, because sitting smack bang in the middle of the front of his desk was a bloody baton. This polished piece of wood was mounted on a stand with something engraved on it. I sat down before I fell down, and it took me a minute or two to get the ugly thoughts out of my head. I wanted to look everywhere but at that object, so I looked around his office. It was large, with what appeared to be police memorabilia scattered all over the place. The room felt quite cluttered with all that stuff in it. I guess top coppers tend to accumulate mementoes and guff as they move up the ranks.

Dewar explained to me that he'd spoken with Ray Sutton, and that Ray had told him about what I had said when he saw me at Mum and Dad's. He then explained that he, not Anna, was taking my statement because of the seriousness of the allegations I was making, not only against ex-cops, but also against serving members of the police.

He then asked me to start from the beginning and tell him about what had taken place in Murupara with Sam Brown. This I did, and as I spoke he wrote down what I was saying on a writing pad. Every so often he would stop me and ask questions, or he would ask me to repeat myself. The whole business of taking my statement went on for about two hours, but by the end of it I felt I'd told him all that had gone on in Murupara, as well as in Rotorua while I was boarding with the Browns. I did it to the best of my memory. Towards the end, I told him that bad things had happened to me with other cops in Murupara, but not in a lot of detail. I also told him about the Rutland Street incident concerning Shipton, Rickards, Schollum and the baton. Dewar listened, but told me that we would just concentrate on the Brown matter for now. He said that we would look into everything else that I had told him later on. OK, I thought. One step at a time seemed to make sense.

Dewar left his office for a while, leaving Mum and me there on our own. I remember making some smart-arse comment about the baton on his desk, and Mum asking me if I was OK. There was not a lot I could do about that baton being there: it was just a matter of trying to ignore it. Dewar returned with the statement that he had taken from me all typed up, asked me to read it through then, if I felt that it was OK, I was to sign it. What I read appeared to be what I had told him, so I was happy enough signing it.

Looking back through that statement today, I'm thinking of the length of time I was in his office giving that statement, recalling in graphic detail all that Brown put me through, and it just doesn't seem possible that two and a half years of hell can be typed out onto five sheets of A4 paper.

A matter of days later, I was sitting in front of Dewar and that damn baton again. I had phoned him to say there was another incident that had occurred in Murupara with Brown that I had forgotten about, and I'd like to make a statement about it. Mum didn't come with me this time. Even though the thought of wandering through the rabbit warren past all those uniforms to get to his office spooked the hell out of me, I told myself that I needed to get hard, I needed to learn to face my fears. On February 2, 1993, I told Dewar about an incident that had happened while I was babysitting Brown's children. Again, Dewar wrote down what I said, questioned me on certain things, then wandered off to get the statement typed up. He again asked me to read it and, if I was OK with it, to sign it. I left the police station feeling like I was finally achieving something for myself and maybe, just maybe, this was the beginning of the end of the whole nightmare for me.

Everyone agreed counselling was not a success in my case. My doctor decided to refer me to a psychiatrist, Dr G. Newburn. In a covering letter, he explained that I felt counselling was not helpful and that the drug Prothiaden, which he had prescribed me, wasn't doing much for me either. The reason the drugs didn't work was because I didn't take them. Ever since my overdose attempt when I was 13, drugs and I did not mix. I steered well clear of them, because I guess I didn't trust myself if the going got tough; and at this stage, things were getting really tough. My doctor also explained in his letter that he was concerned with how thin I was, with my heavy smoking and my drinking substantial amounts of coffee — coffee and tobacco were my staple diet at this point. I had lost some 5 kg over the last four months, so at this stage, at the age of 26, I weighed just 45 kg. The doctor even referred to this as anorexia, and said he would be glad of Dr Newburn's assistance.

I sat down for a consultation with Dr Newburn on 9 February, but it quickly became clear to me that he wasn't going to be much use to me either. I have the letter he sent back to my doctor, in which he tells me what we all knew — I was a quivering mess — and that he thought the answer was a new wonder-drug for depressed people. I didn't rely on his drugs at all, simply because I didn't trust them or myself. I don't think I ever went back to Dr Newburn: I don't recall sitting down with him again, and I have no other notes to suggest that I did.

While all this was happening, I was being kept informed by Dewar about how his investigation was going. On about 15 or 16 February he phoned to inform me that he was heading down to Napier to interview Clayton and Schollum, then he was heading on to interview Brown. He didn't mention anything about the possibility of arrests, so it was a big surprise when he phoned me while he was driving back to Rotorua to tell me he'd arrested Brown and charged him with 'Sexual Intercourse with a Girl Under Care and Protection'.

I was totally speechless, and it took a moment to comprehend what it was that he had just told me. When I pulled myself together, I asked him how the interviews had gone. He sounded really pleased with himself, especially when describing Trevor Clayton's reaction to his taping the interview.

'The look on Clayton's face as I tapped my suit pocket was huge,' he said. 'He was obviously not a happy man after that.'

Dewar was clearly delighted with himself over the whole interviewing saga, and especially the arrest of Brown. After talking to Dewar I immediately phoned Dad and told him. He was somewhat surprised but, as you can imagine, also ecstatic. I was stoked too, but I was also left feeling there was something not quite right. It all seemed pretty quick. What evidence — and I mean hard evidence — did Dewar have that enabled him to suddenly turn around and arrest Brown? When I told Dad of my nagging doubts, he said that Dewar obviously had enough to go ahead with.

'Remember,' he said, 'he's a Detective Inspector, so he knows what he's doing.'

Well, who was I to argue? And after all, this was the reason for coming forward in the first place: to put the man who had raped me before the courts.

On 15 March 1993, I was admitted to hospital complaining of vomiting and headaches. The doctors checked me out, and apart from noting that I was very thin, they reported that medically everything else was fine. In their report they noted that I had been under a lot of stress in my personal life of late, and that I was having treatment for depression. I was kept in overnight for observation, but discharged the following day feeling OK, just so damn tired. I was trying desperately to keep everything at home running normally. Jess was in kindy by now, which made things easier. Kerriann was a much more contented baby and easier to keep amused, so I found myself with more 'me time'. This was a good and a bad thing, as I found myself with more time in which to stew about how things were going to pan out.

This only got worse after John Dewar informed me that a date had been set down for the depositions hearing. I had my first day in court on 4 June.

As the big day drew nearer, Dewar explained to me how a depositions hearing worked. It's very similar to a court case, he told me, but before the case is heard in front of a judge and jury it has to be determined whether or not the police actually have a case for the accused to answer. He told me I'd have to take the stand and tell two Justices of the Peace what had happened to me in Murupara and Rotorua with Brown, and that Brown's lawyer would then have the right to ask me questions about what I'd said. Didn't sound so difficult, I thought. Apparently I would give evidence first, then my mum, and then Mrs Radford, my typing teacher from Rangitahi College.

My nerves became really frayed. I had a lot of contact with Dewar as the day approached, lots of phone calls, and he often visited me at home. I never really stopped to consider how Ross was feeling through all this, though i knew he had his doubts about Dewar. I told him things as they unfolded, but never really asked him what he thought or how he was coping. I was so caught up in the whole process that I couldn't see how it might be affecting Ross until it was nearly too late.

Finally 4 June 1993, the day of the depositions hearing, arrived. With the butterflies fluttering away inside me, I took the stand in the courtroom where the Justices of the Peace were seated, along with the police prosecutor. The hearing started with the police prosecutor asking me questions about Murupara, and from there I just told him what Brown had done, which included what had gone on in Rotorua. Once the police prosecutor had finished asking me questions it was the turn of Brown's lawyer, Les Atkins QC. The questioning started off OK with what felt like small talk. But then he threw a question at me that totally bowled me over. He asked me if I had been picked up by a group of police officers and then whether they had taken me to a house and a baton used on me. I tried to say that that incident had nothing to do with the Brown business we were here to discuss, but he was like a pit bull and wouldn't let it go.

While I was still reeling over that line of questioning, he switched tack and asked whether I'd ever claimed to have been raped by 'five masked men on horseback'. I put him straight on that incident — I'd once complained, at Dad's suggestion, to Trevor Clayton that a bunch of Maori kids had made smutty remarks to me when I was out riding — but he insisted on asking me whether I'd said at the time they'd raped me. I was totally bemused by his approach.

It wasn't long after this that Atkins finally said he had no further questions for me, which I must say came as a huge relief. When I had time to sit and think about what I'd been asked, it became pretty clear that something untoward had gone on. How on earth did Brown's defence know anything about me being picked up by cops and taken to a house? The details were wrong, but it was too similar to the Rutland Street rape to ignore.

During the lunch break John Dewar, Mum, Dad, Mrs Radford and I went to the Steakhouse for lunch. As we sat there, I was going on about the crap that Atkins had brought up. Only I, my family, Ray Sutton and John Dewar knew about Rutland Street. How did Atkins get hold of the information? Dewar said Trevor Clayton must have told Brown, but that didn't ring true. That's when I first had an inkling that Ray Sutton's police notebook, the one in which he had written all the information I had told him, had fallen into the wrong hands. I also wondered where he'd got the bullshit concerning 'five masked men on horseback'. I was laughing at the stupidity of it, and I didn't notice Heather Radford looking sick.

It wasn't until some time later that Dewar told me Mrs Radford had pulled him to one side after that lunch and explained that when she'd first heard my complaint about Brown, I had also told her I'd been raped by some Maoris on horseback. She told Dewar she didn't believe me at the time. She felt that I'd sort of 'thrown it in' at the end because I was afraid she wouldn't believe me about what a policeman had done, but she might believe me about what some Maoris on horseback had done. It sounds far-fetched, but who knows why else I'd said it? After all, Trevor Clayton had said no one would believe the truth, so perhaps I felt obliged to make up something that people would believe. In all honesty, I have absolutely no recollection of that part of the conversation taking place. I don't remember ever saying it, but obviously I did, as Mrs Radford had no reason whatsoever to lie.

The depositions hearing only lasted a day or so, and despite Atkins's questions from left field, the Justices of the Peace decided there was a prima facie case to answer. A trial date was set down for 6 December 1993. I was relieved, as I thought the Justices of the Peace had seen through the defence's bullshit. Before I could get too carried away, though, Dewar told me it was pretty rare for them not to send a case up for trial, as they really don't have the experience a judge has to make any other decision. I wouldn't hear a word against them. As far as I was concerned, they were legal geniuses and they did a great job!

With all my experience of living a double life, I was in danger of becoming two different people. I was having awful nightmares, I was depressed a lot of the time, and when I wasn't depressed I was so irritable that I would fly off the handle at the slightest pretext and throw things around.

I was referred to a senior clinical psychologist by the Rotorua Victim Support Group. The notes confirm I told him I was going through a hard time, as the depositions hearing hadn't gone as well as I'd hoped. The psychologist thought I might be suffering from post-traumatic syndrome, and looked at providing me with support and therapy. Yet I pulled out of the sessions almost immediately, telling myself nothing was wrong and I could cope alone.

I think my problem with therapy and all the professionals who were trying to help me was that I hated being told what to do, where to do it and how to do it; I preferred to try to fix things on my own. Looking back now, I believe that had a lot to do with the abuse. I couldn't shake the feeling that what had happened to me was somehow my fault, and if I was responsible for it, only I could fix the hurt inside.

Then in September, a couple of months after the depositions hearing, I had my first counselling session with Margaret Craig. I have no real recollection whatsoever of what was said, but I had 20 sessions with her. I felt extremely comfortable talking with her. I do know that there was one significant session on 10 November, one that involved John Dewar. I remember Dewar picking me up from my home and taking me to Margaret's. Her notes state that one of the matters Dewar wanted to work through was 'consensual sex', and she recorded his interest in sorting the numerous incidents I had reported into 'consensual' and 'non-consensual' categories. He seemed intent on getting across to me that

I needn't discuss any episodes of consensual sex that had occurred; I should just focus on the incidents where I had not been a willing party. He seemed concerned that I might be too embarrassed to admit that some of what I was alleging was actually consensual.

As she gently tried to make clear to me at the time, Margaret felt he was missing the crucial point of all that had happened to me. Her knowledge and training assured her that the type and extent of abuse I reported could not be considered 'consensual', given the background. I was still a child when the abuse began, and it was on a child's deference to adults that my abusers had been preying. But back then I wouldn't hear a word against Dewar. I was relying on him to make things right — after all, he was the first cop I had ever known who hadn't hurt me, who seemed to believe me and appeared to be on my side. That's why I pretty much ignored other people's views about him, including Ross's and eventually Margaret's. I couldn't see past what I thought was a genuine determination to see a bad man like Brown go to jail.

Phil

I WAS READING THE COURT file almost a year later when I began to get a sense of the game Detective Inspector John Dewar was playing. I also had a set of medical notes that included a record of the counselling Louise was receiving before and after the depositions hearing. Louise told a clinical psychologist a week before the hearing that she was feeling positive about giving evidence. A week after, her mood had changed dramatically. The notes indicated that she'd been given a grilling on allegations that had nothing to do with Brown. The psychologist reported that Louise had been caught out telling 'untruths', and he observed that she was now on the verge of giving up on efforts to see the case through. He also recorded Louise's wish that he talk to Dewar, a certain sign of how heavily she was relying on the senior policeman. Dewar confirmed to the psychologist that 'she was given a fairly rough time at the depositions . . . which she didn't handle well'.

For all Louise's obvious faith in Dewar, I smelt a rat. What the hell was she doing giving evidence in person at the depositions hearing anyway? Sexual-abuse complainants are not required to give oral evidence at depositions. Their evidence is usually presented in written form, and it's incredibly rare — and only allowed at the discretion of a judge — for complainants to give evidence in person until they get to trial. But Dewar had told Louise she was obliged to give evidence in person. He was wrong, and it is inconceivable that a policeman of his rank didn't know he was wrong. So why did he do it?

Only Dewar can answer that, but I began to suspect he had something else in mind other than nailing Sam Brown for rape. It very much appeared that he intended killing two birds with one stone — securing the failure of the case against Brown, and the increased likelihood that nothing would ever come of Louise's baton-rape allegations against the Rotorua trio. By persuading her to front up to the depositions hearing, he exposed Louise to a sustained attack on her credibility by Les Atkins QC, then a highly skilled defence lawyer and now a judge. And, somehow, that attack was armed with an array of potentially damaging information. Somehow, Atkins had learned details of the Rutland Street incident, and he also knew that Louise had complained to Brown's mate, Trevor Clayton, about some Maori boys.

So how did Atkins know all this? The missing Ray Sutton notebook might have had something to do with it, but it's more likely that Trevor Clayton was the source of the information. He had received Louise's complaint about the 'Maoris on horseback' in Murupara, and he had also received — as he hinted to Dewar in their interview — her account of the Rutland Street incident. He was Brown's mate, and had declared his willingness to lie to protect him.

However they had got hold of it, it was fertile ground for the defence to traverse and, thanks to Dewar's faulty advice, Louise got her first taste of what rape complainants face in the witness box. Contrary to what Dewar told the psychologist, she actually handled it brilliantly, given that Dewar had convinced her of the need to steer clear of the Rutland Street episode.

The burning question, and one to which we'll never know the answer, is whether Dewar knew what lay in store for her when she faced up to Atkins at the depositions hearing. If he was hoping, as I strongly suspect, for a win-win — the acquittal of Brown and the burying of Louise's allegations against Shipton, Schollum and Rickards — it's hard to imagine a better way of going about getting it. Louise was made to look unreliable, and the baton-rape incident was placed on the court record for Brown's lawyers to use at the forthcoming trial if her case survived depositions. And he must have had a pretty good idea of how great the chances were that, given a taste of what was to come in the District Court, Louise would walk away from the whole thing.

Louise

JUST PRIOR TO THE START of Brown's trial, I had my first meeting with the Crown Prosecutor, John McDonald. Mum, Dad, Ross and I met at the Rotorua Police Station, then John Dewar and I walked to McDonald's office. He explained how he was going to run our side of the trial, and a little bit of what I could expect from the other side. I was nervous as hell.

The trial got under way on the morning of 7 December 1993. The first part was taken up with the lawyers outlining their cases to the jury, and we were excluded from the courtroom for this phase of things. My family and I had been allocated a little room where we could sit, make coffee and smoke up a storm while waiting for our turn in the box. You could have cut the air in that room with a knife, and not just because of all the smoke.

Eventually, the Clerk of the Court leaned in and called my name. He showed me into the courtroom, where I saw the judge — Judge Paterson — and the 12 members of the jury, as well as Atkins and Sam Brown. My evidence was to be heard in a closed court, which I was relieved about. I didn't really want my family to hear the awful details, and I knew that I would probably get emotional, which could upset them. I was, however, allowed a support person in court with me, and I'd asked my sister-in-law, Karen, to be that person. Thankfully, she said yes. She wasn't allowed to say or do anything other than hand me a tissue or a drink of water if I needed them, but just having her sit there close to me was really comforting.

I was extremely nervous about giving my evidence, going through the explicit details of what had happened in Murupara in front of these complete strangers. Even worse was that Brown was sitting there right in my line of sight, shaking his head or making stupid little noises every time I said something about what he had done. And I was right: I did get emotional when telling the court about what had happened to me, especially the incidents at the police station.

I had spent the best part of 13 years trying to escape from that meal room, and now here I was deliberately going back there, for the benefit of the jury. That was one of the hardest things I've ever had to do, as I could see, hear and even smell all the bad things that had happened in that room. No wonder it upset me, but I did it, and once I'd finished my account of events a huge wave of relief swept over me. For a fleeting moment, I felt I could definitely start to heal.

But then Les Atkins stood up and started questioning me. I was braced for the worst, but he didn't bring up the Maoris on horseback nonsense, and he didn't bring up the Rutland Street incident either. All he did really was call me a liar. In fact, throughout his questioning, everything he said was accompanied by the words, 'and I suggest to you, Mrs Nicholas, that you are lying', or, 'I suggest to you that this is total fabrication, a fantasy . . .' and so on. All I could say in reply was, 'No, Mr Atkins. I'm not lying', 'No, Mr Atkins', 'No', and so on and so forth.

Once I had given my evidence, I was allowed to take my seat in the public part of the courtroom, where my friends and family and a few other people I didn't recognise — Brown's friends and family, I suppose — were sitting. It was now Mum's turn in the box. Under John McDonald's questioning, she spoke about the meeting where Heather Radford had passed on what I'd told her, and about the day the Browns turned up at our home to suggest I go to board with them in Rotorua. She then talked about the meeting she had had with Brown at the police station where he had presented her with the letter Jane had written but then taken it back off her. When McDonald had finished, it was Atkins's turn. His questions were nothing much at first, but then he asked one that totally bowled Mum over. He circled around it, getting her to say yes, she was a bank teller at the Murupara Trustbank for several years, and yes, her boss there was the branch manager, Noel Johnson, and yes, they had a good working relationship, and yes, she was working there at the time the Browns approached my parents to see if I would board with them in Rotorua.

'And is it true,' he then asked, 'that you were having an affair with Mr Johnson at this time?'

I wished I'd had a camera to capture the look on Mum's face!

Noel and his wife Sandy were good friends of Mum and Dad's, and would on occasion socialise with them, either at our place or at theirs. Mum categorically denied any sexual relationship with Noel and told Atkins it was the most ridiculous thing she'd ever heard.

She was fuming when she came out of that courtroom.

'That bastard! That mongrel bastard!' she was muttering. 'What a load of rubbish that is! Where does he get off, coming up with rubbish like that? I never had an affair with Noel Johnson! I wouldn't even contemplate doing anything like that with that man!'

Dad and I did our best to calm her down. It was important that we didn't let them upset us, we told her. She'd told the truth, and that was all that mattered. It was clear, as Dad told her, that Brown was running scared, and this was all part of a ploy to make our family look dysfunctional — Brown had tried to do something similar at the depositions hearing by saying that Dad was an alcoholic — so that the jury would think: look at her family, poor Louise was bound to end up flaky. It took Mum quite a while and a good few fags and cups of coffee before she calmed down.

Mrs Radford gave her evidence after Mum, and then Dewar took the stand to give his. Dewar was impressive as he went through his evidence, as you'd expect a professional copper would be. Then suddenly, right in the middle of it, Atkins got to his feet and objected to something Dewar was saying about Clayton. Judge Paterson ordered the courtroom to be cleared so that counsel could speak to him in chambers.

We sat in our little room wondering what the hell was going on. Next thing we knew, John McDonald was there telling us that the trial had been aborted.

'What? What does that mean?' I asked.

'The judge has abandoned it,' McDonald said. 'He's discharged the jury, and we're going to have to come back and do it all again.'

'Again? Why?' I wanted to know.

I barely took in what he told me. It had something to do with Dewar telling the court that Clayton had said he'd lie to protect Brown. Atkins had cried foul, saying this was hearsay, and the judge agreed. I was stunned.

Dewar appeared then, and explained that he had presumed Trevor Clayton would be giving evidence later. He admitted it was inappropriate for him to have said what he did if Clayton wasn't going to be called.

It was all really confusing for those who don't know how the law works, but as Dewar pointed out, all was not lost as we'd be able to come back and try again. I wasn't too thrilled at the prospect of having to give evidence again, but I told myself that I was being offered a second chance at putting the man who raped me behind bars.

The second trial was set down for 7 June 1994. It was only six months away, but that seemed like a lifetime, given how much I wanted to get it all over with. Dewar kept in touch with me over this period, keeping me up to date with any developments — not that there really were any. He regularly took me out for coffee or drinks, and I always thought this was very nice of him. He made me feel important. The counselling with Margaret fell by the wayside a bit. I guess I didn't need her as much, as I felt I could lean on Dewar. And anyway, I thought I was coping pretty well on my own.

The kids too kept me busy. Jessica was going to be five this year and Kerriann was hitting three. To add to all that, I fell pregnant with our third child in March, and that became a wonderful time for Ross and me. We both hoped for a boy, as we swore this was definitely the last child. I was a little concerned that I would be around three months into my pregnancy when we went back to court, as the first three months is a crucial time for a developing baby. But the doctor was onto it and monitored me carefully. He told me not to stress, and to really look after myself. Again, it helped that Jessica was in kindy and Kerriann was such a placid kiddie. The only real problem I had was morning sickness. Ross was awesome at this time too. If his travels took him past our road, he would drive up in the truck and take either Jessica or Kerriann with him. The girls loved it, and it gave me precious time to myself.

With all that going on, it wasn't long before June was upon us. Once again I found myself in a courtroom face to face with Sam Brown and swearing an oath to tell the truth, the whole truth and nothing but the truth. Everything went as before, with John McDonald, the Crown Prosecutor, kicking off by asking me to tell the court what had happened with Brown in Murupara and Rotorua.

It was like déjà vu until Atkins started on me. This time, he did bring up things that had been done to me by other serving members of the police. I agreed that I had made a statement to Dewar that other cops had done things to me while I was living in Murupara. Even at the time, it had struck me as strange that he had never delved too deeply into what had actually happened with these men. He basically just asked me whether I had complained about the Murupara Four, and he seemed satisfied when I said yes.

Once I had finished in the box the same witnesses were called in the same order as in the first trial: Mum, Mrs Radford, then Dewar. It was déjà vu again — especially when Dewar was giving his evidence and Atkins piped up and objected to something he said. Once again, the court was cleared. And once again, the trial was aborted because Dewar had given hearsay evidence.

It turned out that Dewar had told the court that four other police officers had had sex with me. Atkins had argued, and the judge had agreed, that this was prejudicial to the outcome of the trial.

I did my nut at him. I told him he'd have to take a statement from me about what had happened at Rutland Street and Corlett Street, as it was obviously going to keep coming up in court. I needed the jurors to understand what had happened. But no, Dewar was adamant that it would do no good and we must concentrate only on what Brown had done. There was nothing I could say or do to convince him otherwise.

Yet another trial date was set, this time 19 September 1994 — when I would be about seven months pregnant. I was so damned frustrated that we had to go through it all over again for a third time.

For a while life just continued on with the same old mundane events of being a housewife and mother — until a strange incident one day that still makes me wonder. I was outside watering the garden and Jessica was riding her little three-wheeler bike up and down the driveway. A couple of young guys were wandering down the street towards us. I didn't pay much attention until one of them crossed the road and approached me.

He said something that I didn't quite catch.

'I'm sorry?' I said. 'What did you say?'

'I'll give you five bucks for sex,' he said.

I couldn't believe what I'd heard.

'Excuse me?' I said, and he repeated himself.

I politely said, 'No, thank you', and turned off the hose. I called to Jessica to come inside, and as I turned to walk away the guy started to follow me. I was on the verge of panic, but I tried not to show him he was scaring me. I managed to grab Jessica off her bike and looked towards my neighbour Josie's house. Josie was standing at her dining-room window so I tried to signal to her to call the police. All the while, I was cursing having locked our Rottweiler, Rocky, in the back yard, as I did when Jessica was playing outside. I didn't know if Josie had realised what I meant, but I managed to get to the gate. Rocky was nowhere to be seen. I was really starting to panic now. I closed the gate behind me as calmly as I could and walked inside.

I put Jessica down and immediately phoned 111. The young fella was still standing outside by the gate, and as I asked to be connected to the police I heard Rocky doing his balls, which made me feel a little easier. He'd obviously heard me come through the gate, and when he came around to see me he'd spotted this guy and begun doing what guard dogs do. I explained to the police operator what was going on and he said he would send a police car around. I gave him my details and he told me to stay on the line until the car turned up.

By the time the cops turned up, the two young guys had wandered off down the street. Then suddenly there were cop cars with flashing lights and men in black balaclavas with rifles everywhere. And then, to top it off, John Dewar turned up!

He told me he'd been in the communications room when my call came through. He said I had sounded really scared and he'd immediately thought Brown had something to do with what was going on. He scrambled the Armed Offenders Squad. It had never entered my head that Brown would do anything like this, but I was grateful to Dewar for his concern. Later he told me that the two young fellas were doped up. The police found drugs on them and arrested them and took them to the police station. So far as I know, nothing ever came of the incident, which I thought strange whenever I remembered it. Because Dewar was involved, I figured he must have sorted it out.

After that I became paranoid over the slightest noise, or even seeing a car I didn't recognise in my street. Now that the thought had been planted in my mind that Brown might try to get to me, I became more reliant than ever on John Dewar.

Then 19 September was upon us. It wasn't until four in the afternoon that I was called to give evidence. I'm not sure of the reason for the late start, but I know enough about the court process to know that legal arguments can take a good chunk of the day to hear. I wasn't feeling the best. I'd been having some rather uncomfortable contractions, for which the doctor had prescribed some tablets to prevent the early onset of labour. And in all honesty, by now I was in the wrong frame of mind to put across to the jury how Brown had screwed up my life and how much he had hurt me both physically and emotionally.

I had a been-there, done-that feeling about the whole process, and I didn't feel as emotionally charged as I had in the last two trials. There were no nerves, even when I was in the witness box. I felt detached from the whole proceedings. This time, there were no tears when I had to recall what Brown had done, there was no anger, there was nothing. All I did was tell my story as it had happened, and then answer the prosecutor's questions — basically, just let the day flow.

I must have seemed like a robot. It wasn't a good look for the jurors, but I had had enough, and to top it off I was still having some contractions, which made it hard to concentrate. We only managed to get through an hour and a bit of my testimony before the judge called a halt, and as I lay in bed that night I could only hope that I'd be more onto it in the morning, especially with Atkins having a go at me.

The trial resumed at 10.35 the next morning. This time Dad was allowed to stay in the cleared court as my support person. He sat by himself in the public gallery, but just being able to look at him when the going got tough was enough for me to keep my strength and wits about me. During the cross-examination, Atkins again brought up the Maoris on horseback incident, the Murupara Four and what had happened at Rutland Street with Rickards, Shipton and Schollum. And once again, Atkins continually followed his questions with remarks like, 'It simply didn't happen, did it, Mrs Nicholas?' All I could do was insist, 'I'm sorry, but it did.'

Again, I felt flat the whole time I was in the box. I guess I'd really just about given up. And then, to top it off, once I'd finished giving my evidence Dewar told me the Crown was going to call Rickards, Shipton and Schollum. Dewar suggested it would probably be best for me to stay in the little room outside so that I didn't have to look at them.

I was confused. 'Why would we be calling them?' I asked him. 'They're the bad guys.'

Dewar didn't give me any kind of satisfactory answer, and I didn't get a chance to quiz John McDonald on it. Once again, I just accepted what Dewar told me and figured there must be a good reason for it. As it was, I did see them: at one point, I glanced out of the little room and saw them standing in the foyer waiting to be called into the courtroom one at a time. They were all dressed up in their police uniforms and wearing these big trenchcoats.

A minor miracle seemed to have happened when Dewar got through his evidence without the trial being called off. Then Brown took the stand, and I decided I really did want to hear what he had to say, even though I knew it was all going to be deny, deny, deny! And that's exactly what he did say, to the point where I couldn't bear to hear any more of his bullshit and got up and walked out. I went back in for McDonald's summing up, and I heard Atkins too. That was difficult to listen to, as all he said was that I had made everything up and his client, Mr Brown, was innocent of all accusations. There was nothing surprising there. Then Judge Lance summed up and gave his directions to the jury, and our anxious wait began.

We all wandered off to the Rotorua Citizens' Club. Dewar explained that if the jury returned early, it probably wasn't a good sign. If they took a while to come back, that would probably mean they were more in favour of a guilty verdict. But at the end of the day, he said, jurors were fickle creatures and you never really knew which way they would go.

We'd only been there for about an hour when Dewar's cellphone rang. He listened, nodded, and told us the jury were coming back in. Dad wanted to know whether they'd been out for a long or a short time, but I think we all knew they'd come back too soon. We tried to remain positive: perhaps they'd decided early on that Brown was guilty. Ross gave me a reassuring hug as we entered the courthouse, but I knew deep down that it was all over and I had lost again.

Sure enough, as the charges were read, the foreman called out: 'Not guilty', and Brown swung around and furiously shook Les Atkins's hand. I was absolutely gutted, but I knew I'd done the right thing bringing it to court. Just because we couldn't satisfy the jury, I told myself, doesn't alter the fact that we all know he's guilty as hell. As we left the courtroom I was slightly dazed, but I remember John McDonald giving me a hug and apologising for not getting the guilty verdict. I was surprised, but thanked him for all his help and told him we knew he'd done his best. We all knew it was going to be hard to get a conviction,

I told him, because of the historic nature of the case.

Outside, one of our friends put a consoling arm around my shoulders and said to me: 'Well, Louise, it wasn't the verdict we all hoped for, but at least now you can put it behind you and move on, eh?'

I guess so, I thought, but why was I left feeling that something wasn't quite right about it all?

Dewar called around to the house with a lovely bunch of flowers a few days later, and we had what I suppose you'd call a bit of a debrief. We talked for a while about all that had happened, but nothing he could say would change the fact that Sam Brown had got away with rape and I had to live with it. It was unfortunate, too, that because Brown had been acquitted he was allowed permanent name suppression. To top it off, because of Dewar's hearsay evidence and the two aborted trials, Brown was awarded costs of $20,800.

Dewar played that down with me, offering excuses that sounded plausible at the time. I was exhausted by the whole process. I was past caring, heavily pregnant, and really just wanted to put it behind me and carry on with being a mum, wife and normal person.

Phil

IF I HAD HAD DOUBTS about the sincerity of Dewar's efforts to convict Brown after reading the material leading up to the depositions hearing and learning about how he had handled the hearing itself, they had all but disappeared by the time I'd finished reading through the transcripts of the trials.

As is common with legal trials, the first round took place before the jury was even involved, with a series of 'pre-trial' arguments taking place in chambers about what was and what was not 'admissible evidence'. Behind closed doors, defence counsel Les Atkins QC asked Judge Paterson for permission to question Louise on the baton-rape allegations. The fact that this line of questioning had surfaced at depositions didn't automatically mean the defence could bring it up at trial. Atkins told the judge he had no opinion on whether the allegations were true. But if they were, the extent of Louise's psychological damage could be attributable to more than just the behaviour she alleged she'd suffered at Brown's hands. He didn't need to tell the judge that airing these allegations before the jury would cause them to wonder why she'd never formally complained about them, or if she had, why they'd never gone any further. And Atkins did say that if the baton allegations were false, it said something about Louise's willingness to make wild allegations.

Judge Paterson ruled that neither the Rutland Street baton allegation nor Louise's complaint about Maori boys on horseback was relevant to Brown's case. He forbade Atkins to question Louise about them in court.

That was a victory for Louise and the Crown, but it counted for nothing. The trial had hardly got going before John Dewar scored his first goal — an own goal, if his intention was ever to see Brown convicted. As officer in charge of the investigation, Dewar was called to give evidence. All was routine until he suddenly and deliberately began introducing hearsay. With no prompting from anyone, least of all the Crown Prosecutor, he mentioned his interview with Trevor

Clayton and reported that the former policeman had declared himself willing to lie to protect his mate, Sam Brown. Atkins objected, and the trial was over, aborted.

So why would Dewar deliberately give this hearsay evidence? His excuse was that he'd seen Clayton in court and presumed he was going to give evidence for the defence. Such an experienced policeman would have known full well that anyone present in the public area could not give evidence, as only someone in his own privileged position as officer in charge would be admitted to the courtroom before they were called as a witness. And it's all academic, anyway. Dewar had been in the game far too long to make the kind of rookie error he claimed to have made. He would have known full well that the proper procedure to alert the jury to Clayton's unreliability would have been for the prosecution to let Clayton give evidence, and then to recall Dewar to the box. Dewar would have been perfectly entitled to tell the jury under McDonald's lead that Clayton had told him he would lie under oath.

The defence had lost a vital weapon from their arsenal when they'd been forbidden to bring up Louise's baton allegations and the distracting story about Maoris on horseback. The Crown, on the other hand, had a credible rape complainant, supported by equally strong evidence from her schoolteacher and her mother. So in spite of Dewar's dubious and lacklustre investigation, Brown might have gone to jail. But that wasn't what Dewar wanted. If Brown had gone down, whatever deal had been struck in the conversations that took place outside the recorded interviews would have been off. Brown may well have chosen to take Rickards, Shipton and Schollum down with him, or his mate, Trevor Clayton, might have decided to come forward with what he really knew. Dewar was also in a better position than most to know what a toll the whole proceeding was taking on Louise. How long before she reached the point at which she threw up her hands and simply walked away?

Six months later, the second trial began under Judge Evans. Again, there were pre-trial arguments, and this time it was ruled that potentially compromising evidence could be introduced by the defence. Having been ambushed with the baton allegations at depositions, Louise was concerned that other incidents of her sexual history would be brought up too. In for a penny, in for a pound, she decided: she wanted it all out in the open. Between the first and second trials, she told Dewar she'd been indecently assaulted by other Murupara police officers. Louise considered those alleged incidents — they consisted of mauling and harassment — trivial in comparison to her allegations against Brown and Rickards, Shipton and Schollum. In contrast Dewar, while insisting they let the baton-rape allegations lie, decided that these fresh claims warranted investigation. As with Brown, he went through the motions, but this time concluded there was insufficient evidence to lay any charges.

With the benefit of hindsight, giving Dewar this material was a mistake, because inevitably it ended up in the hands of the defence. Under our legal system, the Crown has to 'discover' its evidence to the defence before the trial; it's just one of the asymmetries of the system that there is no equivalent obligation on the defence.

This time, the trial judge, Judge Evans, ruled that the defence could question Louise about her past, which included not only the Murupara indecent assault allegations, but also the baton allegations. I thought it was hard to see how this was going to help Louise.

The trial began; Louise, her mum and Heather Radford gave evidence; and then, incredibly, Dewar scored at the wrong end of the pitch again. This time, he said Louise had told him about 'incidents' involving Shipton, Schollum and Rickards.

'I have spoken to all those officers,' he told the court. 'They have indicated they had sex with Louise.'

Atkins again immediately objected, saying Dewar had once more given hearsay evidence.

As Louise and her supporters watched aghast, the judge called counsel into chambers again, and again the trial was aborted.

Crown prosecutor John McDonald wrote that he 'could not believe' Dewar gave deliberate hearsay evidence for a second time, and for the first time in his legal career he demanded a report from the officer in charge — John Dewar. This time, even the judge smelt a rat. Judge Evans was so annoyed with the senior policeman's indiscretion that he indicated to McDonald his intention of charging Dewar with contempt of court, although he apparently cooled down overnight. It must have crossed the judge's mind that Shipton, Schollum and Rickards deserved to be on trial every bit as much as Brown, and he must have wondered why they were not. In a memo on the court files, Judge Evans described Dewar's second indiscretion as 'remarkable' given that the case implicated so many police officers, and he stated that Dewar's motives should be investigated.

Certainly, something should have happened. But no one treated the judge's comments as a direction, and instead of being suspended in the face of such damning criticism, Dewar remained at the head of the inquiry. He continued moulding Louise's mind, even driving her to her counselling sessions. Her counsellor was so disquieted by this that she later wrote to the police saying that the relationship Dewar was cultivating with Louise was 'unhealthy' given Dewar's position on the case.

Louise didn't give up, and she was heartened by a letter she received a month before the third trial began. It was a written apology from Brown's Rotorua doctor. This was the man to whom Louise had complained that she'd been raped by an unnamed 18 year old while she was living with Sam and Jane Brown in Rotorua. When I questioned her about this incident, Louise told me that Jane Brown, who had brought her to the surgery, was in the waiting room, so there was no way she was going to tell the doctor that Brown had been raping her in case the doctor confronted Jane. But the doctor did make a note of the story she made up about the 18 year old. Louise said it was a cry for help, and the doctor's apology shows he saw it this way too. He was apologising on two scores: first, for not acting on his intuition, and second — worse — because Brown, meanwhile, had got hold of his notes to use against her at trial: to suggest that Louise was in the habit of making up rape complaints. The doctor reported that Brown had 'misled' his surgery staff to get the notes, and that, as a former policeman, Brown would have 'known the implications of his actions'.

Just before the third trial got underway in September 1994, Dewar discussed the Rutland Street allegations with John McDonald. Louise had complained about baton rape by Schollum, Shipton and Rickards, McDonald recorded, but Dewar said there was 'no substance' to the complaint and there had been 'some consent' by Louise.

Believe it or not, though, Dewar insisted Shipton, Schollum and Rickards be called to the witness box to give evidence to 'support' Louise's case against Brown. The only thing more staggering than that suggestion is that McDonald accepted it.

The trial began with Louise seven months pregnant with her third child. Again, under cross-examination Louise was grilled by Atkins on her allegations about Rutland Street and the Murupara Four. Again she insisted the incidents happened. Then the court was closed. One by one, Rickards, Shipton and Schollum were called to the box and one by one, on oath, each said they'd had sex with Louise. Atkins got them to confirm under cross-examination that the sex was always consensual.

What was going on here? After scoring own goals to thwart the previous trials, Dewar was handing the third to the defence as a win by default. Dewar claimed the decision to call the Rutland Street baton brigade was in Louise's interests — that if the jury heard Louise had sex with the three police officers, it would somehow corroborate her complaint against the ex-cop, Brown. Perhaps McDonald went along with it imagining there was a subtle point to be made about how Brown's treatment of Louise had eroded her psychological defences to the point where she would consent to all kinds of degradation in later life. Other than that, it's impossible to see how hearing Louise insist she had been baton-raped by Schollum, Shipton and Rickards, and then hearing each of the three policemen, impressively togged up in their smart uniforms, explain this had been consensual, would help the jury to believe Louise's allegations against

Brown. Only if the three had admitted they'd raped Louise was there any real prospect of corroboration, and what were the chances of that?

Yes, Schollum, Shipton and Rickards each said in the box, we had sex with Louise. Yes, Shipton and Rickards said, on occasion it was group sex. But no, all three protested, they'd never used a baton, and the incident that Louise described at Rutland Street never happened.

So why did McDonald allow it? To his credit, he admitted it was a mistake and later said calling the three policemen was his biggest regret. It was, he said, a lapse in judgement. It was. The jury took an hour and a half to find Brown not guilty.

The Brown matter was all over for Louise Nicholas but not for Sam Brown. He had name suppression, and under the 'double jeopardy' provisions of our system he could not be charged again with raping Louise. He'd clocked up substantial bills along the way — through the investigation, depositions and then three trials. He made an application for the Crown to pay his legal costs. Nine months later, a costs hearing was held. Judge Lance presided, and he devoted much of his decision awarding $20,800 to Brown to slamming Dewar. Not only had he twice and apparently deliberately given hearsay evidence, thundered Judge Lance, but he had failed to do his duty in the matter of Louise's serious allegations against Schollum, Shipton and Rickards.

'The failure to record and detail these allegations was not only remarkable,' Judge Lance wrote, it was utterly incredible. 'During his interview with the complainant he is told of allegations of potentially serious sexual offending by three other named and currently serving police officers.

'Such disclosures should have triggered alarm bells that would have permanently silenced Big Ben. Even more surprising than the failure to record is the officer's deliberate advice to the complainant not to make a statement about her allegations against these officers.

'That a then non-serving officer is pursued with vigour and the allegations against currently serving police officers are not recorded and the complainant advised not to make a statement,' he wrote, supported an argument that Brown was 'a sacrificial offering'.

At that time, Judge Lance wasn't in a position to know how incomplete Dewar's investigation into Sam Brown was. He might have suspected Dewar was playing a double game, but because Dewar's motives weren't investigated when he first gave hearsay evidence — as Judge Paterson had suggested they should have been — he lacked the evidence to support him in saying so.

When a judge makes such a withering criticism of a police officer, the police are required to act. Dewar's boss asked for an internal police report into the botched trials. Detective Chief Inspector Rex Miller was brought in to head the inquiry. At the same time, the police received a string of minor complaints about Dewar, mostly from other Rotorua police. Battle lines formed in the Rotorua station, pro- versus anti-Dewar. A senior detective investigated the minor complaints and eventually, kicking and screaming, Dewar was shifted out of Rotorua to run police communications in Auckland. Nothing much out of the various complaints about him was substantiated, although he was found guilty at a police disciplinary hearing and fined for asking if a female Rotorua detective who'd received some work out of the district had been 'bonking one of the bosses'.

That policewoman said that one of Dewar's staff tried to intimidate witnesses for the internal inquiry. 'If a gang member did anything like this he would have been arrested,' she said. 'I now know why some people hate the police. I am totally disillusioned and feel that some sections in the New Zealand Police are corrupt,' she told Miller. The police are often rightly critical of gang members who refuse to co-operate with police inquiries. Miller's inquiry team found themselves in the same boat. They encountered 'extreme resistance' by serving police officers to 'disclose information', and it wasn't just the policewoman who was intimidated. Several others interviewed by the inquiry team felt intimidated by police officers after speaking to the inquiry.

Around this time, Sam Brown complained to the Police Complaints Authority (PCA), accusing Dewar of prosecuting him because he had complained about other police officers and in order 'to cover up the allegation [Louise] made against Shipton, Schollum and Rickards'. If Brown was ever part of the jack-up surrounding his own trial, he played his role to the limit, covering up the cover-up. It's more likely that he simply lacked the perspicacity to see how great the favours Dewar did him really were. Indeed, by giving deliberate hearsay evidence and insisting on calling Rickards, Shipton and Schollum, Dewar was doing everything in his power to get Brown off. But in making his PCA complaint, Brown seems to have interpreted Dewar's disgraceful behaviour as somehow calculated to get him convicted.

The PCA must have been scratching their heads over this one. In 1996, they told Brown that Rex Miller's inquiry had concluded that 'far from frustrating the defence case, [Dewar's behaviour] had a serious impact on the prosecution'. But they did agree with Brown on something. They told him they shared his view that Dewar had failed in his duty to investigate Louise's allegations about Rickards, Shipton and Schollum.

It was around the time of Sam Brown's costs application hearing that I received the first phone call from my anxious police source, telling me that all had not been right in the investigations and trials. But, like Dewar, I failed to follow up properly.

Louise

MY LIFE HAD BEEN A gigantic rollercoaster since I was 13, and now that everyone had tried their best to see justice done to Sam Brown, I was determined to put it all behind me. No more surprises; no more contact with the legal system or the police.

It didn't quite work out that way. In 1995, John Dewar phoned me and said he was being investigated by the Police Complaints Authority over his handling of the Brown trials and the way he had gone about investigating my complaints. I was a bit taken aback at this, and told him that I would help him in any way I could. He told me I could expect a phone call from whoever was heading the investigation, and that I should be honest but careful with anything I said. He made it quite clear that 'they' were out to bring him down. That didn't seem right to me, so I prepared to do my best to help someone I considered a mate.

Sure enough, not long after this I received a call from Detective Chief Inspector Rex Miller. He explained that he would like to talk to me about John Dewar and how he had handled my complaint, and he asked me to report to Police Headquarters in Rotorua. He said I could bring someone along for support, and I told him I would be bringing my father. It was arranged that we would meet on 25 May 1995.

Here we go again, I thought. Dad and I showed up at headquarters at around 11 in the morning, and I was introduced to Rex Miller and another policeman called Bruce Raffin. My first impressions of Miller weren't that favourable. He was a big, scary, gruff man — not at all like the kindly John Dewar — and I felt quite intimidated by him. When we got to his office Miller explained that he would be taking a statement from me so that they could get an overall picture of the events that had taken place not only in Murupara and Rotorua with Brown, but also what happened at Rutland and Corlett streets. It took about an hour and a bit to cover the Murupara stuff, then we stopped for lunch. Dad and I returned to headquarters at two, and I carried on with the next statement. I took Miller through the events at Rutland and Corlett streets, and I also told him that I had told Dewar about all this during the first meeting I had had with him. This statement took about an hour to do, and along the way, at my insistence, several versions were shredded, as I wasn't happy with how they were worded.

Miller then asked me to show him and Raffin where the house was in Rutland Street. Dad asked me whether I wanted him to come along for this, but I felt I could cope. Miller, Raffin and I got in a car and I gave them directions. As we pulled into Rutland Street, I explained that the house was on the left-hand side towards the end. As we got close I shut my eyes for a few seconds just to put that house back in my head, and when I opened them, there it was. I don't know that it would look as evil to someone else as it did to me, but this was where unspeakable horrors had been performed on me. I had no hesitation in telling them this was the house. They asked me several times if I felt I had the right house, and I just kept nodding and saying this is it, this is where it all happened, you never forget. They also asked me if I had ever been back after the incidents of 1986, and I told them no. As I said, you never forget: it doesn't matter how many years have gone by, you never forget. Miller and Raffin seemed satisfied, and the interview was over.

Although Miller had told me I shouldn't tell Dewar what I'd said in my statements, I couldn't help myself. I phoned him and told him what had gone on. Soon afterwards, Dewar contacted me again and asked if I would go on TV3's *20/20* current affairs programme and say publicly that I thought he had done a good job with my complaint. I had no hesitation whatsoever, and told him I'd be more than happy to do that. It was arranged and I told the public of New Zealand that, 'As far as I'm concerned, the way John Dewar dealt with my case, the way he handled me and how he helped my family — I can't speak more highly of the guy. At the end of the day, if he's cocked up then he must pay the consequences.' I meant what I said. I regarded Dewar as a friend and as the one good cop I had known — someone who had believed me and done his best to see justice done for me. As far as I was concerned, despite his mistakes in court, Brown's acquittal had been as much a blow to him as it was for me.

Miller phoned once or twice in the days following my interview to ask further questions or to check details. As soon as I got off the phone I'd call Dewar and tell him everything that had been said. A couple of weeks after the TV appearance, Dewar phoned and suggested I make a further statement to him about the way he had carried out the investigation and the way Miller had been behaving. I was willing. It was arranged that I would meet Dewar in his office at the Rotorua Police Station to do this statement. When I got to his office, the statement had already been done. All I had to do, he told me, was read it through and make any changes I thought necessary. Suffice to say, I skimmed through it, picked up on a few sentences that I thought sounded rather good, considering I didn't even know the meaning of some of the words I was supposed to have used, then signed the statement with no qualms whatsoever.

I left the station satisfied I'd done my bit for Dewar, just as he'd done his bit for me. And that was the last I heard for a long, long time.

Ross and I and the girls had shifted back out into the country shortly after the trials had finished. At first we lived on the same property as Ross's parents at Horohoro, but in July 1999 we shifted to a bigger house that we rented off the church in the little village of Ngakuru.

Ross had got a job driving milk tankers with the Reporoa Dairy Factory, and the money was pretty good. It meant working shifts — he would do three days, then three nights, then have three days off — but, with the awesome neighbours we had, I wasn't worried about being home alone at night. We still had Rocky the Rottweiler, and even though he was getting on a bit, it was always a comfort to know he was there when Ross wasn't around.

These were happy years — far happier than any of us could have imagined they would be just after we'd watched Sam Brown walk free. The girls thrived on country life, and it taught them all sorts of life skills at an early age. They were forever out and about on the farm, making huts, catching koura (which they brought home for me to cook — and, yes, they did eat them!) and helping Grandpa with jobs around the farm, such as grubbing thistles. Our youngest daughter, McKaela, was attending kindy in town, but between us and our neighbours — Louise and Paul Doust just down the road, and Bridgid and Andrew Drysdale across it — we arranged a kind of roster system for driving them in. It was easy to combine the trip with your shopping day, so after I'd dropped the kids off at kindy I could take it easy doing the rounds of the shops, picking up groceries and supplies and the odd thing I'd stash in the wardrobe and tell Ross about later! It was a great arrangement. Jessica and Kerri settled into school just fine. Ngakuru School was pretty small in those days, with just 90 kids, so the teachers had plenty of time for everyone.

So, we had happy kids, neat friends and, for me, a sense of peace at long last. By the time McKaela started school, however, I was starting to get itchy feet. As much as I enjoyed wandering over to see my friends Bridgid and Louise for cups of coffee and pigging out on their amazing home baking, I was getting bored. I didn't want to find a job that meant travelling into town, but felt that if I could find something to occupy my day that was close by I would feel a hell of a lot better. Not only would it keep the old brain active, it wouldn't hurt to add a few bucks to the bank account.

One day I was chatting to Anna Davies at school. She and her husband Peter owned a couple of dairy farms, one of them straight across the road from us. I told her that if she ever needed a hand, she should just sing out, because I'd love to come over and get my hands dirty. Anna spoke to Pete about it, and that was where my career as a relief milker started.

They only milked 100 cows on the property across the road, but how convenient was it! It took me a wee while to get the hang of milking again, as the last time I'd set foot in a cowshed was way back when I was a kid going to stay at a friend's uncle's farm at Galatea, just outside Murupara. That's where I learned to milk, and even though it was a long time ago cows still had their bits in the same places, and it didn't take me long to get back into the swing of it. Before long I was milking that little shed all on my own. Because it was just across the road, I was able to be home to get the kids out of bed and off to school by nine o'clock. The only days I couldn't milk were those when Ross was working dayshift, as he was up and gone by 5.30.

Word soon got around the district that I was looking for relief milking jobs, mainly on the weekends, and soon I had several farmers booked in. I'd found a real niche, because if there was one thing the district lacked, it was relief milkers. I soon built up a good reputation with the farmers, who knew they could rely on me to be in that cowshed at the right time and with the right attitude. The last bit was the most important part of the job: if you're happy in your work then the cows are happy, and if the cows are happy then they milk well, and if the cows milk well, then the farmers are happy. It got to the point where I needed a diary to keep track of all the relief milkings I'd booked in. I asked Bridgid Drysdale if she wanted to take some of my weekend milkings. She was as keen as, so with Ross's help I taught her to milk cows too, in the little shed across the road. Soon she was away on her own.

What an awesome life I was living. Once I'd finished my stint in the shed and packed the girls off to school I found I had a lot time on my hands during the day. I asked my father-in-law Lin if I could help out with any jobs on the farm. He was happy with that suggestion, so soon I was milking some mornings, getting the kids off to school, then heading off to help Lin during the day, back to the shed for afternoon milkings or home at 2.30 in time to collect the kids from school at 3. If for any reason I couldn't make it in time, Louise Doust would take the kids down to her house after school until either Ross or I got home from work.

This kind of community spirit convinced Ross and me that if the chance came up, we would really like to stay here permanently, which meant looking for a property to buy. It so happened there was a piece of land, around half a hectare, for sale across the road from us. I told Ross that we should look at buying it and building our own place. It had been on the market for ages, so we decided to be cheeky and put in a ridiculously low offer. To our absolute delight the owner accepted.

Once we had the finance sorted out, all we had to do was decide what sort of house to build. We'd never done anything like this before: Ross and I had an absolute ball going around show homes and making decisions on what sort of heating to install, what interior colours to choose, what exterior look we wanted, landscaping, the whole nine yards. It was exciting as hell watching it all take shape. We finally shifted in around October 2001.

After a few years of relief milking I decided to accept an offer to work full-time as a milker for Dave and Leigh Hannah. Their cowshed was only a couple of years old, a 45-a-side herringbone, and it was an absolute dream to work. I would be at the shed at around 5 in the morning, getting it set up while waiting for the cows to come in, then back again between about 2.30 and 3 in the afternoons. It would take us around three hours to milk between 650 and 700 cows and get washed up, which meant I could still do my shift and be home for breakfast. The Hannahs were awesome to work for. We had so many hard-case days milking — there was always laughter and joking around.

One morning, Dave couldn't understand why the cows weren't going into the shed properly. He thought maybe I'd fallen over or something major had happened, so he rushed in to find me sitting very still at one end of the pit with a horrified look on my face. He asked me what was wrong, and I said there was no way in hell I was going down into the pit to move the cows up until someone killed the big huhu bug that was flying around the lights. They scare the crap out of me! Poor old Dave didn't know whether to laugh or cry or just bash me. He eventually killed the beast and it was business as usual.

Another morning I saw Roger, the Hannahs' full-time worker, high-tailing it as fast as he could after a calf. The little critter had only been born a few hours earlier, but it had some major speed going on in those skinny little legs. I couldn't help myself, and had to yell out to Roger, 'Run, Forrest, run!' because that's exactly who he looked like. Well, the poor bugger started laughing, then he totally lost all balance and speed and fell flat on his face and got covered in cow shit. Dave and I were rolling around the paddock in absolute hysterics. It was hard, tiring work but, hell, did we have fun.

Meanwhile, my children were adding years to my life, the way kids do. Jess was first, with a pushbike accident that left her with two broken wrists. The worst thing about it was that because she had broken our rule about staying on the property when Ross and I weren't home, I was mad as hell with her. The poor kid was in all sorts of pain that night, but I had no sympathy whatsoever. It wasn't until an x-ray the next day confirmed she'd busted her wrists that I started to believe her. But I was still furious. She had both arms in plaster, and we were on the way home when she piped up and said, 'Bet you feel really stink now, eh, Mum?' The look I gave her showed her I wasn't quite ready to admit it yet.

Kerriann was the next casualty. She had to be rushed by ambulance to Rotorua Hospital with suspected neck injuries after the neighbour's horse she was riding bolted and she got her foot caught in the stirrup. She was dragged a fair way before smacking her head against a post as the horse swerved through a gateway. The riding helmet she was wearing saved her life. Her foot came free of the stirrup, and she managed to get up and walk the short distance home. I got her into the car, but she kept blacking out on me, so I phoned the ambulance and they met us halfway. She spent a night in hospital but thankfully had no serious injuries apart from a thumping headache.

Not long after that, the poor little bugger ended up in hospital with suspected meningitis. They had to do a spinal tap, and it took the useless doctor three goes to get the needle in the right place. Kerriann was screaming, I was crying and the nurse was having problems holding back tears as well. After several hours of waiting, the nurse came in around midnight and told me all was well.

And last, but not least, there was the time McKaela had the whole village on tenterhooks. She had wandered down to her friend Jesse's house to play after school, and about an hour later one of the kids came screaming up to the house saying Kaela had fallen out of a tree and wasn't moving. I ran the several hundred metres in record time and found Kaela awake but motionless and in an awkward position. I knew straight away this wasn't good. She wasn't really crying, but kept saying, 'I can't feel anything, Mummy, except the sandflies are biting my ankles.' The ambulance was there within 20 minutes, and Ross came home from work too. I'd had enough of bloody hospitals, and I didn't want to be there when a doctor concluded my youngest daughter was never going to walk again, so we decided Ross would go with Kaela.

The silver lining for Ross was that he had decided he didn't like what was happening — or not happening — with Kaela and they had sent for the rescue chopper. Despite his anxiety, Ross came back to me with a bloody great grin on his face. For a moment I thought he'd been told everything was fine, but it was sort of the opposite. He told me that it looked too serious for the ambulance, so he and Kaela would have to go by chopper.

'Typical, mate,' I told him. 'You get all the good jobs, you bastard!' We both laughed, but we were worried sick. No one had said what they thought the outcome would be, but I was assuming the worst.

The chopper arrived, landed in our paddock, loaded Kaela and Ross aboard and flew off to hospital. I couldn't even bring myself to go in and be with them, couldn't bear to be that close to the bad news. Ross phoned regularly and kept us all updated. He told us the doctors had booked another chopper to take Kaela to Starship Hospital in Auckland if no feeling had come back by midnight. I just went numb. My life has been full of excruciating waits, but this was the worst I'd known.

Then, around 11.30, Ross phoned to say she was starting to get feeling back in her legs and the chopper had been cancelled. She spent a couple of days in hospital, but it wasn't long before she was running around again with her friends and enjoying life as one her age should.

By now I felt I deserved peace and tranquillity for the rest of my days. But no, the big guy upstairs was clearly determined that I should never have a normal, settled life. There were plenty more rollercoaster rides in store for me.

On 25 November 2003, I was attending a farewell for one of Dave and Leigh Hannah's workers when I got a phone call from Kerriann telling me I had to ring Nana (my mum) as soon as possible. I asked her if Nana had told her what it was about and she said no, but it was important.

I phoned Mum, and she told me a reporter had been trying to find me so that he could give me some information he had uncovered about John Dewar and the court cases of 1993/94. 'What on earth would he have found after all these years?' I wondered, but I told Mum she could phone this guy back and tell him I'd listen to what he had to say. She called back and told me she'd arranged for us all to meet at their house the following night.

When I got home that night, I told Ross that this reporter wanted to talk to me about Dewar and the trials. His reaction was the same as mine.

'What the hell for?' he said. 'Why drag all that up again?'

'I'm meeting him at Mum's tomorrow night,' I told him. 'Do you want to come too?'

'Nah, hon,' he said. 'You go in and see what it's all about. I'll stay here with the kids.'

The next night, after tea, I wandered into Mum's and was pleased to find I'd got there before this guy. That gave me an opportunity to talk to Mum and Dad about what he wanted. Dad had spoken with him the day before.

'I had a yarn with him yesterday,' Dad said. 'From what he knows, it looks like Dewar did the dirty on us.'

'Bullshit he did!' I said in absolute disbelief. 'He did a bloody good job! Where the hell's this guy coming from?'

Dad shrugged.

'Wait and see what he has to say,' he said. 'It'll surprise you.'

Soon after that there was a knock at the door. Mum got up and answered it, and in wandered this scruffy-looking bugger who needed a damn good haircut. He introduced himself as Philip Kitchin, a reporter from *The Dominion Post*. None of us had ever heard of it.

I stood up and shook his hand and said: 'Gidday, I'm Louise.'

As I settled back down in the chair I quietly picked up my tobacco, rolled a smoke and waited for him to start. There was a fair bit of tension in the lounge — whether because he was nervous we would chuck him out or because we didn't really want to hear what he had to say about a man we all held in high regard, who knows? But, thankfully, we gave the poor bugger the benefit of the doubt and let him talk.

He talked about the two scenarios that were possible around what Dewar had done for us. There was either the good Dewar or the bad Dewar. I raised my eyebrows, took a long drag on my smoke and let him continue. Scenario number one was that Dewar had done a good job investigating my complaint, he said, but had been shafted by the police bigwigs because of it. I nodded.

Then there was scenario two. Philip then produced police job sheets and asked me to read them. I'd never seen these documents before. Didn't I find it incredible, Philip asked me, that not once did Dewar ask Schollum when he interviewed him about the baton allegation I had made. Philip then asked if I had definitely told Dewar about this.

'Of course I did,' I said. 'I told him all about it the first time he took a statement from me about Brown.'

Mum piped up then, and said that I had definitely told Dewar about those three men because she was there when Dewar took my statement.

Philip went on talking about other discrepancies he had discovered in the way Dewar had conducted the interviews with Clayton and Schollum, but I really wasn't taking too much in at this point, as anger came welling up inside me. It was the strangest feeling sitting there listening to all this, but finding myself going all the way back to 1993/94. I remembered someone telling me as we walked out of the courthouse after the third trial: 'Well, it's not the result we wanted, but at least now you can put it behind you.' Listening to Philip, I knew why I had felt something was not sitting quite right with me after Brown was acquitted.

I looked at Philip, then at Mum, then Dad, and said: 'The bastards have shafted me again.'

Philip explained to us a bit about what it would take to put the story together and bring it out into the light. He told us we would need to trust him.

I remember looking at him, still thinking he was a scruffy-looking bugger, but thinking that at least he had the face and the eyes of an honest and trustworthy scruffy-looking bugger.

'Do we have a deal?' he asked.

My blood was still boiling.

'Damn right we do!' I said.

I got home that night, walked into the lounge, sat myself down, looked at Ross and shook my head.

'You're not going to believe this, hon,' I said, 'but you know the court cases back in '93/'94?'

'Yeah,' he said, 'what about them?'

'We were shafted big-time!'

'What do you mean shafted?'

'That mongrel Dewar screwed those trials to protect his mates — Shipton, Schollum and Rickards.'

Ross just looked at me, and a big, silly grin spread across his face.

'I told you, didn't I?' he crowed. 'I said to you lots of times I didn't trust that bastard! That there was something screwy about him. But would you believe me? Nooooo! Eh, missus? So there you go! Once again, I'm right and you were wrong, eh missus?'

Much as it killed me to admit it, he was right and I had to say so. Then he just said: 'So tell me about this reporter.'

For the next hour or so I told Ross about Phil and all that he had uncovered. I told him Phil wanted to run a story about it all in *The Dominion Post*. Ross wasn't all that keen for that to happen, but I said that unless Phil could substantiate his suspicions of what appeared to be a cover-up, I didn't think there was a story. I suggested to him that we wait and see what developed.

Still, I told him, I'd agreed to go back into Rotorua to meet Phil again and get down on tape all that had happened both in Murupara and in Rotorua.

I could tell Ross was still uncomfortable, but finally he shrugged and said, 'Oh, well. Let's see what happens.'

Over the next few days I spent several hours at Mum and Dad's house going over absolutely everything with Phil. Even though he came across as a nice, trustworthy guy, I was still a little cautious about having to tell him all that had happened. But I needed him to understand that I had done nothing wrong, that everything I was saying was the truth, even if I cocked up dates and details like that. He had to understand that it's easy — too easy — to remember the bad things. You never forget the what, when, who or how, but trying to get the in-betweens in the right order wasn't that easy at all. He said he understood where I was coming from, and not to worry too much about getting everything spot on. I'd remembered the important points and that's what mattered. Having Dad there helped — I felt better having him not too far away — and altogether it worked pretty well.

With the help of statements and documents I'd kept over the years, Phil was able to put together a picture that was proving more and more that there were huge discrepancies in Dewar's handling of my complaint. But I could tell he thought the statement I had signed with Dewar on 20 June 1995 might be a bit of a spanner in the works. He asked me if I knew what I was signing at the time. I said that because Dewar told me it just said he had done a good job with my complaint, I hadn't really read it, just skimmed over it. I remember Phil just sitting there, shaking his head. This could have been disastrous for me, he said, because I'd signed it. But it was obvious to him and to anyone else who knew me that I didn't write it, so it could even work in my favour.

Phil asked me if I knew what Shipton, Schollum and Rickards were up to. I told him I didn't have a clue what they were doing now, didn't even know if they were still alive. He told me that Schollum was a car salesman in Napier, Shipton was a city councillor in Tauranga, and Rickards was Assistant Commissioner of Police and about to take up a new position as the big police boss in Auckland. I sat there with my mouth open — not so much because of Shipton and Schollum, but hell, if the story ran, I was about to take on the Assistant Commissioner of Police! Phil then explained to me that several serving members of the police had approached him and told him they weren't happy with Rickards's fast rise through the ranks. They were concerned that if he did get to the top job of Commissioner (for which he was apparently being groomed) it would cause all sorts of problems for police morale.

I asked Phil if he knew about the family situation of these guys. He told me Schollum had remarried, to a woman named Karen, and that they had two little kiddies. Shipton was still married to Sharon, and had one child who was about 10 years old. Rickards and his partner Tania had one child between them but he had other children from previous relationships. Dewar had separated from his wife and was in another relationship; they had two little kiddies too.

That made me stop and think. I'd have to take into account what effect my coming forward would have on these families. I didn't give a rat's arse about the men, and I knew that the wives would hate me with a vengeance, but to put their children through something like this weighed heavily on my mind. I began to wonder whether it was worth proceeding. This was when Ross sat me down and gave me a lecture on priorities. He fully understood where I was coming from, but he said that I had to get hard and put our family first, not theirs. He admitted that his major concern was how going ahead would affect our own children. This was something he had obviously thought long and hard about.

In the end we decided that as long as we were open and honest with the girls, and Phil kept his word about protecting them at all costs, then we should have no worries about putting the allegations into the public arena. As Ross pointed out, there had been a miscarriage of justice, and it should be brought to the public's attention that New Zealand's next top cop was a rapist, that Tauranga's city councillors had a rapist sitting among them, and that Napier people were buying cars off a rapist. Worse, we had lately found out that Sam Brown was a nurse in a hospital somewhere in the North Island, so there was a rapist dealing with vulnerable people in our health sector. And the public also had the right to know that there was one cop who, if he had been on the level, could have put all these rapists behind bars but had chosen not to simply because he was their mate.

I was blown away with how Ross felt, and very proud of him. I knew that what we were about to do was the right thing, and with him standing next to me I felt I could take on the world.

Phil was of the same mind as Ross. They should have thought about their families before assuming it was their right to play havoc with the lives of innocent victims, he said.

The stakes were raised when Phil came to us one day and told us he'd been offered a job with TVNZ as an investigative reporter. It meant he'd be leaving *The Dominion Post*, but after negotiations between the two organisations it had been agreed that they would run my story together. Phil asked if I would be prepared to go in front of a camera and tell my story on television as well. He said that if I wanted they could blob me out so that no one could identify me, which meant no one would be able to identify my family.

I asked him if I could think about it before making a decision, as this was something that Ross and I needed to consider seriously. In fact we spoke to the whole family about it. Some of them were concerned that putting my face out there could backfire on us. Ross's sister Karen phoned me and told me point-blank that I shouldn't just think of myself, but should think of what I could be doing to the girls. I thanked her for her concern. After all, this was a family decision, and if the girls weren't happy with it then Ross and I would reconsider my involvement.

Finally, Ross and I sat the girls down at the dining-room table, and Ross just said, 'Mum has something to tell you.' I had rehearsed how I was going to tell them and thought I had it down pat, but it all fell out the window when I had these three pairs of big, beautiful eyes fixed on me. They were expecting something wonderful, to learn that something amazing was about to happen, something that would make them really happy. Instead, I was going to say something that I really believed might make them hate me. Still, I had to take that risk.

I decided that beating about the bush wasn't the way to go, so I just told them straight up that I had been raped by policemen at the age of 13, and that they did this awful thing for a couple of years while I was living in Murupara. I then told them that I had been raped when I was 18 by three policemen in a house in Rotorua, and that they also used to come around to my flat and rape me there. I told them, without going into any detail, that they had used a police baton on me. Ross and I then explained about the court cases of 1993/94, and how the man who had raped me back in Murupara didn't go to jail because of John Dewar. We told them about Phil, and how he wanted me to go on TV as well as put it in the papers about these bad things. We then told them that they had to be OK with me doing this, and if they didn't want me to, then that would be fine. We explained that people would know who we were, but nobody was allowed to talk to the girls, or photograph or pester them, unless they wanted to be in big trouble.

There were many tears shed at the table that night but the girls, who were only nine, 11 and 13, told me that I must do the right thing, and that was to tell people about what had happened to me so that these bad men couldn't hurt anyone else. My heart just about burst with pride. The love and the honesty that these three amazing girls showed me that night brought home to me the reality of what had happened over 20 years ago. I knew I had to step up and tell the world it was wrong. Bad people got away with telling lies, and when they got away with it they were free to hurt others. Because although I didn't know who or when or what, I knew I wouldn't be the only victim of these men, and it was my duty not only as a victim, but as a woman, to make them accountable for their crimes.

Several days later, McKaela came up to me while I was getting dinner ready and said, 'Mum, can I ask you a question?'

'Of course, sweet,' I replied. 'What is it?'

'You know when you told us that those policemen hurt you with that baton? Did they hit you with it?'

Oh, my God. My blood just froze and my heart sank. How on earth do I answer this without having to tell her the whole disgusting story of what those bastards did to me? Ross and I had decided before we told the girls that we wouldn't go into the nasty details. So how the hell was I going to get out of this?

I managed to pull myself together, put down the potato peeler, then I turned and looked down at her beautiful, innocent little face. I fought back the tears, and with a smile I said to her, 'No, sweetheart. They didn't hit me with that baton.

They just did some nasty things to me with it.'

I watched her little face as she absorbed this and pondered, obviously turning my answer over and over in her little mind, while questions raced around my own. What more could I say? Did I say the right thing? Should I tell her the whole gory truth?

Then she looked up at me and said, 'They really are bad men, aren't they, Mummy?'

'Yes, sweetheart. They are.'

With that, she just turned around and wandered off outside. I couldn't finish those spuds. Instead I went into the bathroom, closed the door, turned on the shower and cried and cried and cried.

Phil

BY NOW IT WAS DECEMBER 2003 and I was almost living in Rotorua. Thoughts of a summer holiday had long since evaporated. I felt acutely that we needed more convincing evidence before we could publish. In an ideal world, we would get access to the report of Rex Miller's internal investigation, but this kind of report is secret and cannot be obtained under the Official Information Act. I had copies of the statements Louise had made to Miller's inquiry, but while they largely confirmed many of my suspicions, they stopped short of being the smoking gun I thought the story needed.

I had considered approaching Rex Miller himself, but Louise's mother had made me doubt how sympathetic he was toward Louise. The last words he had spoken to Barbara were: 'Your daughter needs help.' Barbara took this to mean Miller didn't believe Louise and thought she was deranged. Of course, when Miller spoke to the Crawford family, they (including Louise) were still very much of the opinion that John Dewar had done a good job for them. They were therefore inclined to mistrust Miller and what they viewed as an attempt to shaft the only friend they had in the New Zealand Police. They had never seen Miller's report.

I was getting some explosive stuff down on tape. The statements Louise had made to Miller's team included sickening details of the Rutland Street allegations she'd made against Schollum, Shipton and Rickards, and I tested her on these. It was, needless to say, an incredibly sensitive area for her. Her answers were staccato, as though she was forcing them out.

'I didn't tell anyone about this incident at the time,' she said, 'as I felt no one would believe me because they were police officers.'

And later: 'I never ever gave consent to any of these people. It was always taken for granted.'

Significantly, she said: 'I told Detective Inspector Dewar there was no way

I had consented to these acts.'

There had been four people at Rutland Street during the incident, she said, although only the three she knew raped her. She believed she might still be able to identify the 'fourth man' who'd watched, if she saw him again.

I asked what had happened after the alleged baton rape. 'I was shown to the shower . . . they just continued drinking . . . and I said to Bob, take me home . . . he said: "I'm sorry, Lou."'

Were there injuries?

'Even if there had been injuries, I doubt if I would have gone to a doctor.'

Why not?

'I wouldn't have wanted to tell a doctor.'

She told me about Corlett Street, about how Shipton and Rickards would turn up in uniform at her flat, parking an unmarked police car outside and demanding sex in spite of her protestations. It was difficult for anyone who doesn't appreciate the psychology of sexual-abuse victims to understand how this worked, and I quizzed her on it.

'Sure, I didn't scream and I didn't fight and I didn't do what people think you should do. I was shit-scared. I don't know how else you can explain it. You just go into . . . you just fold into yourself when all these things are happening. You are not even there. You just go away from your body. You are not even there.'

So there was no actual force used?

'I was pushed into positions,' she told me, 'but no actual . . . they didn't beat me up or get angry.'

She told Miller that she'd complained about Brown raping her, 'but it was not acted upon and I felt that I had no way of stopping [Shipton and Rickards] this time . . . they used to ignore my protests.'

Did she tell her flatmate, Sue, about what was going on?

'I never told her anything, no.'

What were the men saying while the group sex was going on?

A long sigh followed this question.

'It's my turn. Give her to me. You've had long enough. Are you enjoying that?'

If they were to say this sex was consensual, I asked, they would be . . . ?

'Sick,' she interrupted.

Then I asked the question that everyone wants to ask complainants in historical rape complaints.

'You knew what you said was happening to you was wrong. Why didn't you complain back then when you were aged 17 or 18?'

Her voice rose, partly anguished, partly pissed off with me. She told me she'd had the fear of God put into her by the police from an early age. Policemen could do no wrong. Policemen can't get into trouble, she said.

'There's just . . . there was just no way, not a shit-show in hell that anyone was going to believe me about cops. Cops are the good guys. Whenever anything bad happened with them, you'd shut up and say nothing. You just hoped they'd get it . . . do it and that that would be it. It would be all over, red rover, and the sooner the better.'

Louise told me about Dewar's requests for her assistance in defending himself against the Miller inquiry. As a senior policeman with 21 years' experience, he knew he shouldn't be talking to a key internal inquiry witness, let alone taking a statement from her. But his seemingly impregnable arrogance saw him take the risk.

Six times in the five-page document that Louise signed, she says she didn't complain about the Rutland Street baton rape to Dewar. I asked her to explain how it was that she signed this statement, whereas she'd made the exact opposite assertion in a statement she'd made to Miller a month beforehand.

'Those aren't my words,' Louise replied. 'I was made to believe that I was a consenting adult, because I was over the age of 16.'

'You were made to believe that by who?' I asked.

'John. Probably myself, too. How do you bring policemen up on charges like that when I'm over the age of 16, I'm a consenting adult and it's my word against theirs? I remember saying that to John. And he agreed with me.'

'Do you remember ever saying to him that it was not consensual?' I probed.

'That's what I said all the way through,' she said, exasperated. 'But how the hell do I prove that?'

She was also still angry about the interviews she'd had with Rex Miller about the alleged Rutland Street baton rape. She thought Miller didn't believe her. In the statement she made to Dewar, Louise says she believed Miller behaved unprofessionally and unsympathetically to her and she thought he was trying to discredit Dewar. 'He seemed more out to get John Dewar than resolve the baton incident.' Cleverly, too, the statement covers off the fact that Louise had also told Ray Sutton about the baton-rape allegations, saying: 'It was not made in the nature of a complaint, it was by way of background information only.'

The statement ends by praising Dewar's 'vigour and enthusiasm' in pursuing Sam Brown.

This was an incredible document. It was obvious to me that Dewar wrote it — I'd spent enough time interviewing Louise to know she wasn't familiar with the vocabulary and phrases in it, let alone accustomed to using them. I wondered if she had even bothered to read it before she signed it. She told me she did not think she would have read it carefully, because she trusted Dewar.

Any doubts I had that Dewar had duped Louise were being knocked over one after the other. Louise, meanwhile, was reaching the same conclusion.

'There's been a cover-up, a huge cover-up,' she said on my tape. 'It's pretty obvious John was just a typical copper looking after his mates.'

She was still referring to Dewar as 'John', but not for much longer. Soon she only ever spoke of him as 'Dewar'.

I asked Louise to take me to the Rutland Street house. Out of the corner of my eye, I watched her as we turned into an unremarkable Rotorua suburban street. She was quiet but calm as we drove slowly to the end, then she said firmly: 'That's it.'

We looked at the house. 'They were sitting on the balcony. The doors were open. You walk through the back door and into the kitchen which goes into the dining room which leads to the lounge. The bedroom was in the far corner at the back of the house.'

'That's the only time you went there?'

'Yes, except for when [Miller and Raffin] took me there.'

We retraced the route Louise had been walking when Bob Schollum pulled up in his car on the day of the Rutland Street incident. Then we went to look for the Corlett Street flat. Louise couldn't positively identify it at first because a high fence had subsequently been built in front of it. She told me it still puzzled her how Rickards and Shipton knew she was at the flat and not at work each time they came around to rape her.

My next move was to trace the ownership of the Rutland Street house. I discovered it was a police house that Shipton and Schollum were living in at the time. Then I went to see Heather Radford, the schoolteacher Louise first complained to back in Murupara. Mrs Radford looked and behaved like a retired schoolteacher. We exchanged small talk, and she predicted — pretty accurately, as it transpired — the scale of the repercussions should we ever publish the substance of what I was investigating. We had a cup of tea and chatted about Murupara. Her memory was sharp, and she told me about the day she called Louise in because of her sliding grades and deteriorating classroom behaviour. She told me how stunned she was when Louise said she'd been raped by one of the town's local coppers.

I asked her whether Louise had told her she'd been raped by Maori boys on horseback. Yes, she did say that, Mrs Radford said, but hastened to add that this was a 15 year old who'd just told her teacher about terrible and traumatic things that had been done to her. She'd been around school children long enough to know lies when she heard them, so when Louise then told her she'd been raped by Maori boys on horseback, 'I didn't believe her . . . I think she felt she needed to embellish because she was worried I might not believe what she'd said about the police officer. She thought it might somehow reinforce what she'd just told me.'

As for Louise's allegations against Brown: 'I believe her,' Mrs Radford said.

Soon after this I went out to Ngakuru to meet Louise's husband Ross. Louise introduced us. I'd heard a bit about him, and as we shook hands we sized each other up.

'Jeez, you don't look like a reporter,' he said. 'You should get a bloody haircut or something, ya scruffy bugger.'

We laughed.

Ross liked gardening, and so do I. He had a farming background, as I do. It made for common ground and helped us out in those moments when Ross was silent, hearing the most repugnant, intimate details of his wife's allegations. He was deeply concerned for Louise, I could see that immediately. And regardless of how disruptive it was to his family life, he was supportive.

'Well, you got to do what you got to do, missus,' he said, 'because you're never going to feel peace till you've put this bloody thing to bed.'

But I sensed confusion and considerable anxiety at what was still to come. He'd been there when Louise had been done over in the courts, and he'd helped her to pick up the pieces and get on with things again. He confided some of his doubts to me. Was she really doing the right thing bringing this all up again? Could they trust the media? What would all this mean for their kids, and for his family's financial situation? What would the police do? These were all valid questions, and I tried to answer as best I could.

Ross opened a couple of beers and a bottle of some terrible purple muck that Louise was drinking and we carried on talking. Dewar's name cropped up.

'I was the only one of the lot of us who never trusted that bastard. Wasn't I, missus?' he chirped to Louise.

I met the three girls too, and when I next got home, my wife Nicky asked about Louise's family. I used descriptions from days gone by to describe Ross — a good Kiwi bloke, salt of the earth, straight up and down — but I told her that what had struck me most about the Nicholas family was the relationship Ross and Louise had with their three daughters. They were children any parent would be proud of, I told Nicky.

The weeks were flying by. It was close to Christmas and I was due to start at TVNZ. I'd been briefing *The Dominion Post*'s lawyer Peter McKnight on the story and was in daily contact with *The Dominion Post*'s editor, Tim Pankhurst. Tim wanted to publish before I left the paper, and we were then still talking of a story with no names. New information was trickling in, but there was a wall around Rickards. When I mentioned his name, even to close, long-standing police contacts, it was: 'Nah. Nah. Can't help you there, mate. Don't know anything about that.'

Nor, despite extensive research by myself and the staff of the newspaper's research library, had I found the former policewoman, Caroline, who my source had told me had lost her baton and then had it returned to her by a cop who said it had been used sexually on a young woman. I'd been reluctant to approach serving Rotorua policewomen to help trace her, even though they probably would have been able to lend a hand, because I didn't want what I was investigating to get around police circles. And lastly, I wanted to find Margaret Craig, the counsellor Louise had spoken to in the mid-nineties.

So I resisted publishing, as I felt there were still some gaps in the story. By now the pile of copied tapes and documents I was safekeeping was growing by the week.

While he was anxious to publish, Tim Pankhurst also had his reasons for holding off. A year earlier, we'd dropped the Donna Awatere Huata story on the public two days before Christmas. From a media perspective, that's probably the worst possible time to publish a huge scandal. Your readers are going on holiday, Parliament's shut down and 'silly season' reigns, with everyone — news gatherers and consumers alike — preferring 'soft' stories to shock-horror. We'd all learned from that experience.

Avoiding the Christmas period, however, meant pushing things out to after my starting date with TVNZ. To accommodate the aspirations of both organisations, I suggested to Tim that I sound out TVNZ news boss Bill Ralston about the possibility of breaking the police rape story in *The Dominion Post* in the morning and then on *One News* the same night, probably in late January. He agreed it was worth a go.

I phoned Bill. I asked if he remembered that when he'd first asked me to come and work for TVNZ, over one of those long lunches for which he was famous, he'd seen me carefully lock a set of files in the boot of my car. He told me he hadn't forgotten. I said the files were about the next Commissioner of Police, a local body politician and a former police prosecutor who'd all been accused of pack-raping and violating a teenager with a baton. Bill was on a plane to Hawke's Bay the next day to see the evidence. He was pretty excited by what he saw.

I asked him who he'd get to front the story on telly if he and Tim could agree.

'You will,' he said.

I nodded, and tried not to show it, but the thought of reporting on camera freaked me out.

The next day Tim and Bill spoke and they cut a deal.

Christmas came and went and on 2 January 2004 I was back in Rotorua, now working for two bosses. Ralston had assigned one of his most experienced current-affairs producers, Chris Harrington, to put the story together for a *One News* special. Knowing how complex it was, I got the hotel to put a whiteboard in a meeting room and waited for Chris. Chris — or Harry, as he is better known — listened for the thick end of an hour as I squeaked away on the whiteboard tracing the links, the plots and the strands that made up the story. We went over the documents, then got down to the guts of television reporting: getting pictures. There was one picture the story needed above all, Harry told me: Louise's face.

I'd spoken at length by then to Louise, Ross, Jim and Barbara about how New Zealand law protected Louise's name from being published. All sexual-abuse complainants are granted automatic name suppression and that remains set in stone unless they choose to waive it.

Harry gave me a crash course in the business of television, however. Louise would come across as far more credible, he told me, if her face could be seen on screen instead of being blacked out.

That night, I took him to meet Louise. I was in the midst of a spiel about how I'd hoped she'd think once more about showing her face for the newspaper and on television when Louise cut me short. She and Ross had already made their decision, she said.

'I don't want to be seen to be hiding in the shadows throwing stones. If I'm doing this, then people need to be able to see who I am. I'll do it, but my children are not to be identified.'

I could tell Harry was rapt. I think it was her decision to flag her anonymity away that convinced him Louise was telling the truth.

The next day the cameraman arrived. The piece I did with Louise was a pretty fair effort for my first stab at doing an interview for the box. When it was finished I overheard Harry talking to Bill Ralston on the phone, saying: 'She's absolutely believable.'

Then we went to film in Murupara. Just before the state highway turn-off,

Louise sighed and chuckled. I asked what was funny. She pointed to some dramatic steaming cliffs, and said that whenever her father drove her and her brothers past those cliffs when they were kids he'd say, 'That's the place where the dragonflies are born.'

We filmed outside the Murupara Police Station as discreetly as we could. I did a short walking interview with Louise, asking what had gone on in the station all those years ago. A couple of locals got nosy and asked what we were doing, but Harry blew them off with some story about a documentary. Then we drove back to Rotorua, where Harry also wanted a short interview outside the house in Rutland Street. We shot the interview and a short piece of me speaking to the camera. This was remarkable as the one and only time I wore a suit in my television career.

The proposed date for publication of the story was the last Saturday in January. There were a frantic couple of weeks as Harry and I got the pictures we needed and I tried to track down the remaining people I believed we must talk to.

I spoke to certain people from Rex Miller's internal inquiry team. They agreed to talk only if their names were kept out of any story I did. What they told me was useful, but I found I couldn't use it, as even to say how I'd got it would risk revealing their identities. None was prepared to say if they believed Louise had been raped, but they used strong language to condemn Rickards, Shipton and Schollum. They said that as serving police officers the three would have known she was a sexual-abuse complainant, and vulnerable to a police officer's power. One of my informants suggested I speak to Miller himself, because they'd heard Miller had warned the police hierarchy not to advance Rickards through the ranks because it might come back to bite them.

In mid-January I learned Miller had retired to Hamilton, and easily found his address. I wandered up his driveway one day soon afterward. I found him outside, and I cut to the chase. I said I had transcripts of the two interviews he'd done with Louise in 1995, and the contradictory statement Dewar had taken a month later. I said I knew his internal inquiry had caned Dewar, but wondered what had happened to Rickards, Shipton and Schollum.

Rex chuckled.

'I knew all this would come up again sooner or later,' he said. 'But I don't know you from a bar of soap.'

I said I could give him the names of certain police officers and he could check me out. We kept talking. Miller suggested that someone might show me a copy of his secret report. I played it cool.

'That would certainly be helpful,' I said. I desperately wanted to see that report, but I didn't want to let on. I asked Miller if he'd do an interview, regardless of whether I could get access to his report. To my immense relief, he said he would.

As the camera was set up, we continued chatting. I sensed that, even after all those years, Miller was still deeply uneasy at Dewar's decision to take over an investigation that involved his mates Shipton and Rickards. And I could see he believed Louise Nicholas. We recorded a compelling and important interview.

Miller didn't beat around the bush. He said Rickards, Shipton and Schollum 'to some extent' corroborated Louise's allegations. He confirmed that Ray Sutton's notebook did record Louise's rape allegations and that it 'mysteriously disappeared from his desk'.

'You knew that Dewar, who decided to take over this inquiry after Sutton received those complaints, was friends with Rickards and Shipton?' I asked.

'Yes, well,' he replied. 'They'd been in Rotorua together for some time and they were friends, yes.'

'Is it appropriate police procedure for an investigating officer to investigate serious allegations against police officers when the men who have been named as rapists were his friends?'

'It's not professional, and if that does happen, you disqualify yourself. Same as a judge in a court case has to do.'

I also got an answer to the nagging question of why Miller, when he had completed his inquiry eight years earlier, had told Louise's mother, 'your daughter needs help'. He said the comment was made after he'd spoken to Louise's counsellor, Margaret Craig.

'She was worried that Louise was in a position where she had been, well, to use a loose term, brainwashed,' Miller said.

'Did she ever say who she felt had brainwashed Louise?'

'She thought perhaps it was Dewar.'

He said when he'd interviewed Louise she'd been deeply distrustful of the police. 'She'd been slippered that many times over the years, and it had always involved police members, that she really didn't trust anyone.'

'Because she'd complained about sexual offending by police officers in the past and had been told . . . ?'

'Nothing happened.'

'Is that an understandable state of mind for a rape complainant?' I asked.

'Hell, yes,' Miller replied. 'Totally understandable.'

We turned to Rickards's rapid promotion to the top of the police, and Miller told me Police Commissioner Rob Robinson would have known of the allegations and should have seen his report. Miller said there would be a note on Rickards's police file saying he'd admitted having group sex with a teenager. He said internal police disciplinary rules had a time limit that meant the police would be unable to charge Rickards for that behaviour, so the stiffest penalty available was a dressing-down. Miller said he'd given him just that. However, he said, if anyone could unearth evidence that the sex was non-consensual, Rickards and co could still be charged under the Crimes Act.

I ended the interview with this question: 'Are you able to give us a view on whether you think Assistant Commissioner Rickards would make a suitable Commissioner?'

It was one of those golden television moments. Miller stared at the camera for several seconds in silence before quietly answering, 'Perhaps my silence will answer that.'

On 13 January I spoke to former Detective Inspector John Dewar, who by now had left the police and was a manager for St John Ambulance in Hamilton. We met in his office, and I plugged the line that he might want to talk about why he was run out of the Rotorua CIB by the police hierarchy. Dewar was approachable but cautious, asking nearly as many questions as I did. His office was chock-full of memorabilia from his police career — a taiaha, a sword, medals and a baton all prominently displayed. He mentioned the names of police officers who had backed him and, as we fenced, he said it would be better if I got the story of his demise from other cops, because he didn't want to 'bag the police'. I smiled inwardly, as only a few seconds earlier he'd slammed Rex Miller's investigation of him as 'absolutely incompetent'.

I told him I'd spoken to Louise, but talked about her allegations in a roundabout way to gauge his reaction. He tried to steer away from the topic but I brought him back around.

'I'm trying to think of [Brown's] name,' he said. 'He was friends of the Crawford family and was known as "Horse Cock".'

Though I knew all about Dewar's dealings with Trevor Clayton, when I said I'd heard there was an officer who'd told Dewar he'd lie under oath to protect his mates, Dewar clammed up and refused to say who that officer was. Then he started lying. He said Crown Prosecutor John McDonald had agreed that Dewar should tell the jury about Clayton's statement that he would lie to protect his mates in the first Brown trial. He said McDonald even agreed at which point in his evidence Dewar should drop that particular bomb. That a Crown Prosecutor would plan for a senior policeman to give deliberate hearsay evidence beggars belief.

When I mentioned Rickards's name, Dewar told me Rickards 'knows something, but I don't know if he'd help'. Shipton, he said, was 'a power lifter and a bloody good detective'.

I asked about the baton rape, and this was what Dewar said: 'There was a baton involved, inserted in her', but 'Louise was a willing participant in the later issues [that is, in the sex that happened after Sam Brown] . . . she enjoyed being close to police and was too loose with her favours. Despite her views, there was no way to proceed [with a case against the three policemen].'

I had been told by a reliable source that Shipton, Schollum and Rickards had denied ever using a baton in that way, but they'd also denied on oath in the third Sam Brown trial that they'd used a baton on Louise.

From my interview with Dewar, I went to a place where I was shown the secret Rex Miller report — I can't say where or by whom. At first, I was only allowed to read it. Later I was given a photocopy. We were busy filming during the day at the time so I'd sit up late reading and rereading the hefty report, flagging important passages with dozens of Post-it notes.

The report slammed Dewar's investigation into Louise's allegations, his conduct in the Brown trials, and his performance as head of the Rotorua CIB. It reinforced much of what we already knew, and confirmed much of what I'd suspected. In effect, it said Dewar had lied about his relationship with Schollum, Shipton and Rickards. In fact, he had spoken to Shipton and Rickards several times while he was being investigated. It was at Shipton's request that he took over the Louise Nicholas investigation, and he had kept from his superiors the substance of Louise's allegations against Schollum, Shipton and Rickards.

In some passages, the man whom Louise had once considered to be the only friend she had in the police showed his true colours. He told Miller's team that he 'enjoyed a very good relationship with Mrs Nicholas throughout both the investigation and the three trials', but when Miller told him he wasn't going to be charged with conspiring to pervert the course of justice, he relaxed, dropped his guard and said: 'She's just a police slut. I like my women young and fresh.'

Exactly how Dewar set about stuffing the chances of a successful prosecution of Sam Brown is contained in page 20 of Miller's report, never previously published. According to Miller, Dewar told the Deputy Commissioner of Police in 1994 that Rickards and Shipton heard Brown admitting his 'sexual contact' with Louise. Because Louise was under the age of consent at the time, this admission would effectively be a confession of rape.

Miller asked the Crown Prosecutor John McDonald why Rickards and Shipton didn't give evidence to this effect when they testified at Brown's third trial. McDonald said he asked Dewar the same question, but Dewar's response was that Rickards and Shipton had told him they'd lie — just as Clayton had said he would — if they were asked about Brown's admissions.

Miller put the question to Dewar himself: why didn't Rickards and Shipton give evidence about Brown's admissions at trial? Dewar changed his story. He said he'd got it wrong — it was actually to Schollum that Brown had confessed. Schollum told him this, Dewar said, in an off-the-record conversation. So Miller asked Schollum. Schollum denied Brown had ever made any such confession to him. He even rejected Dewar's statement that he and Dewar had an off-the-record discussion about it.

Still looking after his mates, Dewar told Miller that he was sure Rickards and Shipton didn't even know Brown and therefore couldn't have heard him making any admissions. Miller asked Rickards and Shipton if they knew Brown, and they affirmed Dewar's assertion: no, they didn't know Brown.

I found out later that they did. Brown himself told me (and I have it on tape) that he'd worked with Rickards and shared coffee with Shipton on his verandah back in Rotorua.

So far, so good. But then I got to a passage that froze my guts, and for a moment I saw years of work disappearing down the gurgler. The report contained some, but not all, of the details of Rex Miller's interviews with Sue Grant (not her real name), Louise's Corlett Street flatmate. It was the combination of what Grant told him and Louise's statement to Dewar that had convinced Miller back in 1993 that a charge against Rickards, Shipton and Schollum would be unlikely to succeed.

Miller and an Australian police officer, Detective Inspector Ray Platz, picked Grant up from her job in Brisbane. First she told Miller she didn't even know Shipton and Schollum, but Rickards's name seemed familiar. Then she did a U-turn and said yes, she knew Shipton and Schollum. She and Louise had had group sex with them, and Louise 'certainly wasn't saying no'.

At that point I got straight on the phone to Miller and expressed my concerns about this remark and how it could kill any potential story. Miller waited till I'd finished, then said flatly: 'She wasn't telling the whole truth. I didn't believe her and neither did the Aussie officer with me.'

Miller said he believed Grant might have been involved in non-consensual sex with one or more police officers, but she was of a very different disposition to Louise. She just wanted to forget about it all, and could have reasoned that telling the investigation the sex had been consensual would be the quickest way to make it all go away. She said she would refuse to come back to New Zealand to give evidence if Shipton, Schollum and Rickards were charged with rape. In contrast with Louise, Miller said, Grant 'was very evasive . . . She told us what she thought we wanted to hear, not what happened. Louise Nicholas was more believable and she hasn't faltered from day one and she's still telling exactly the same story today.'

Louise Nicholas — My Story

The story was coming together, with Miller's report filling in many of the gaps. I had more than enough to publish, but there were still some finishing touches to put on the television piece. We'd decided to try covertly filming Louise as she confronted Dewar. A cameraman and I went back to Hamilton to scout the St John car park that we expected Dewar to drive into. I'd noted the make and registration of Dewar's car on my earlier visit. Just in case Dewar was thinking the same way and had clocked the registration of my car, and got suspicious when he saw Louise getting out of it, we hired a car.

We set up a camera in some shrubbery across the road from St John and wired Louise with a hidden microphone taped around her back. Then she waited in the hire car. It was a hot day, and our adrenalin was going for it. Finally I saw Dewar's car approaching and alerted Louise by cellphone. Dewar parked, got out and was on his way into the building when Louise called out: 'John! John!' The camera had a clear shot of Louise approaching Dewar. He reached out and put his arm around her. He missed the microphone by millimetres. I could hear Louise through headphones as she told Dewar she'd been approached by a reporter and wanted to 'see what you make of it'.

Dewar said it was obvious there was 'no news happening'.

Louise said she also wanted to talk about 'Shipton and bloody Rickards and all them'.

'That's what, you know, adults do in the privacy of their home,' Dewar said coolly. 'There were some issues of that, that . . . um . . . would perhaps, um . . . were disconcerting.'

'It wasn't consensual,' Louise pressed him. 'This is what hacked me off. It was not consensual. How did he, I mean you knew that. And this is what really, you know, bugs me.'

'Yeah, well,' said Dewar. 'I mean, I certainly knew that the part regarding the baton wasn't consensual. I . . . it would be hard to understand why you would consent to that but, um . . .'

'Exactly,' said Louise.

'He's hung himself,' said the cameraman, as this came through our headphones.

A couple of kids walking through the park started asking us what we were doing. I told them to scram.

Dewar confirmed that Trevor Clayton had said he'd lie for Brown, but Louise's questions were starting to unsettle him. Still, he must have imagined he still had some power over her, because he offered her his card and suggested they have a chat at some stage. Louise kept him talking. She told him she'd had the impression that 'these guys [Shipton, Schollum and Rickards] were your mates'.

'They were,' said Dewar, 'and still are.'

The cameraman nodded enthusiastically.

'It was rape . . . Whenever I hear those names, I cringe,' Louise said angrily.

'Well . . . I mean, obviously you haven't got over it,' Dewar said. 'You've got to move on . . . You can't allow it to persecute you.'

'Yeah, but it's just . . . it's a bit hard. You know these guys treated me like an animal . . .'

'You're not the only one,' Dewar nodded.

'I know I was never the only one, and that's sickening,' said Louise. 'To know there's somebody else out there who these guys did.'

'No doubt,' said Dewar. 'I mean, I couldn't give you names, 'cause I don't know. But I know . . . all I'm saying is . . . that's probably not right. But there's reputation, you know. Rumour and all that sort of stuff — I'm sure there's substance and foundation to . . . They boozed up, they bloody got into stray rooting, and all sorts of things.'

As she questioned him about how the defence had come to know about Shipton, Schollum and Rickards and why those three had been called to give evidence at the third trial, Dewar let slip another clanger.

'They were all mates at that time. What one was doing the other was doing or had known about it. They were talking. Mostly about all that information . . . I suspect there was probably a certain amount of collusion behind the scenes. And I know they were all pretty concerned about it, obviously.'

He finished up telling Louise to phone him.

For a covert interview, it was a dream. We'd struck gold.

I took Louise to Auckland to meet *The Dominion Post* lawyer, Peter McKnight, on his yacht at Westhaven Marina. We sat in the galley as Peter flicked through the Miller report. 'This is good, Phil. This is good,' he was saying. He questioned Louise closely and asked me to phone him in the next couple of days.

By now we knew we had one hell of a story to publish, and all the lights were going green.

On the road back to Rotorua afterward, Louise talked about how Ross took her away from her nightmares when they were first married, how they travelled around the North Island in the stock truck he drove. Good days, happy days, she said. I told her how lucky I was having my wife, Nicky — how even if she was asleep when I got home, she'd get up and listen while I had a glass of wine and we'd talk about new developments. If you couldn't unload like that, you'd burn out, I said.

There had been a few of these late-night sessions lately. I talked often with Nicky about how the lives of those four men and their families were about to be changed forever. We'd been there with other stories that led to people being criminally charged, but that didn't soothe the sorrow and anxiety I felt for the innocent people who were about to be caught up in the media firestorm.

It was 21 January, ten days from publication. Thanks to Miller's report and the footage we'd got in our stake-out, I knew we'd be able to name Dewar. A final decision on whether we would name Rickards, Shipton and Schollum hadn't yet been made.

I still wanted to find Margaret Craig, Louise's counsellor from the mid-nineties, and the policewoman whose baton was used for sex on a young woman. There were two key things we wanted to know from Margaret Craig. Had Louise been credible? And, if so, could she offer a sexual-abuse expert's explanation as to why a teenager practically accepted what police officers did to her? By now I'd been to the homes of every Margaret Craig listed in the Bay of Plenty. Eventually I got a lead for a seaside address near Tauranga, and I was confident we'd tracked Margaret down at last.

I knew an ethical counsellor would never talk to me without approval from their client, so we took Louise with us the next day to try for an interview. I knocked on the door, and the surprised-looking woman who answered confirmed that she was, indeed, the Margaret Craig who had worked as a sexual-abuse counsellor in Rotorua in the 1990s. She invited me in. I explained what it was I was investigating, and asked whether she would grant an interview if Louise gave her permission. Margaret thought carefully, then said she'd need to speak to Louise before she could say.

I told her Louise was out in the car.

'What, she's here with you?' Margaret said.

I brought Louise in and she and Margaret hugged. Then we got down to business, and Margaret agreed to talk. Harry wanted the interview done on the spot.

With the camera rolling, I asked Margaret why people should believe Louise had been sexually assaulted by police officers when she herself admitted she'd never put up a fight or gone to complain at the nearest police station.

Margaret replied that Louise's behaviour was typical of someone sexually abused as a young teenager. She was reiterating the explanation I'd first heard from my police source about sex-abuse victims. Margaret's answers were critically important, because they countered the view of many who say abuse victims who don't complain at the time of the abuse are probably making it up. And as for why Louise would want to bring it all up when she was living a happily married life with three children, Margaret had this to say:

'I imagine she began to see the absolute injustice of her situation. That it didn't matter who she told, nobody seemed to want to listen. We are not talking about a church leader or a schoolteacher. We are talking about the New Zealand police force. And there isn't anywhere else that I know of where you can go, other than the ombudsman or someone like that, if you have a complaint of that nature. I think she must have felt completely let down by the system, really, the investigative system the police instituted in her case. I guess that's stayed with her all these years.'

I was now having regular briefings with Tim Pankhurst and Bill Ralston. With publication just days away, Pankhurst told me that I should tell Louise she could still pull out of the story. I'd done that several times already, but in a relaxed way, making it clear the final decision on whether we published or not was her choice. But I agreed with Tim: I needed to do it differently this time. I phoned Louise.

'As you know, we're not far from D-Day,' I said, 'and I want you to tell me if there's anything you haven't told me.'

'No,' said Louise, sounding confused. 'No. What do you mean?'

'Louise,' I said. 'I've got a family. My bosses have family, and there are a bunch of people whose jobs are on the line for this story. If you've lied to us or if these things didn't happen then it's never too late to drop this and walk away.'

From all that I'd seen and read and heard, I believed her. But I carried on regardless, hardening my tone.

'If you've got things wrong, I need to know. Because I can tell you that if you aren't telling the truth, I am down shit creek without a paddle. *The Dominion Post* and TVNZ will be liable for damages of millions and millions of dollars. My bosses will be finished. A whole lot of people will be gone. Down the road.'

There was silence on the other end of the line. Then, for the first time since I'd met her, I heard Louise Nicholas crying.

'Do you not believe me?' she asked. 'Are you saying you don't believe me?'

'Louise, I'm just saying people's lives are on the line here. Not just your family's, but those being accused, my family, and others as well.'

'I've never told you a lie,' she said. 'Nothing I've said to you is a lie.'

'OK,' I relented. 'OK. But I need to know, OK?'

The scramble continued. I was really at the sharp end by now. Word was getting out about this huge story that was about to break, and it reached Sam Brown. I got a call from him out of the blue. He was in the clear, having been found not guilty, and could talk with a certain amount of freedom. It seemed clear that he hated Dewar, but it was hard to get a handle on what he thought of Rickards, Shipton and Schollum. Such was his dislike of Dewar that he provided me with certain documents, and these had the effect of implicating the other three as well.

Four days from deadline, I put in calls to Shipton, Schollum and Rickards, which I recorded. Schollum was polite but firm. He said he'd like to tell me his side of the story, but couldn't because his name was suppressed. I told him I wished to speak to him about aspects of Louise's allegations that in my view were not suppressed. Schollum remained completely calm and polite and said he'd talk to his lawyer.

Shipton started the same way, and said the allegations had been investigated twice and had no substance. Then he started getting a bit wound up.

'I will say this, mate,' he blustered. 'If you defame or slur me in any way, I will follow through with the legal proceedings because it's just rubbish.'

I told Shipton the allegations were being made by Louise, not me. He again threatened legal action, but said he would not be interviewed and had nothing to say.

I tried to reach Rickards at his new office, from which he headed the Auckland Police District, but was referred to his public relations boss. I told her that unless I had an assurance that she had Rickards's approval to talk to me about the allegations, I wouldn't put them to her. They were so serious and sensitive, I said, that he should hear them before her. She told me she had that assurance. Then she said that Rickards would not be interviewed.

On 27 January, I put another call in to Dewar and hit the record button. He denied he'd told Louise the baton incident was not consensual, but said: 'It's hard to understand someone would consent to that kind of treatment'.

He said on one hand that he didn't doubt Louise, but then he claimed she didn't want to pursue criminal action against the three men. Dewar denied he was friends with Shipton and Rickards. I pressed him on that point. He said if anyone said they were friends, they'd be wrong. Then he lied, saying his investigation had been reviewed and that the police inquiry had ruled he'd done a proper investigation. I couldn't believe what I was hearing.

'So you say you and the police were satisfied you investigated these allegations vigorously and properly?' I asked.

'That's correct,' replied Dewar.

He began to make insinuations about Louise's character, telling me how 'strange' it had been hearing Louise speak in front of her parents about intimate sexual details. Then he paused, and said: 'We're not taping this, are we?'

'Yes, I am,' I replied. 'I'm also taking notes, Mr Dewar.'

Dewar got edgy.

'Anything that you have recorded without my consent in relation to this matter is not to be used.' He hung up.

The cat was out of the bag, and the police moved to determine the extent of the damage that was about to be done and when they could expect the blow to fall. I learned that Commissioner Rob Robinson had booked a meeting with Tim Pankhurst. I wanted to question the Commissioner, and at the request of Police HQ I put my questions in writing. I sent seven in all, including one asking Robinson if he was satisfied Louise Nicholas had been treated the same way other rape complainants can expect to be treated by the police. In his reply, Robinson said he too was snagged by suppression orders shrouding the Brown trials. He did say that if the story had fresh information and questioned the integrity of the police, he'd look into it.

We received statements from lawyers acting for Rickards, Shipton and Schollum, all saying they absolutely denied Louise's allegations. We put their denials into the stories being prepared.

Harry was working like a demon getting what turned out to be an eight-minute news special together. I didn't have a clue what was involved in editing a story for television, so I left the mechanics of getting it all to air up to him. That left me free to continue my search for Caroline, the policewoman who'd allegedly owned the baton used on Louise. The day before publication I got a breakthrough from police sources. The woman I was looking for was Carolyn Butcher, not Caroline: fortuitously, she lived in Auckland.

I went to the address, taking a tape recorder. I was feeling physically and mentally exhausted, but strangely hyped. After identifying myself, I told Carolyn Butcher I'd been looking for her for several years and outlined what I'd discovered and what I'd been told about her baton. She listened without saying anything. Then she thought for what seemed a very long time. I felt like a rubber band stretched out to breaking point.

'Yes,' she said at last. 'That's pretty well what happened.'

I was surprised at myself. My eyes misted.

'There's a woman out there who's waited a long time for this to come out,' I said, 'and she's going to be incredibly thankful for your honesty.'

I explained that the last few months had been long and stressful. 'And if anyone asks, you didn't see my eyes water, did you?'

Butcher wanted to talk it over with her husband before agreeing to an interview, but in the end she refused to go on camera. Unfortunately, that's where television needed her.

We were on the eave of breaking the story. Nicky and I were so wound up emotionally, and God only knows what the Nicholas family — and the families of Shipton, Schollum, Rickards, Dewar and Brown — were going through. To pre-empt the possibility of a last-minute injunction being sought by lawyers for the various interested parties, Peter McKnight notified courts in Auckland, Hamilton, Rotorua, Tauranga and Wellington that he was on stand-by to argue against any gag. Surprisingly, perhaps, none was made.

Meanwhile, the fantastic teams at *The Dominion Post*'s offices in Wellington and at TVNZ's in Auckland were furiously editing and helping me to put the two stories to bed. I finished late — Harry and Bill Ralston packed me off to my hotel room — and it was there that I took a call from Tim Pankhurst, 600 kilometres away. He didn't say it, but his arse was on the line too. He later sent me his speech notes from an investigative reporting seminar, in which he recalled those final moments in his office before the presses ran with the biggest story he'd ever be likely to break as an editor.

'I've never seen anything like it. You could see the fear and doubt in people's eyes. I felt very much alone.' He wrote that he'd notified Peter O'Hara, the boss at Fairfax, which owned *The Dominion Post*, about the potential risks. O'Hara backed him, saying, 'If we hang, we'll hang together.'

Tim's wife Sue had seen the toll it was taking.

'Why do you do this to yourself?' she asked.

'It's what we do,' he replied.

Tim asked if I had any last-minute doubts. Everything had been done, and I felt oddly relaxed.

'Don't worry,' I told Tim. 'We're shedding light on allegations and a conspiracy that should have come out years ago. You should be proud.'

I rang Nicky and had a long talk. I rang Hemi Hikawai, my closest friend and a former cop who'd given me invaluable advice over the past months, from the moment I'd first met Louise. Then, of course, I rang Louise.

We'd now reached the end of the road. I tried again to explain how big this story would be media-wise, but I'm not sure Louise could comprehend it. Either that, or she was too preoccupied with the effect it would have on the families of those we were about to uncover. We talked about that at length, satisfying ourselves that it was regrettable, but the price of justice. Then that was it. Finished.

In the hotel restaurant, the waitress asked if I'd had a long day. It must have shown. I said it had been a long four months and eight years and I was going to sit with the bottle of wine that was in front of me and get quietly drunk.

As a reporter, I could appreciate her curiosity.

'Why?' she asked.

A story, I replied. A story I'd been working on for a long time. It was about to be published, and she'd know what I was talking about when she saw it. Tomorrow.

Louise

IN JANUARY 2004, I MET Phil and Chris Harrington, a producer from TVNZ, at the hotel where the television interview would take place. I was extremely nervous about being in front of the camera, but Phil assured me that if I ignored the lens and just concentrated on him and his questions, it would cease to exist. He was right. Once we got going I felt myself relax and was able to totally ignore the camera. By now it was easy talking to Phil, and that's how I managed to get through the interview. I just sat and had a conversation.

The hardest part of the day was going to Rutland Street and doing an interview in front of the house. That's when it really hit home that this was happening. I was about to put to the public a story that would probably seem slightly unbelievable to some and a load of bullshit to others, but hopefully the majority would see that I wasn't lying, I had nothing to hide and that a travesty of justice had occurred over a period of 20-odd years.

The other thing that made the Rutland Street interview hard was that Phil, who normally gets about in jeans and a sloppy shirt, had put on this suit-and-tie job and, I tell you now, he looked bloody stupid. So as we walked towards the house, while the camera filmed us, I whispered to him that he looked really ridiculous. He whispered back that he felt ridiculous, and from there it was hard for us both to keep a straight face.

Chris Harrington wanted us to go back to Murupara and film where I had grown up, showing the house I had lived in with my family, the high school I had attended and also the police station where Brown had done those bad things to me. We did it, but it was really hard for me to go back and recall those awful days. But again, I found a way to cope. I just remembered the good bits of Murupara — my family, my friends, and my old mate, Dolly the horse. It was a hard day, sure, but it was also a good day, remembering the good times.

Ross, the girls and I headed over to Mount Maunganui for a week's holiday in Ross's parents' caravan. While we were there, Phil called to say he thought they'd found Margaret Craig and they were heading over to see if she was willing to be interviewed. He asked me to go with them, as I would need to tell her that it was OK to put aside client confidentiality and speak freely about me and what had gone on in our counselling sessions. I was stoked to think they'd finally found her, as she held some important pieces of the jigsaw. I prayed she'd be willing to help put it together for us.

When the crew joined us at the Mount, Phil asked if we could do a beach shot showing me walking with Ross and the girls. I wasn't keen for the kids to appear, but he explained that their faces would be hidden and only Ross and I would be seen. Ross was a bit stand-offish, but the kids thought it was a cool idea. It didn't hurt a bit. Mind you, people sitting on the beach were looking and probably wondering who the hell we were to have a TV camera following us. If only they knew — and soon enough they would!

We headed over to where Margaret lived, with our fingers crossed it was her. We pulled up outside the house and Phil went and knocked on the door. A lady answered the door, but I couldn't tell if it was Margaret or not. After a short time, Phil came and got me. It *was* Margaret, and she was really happy to see me. The hug she gave me was so warm and welcoming that I knew all would be well.

Phil explained why we were there. Margaret listened with absolute astonishment. After I'd given my consent for her to discuss my case, she went to a cupboard to find my file. She explained that when she and her husband decided to move away from Rotorua she had destroyed the files of any clients she no longer had anything to do with, but after the court cases of 1993/94 she always felt that things could possibly raise their ugly heads again. As she rummaged through the cupboard looking for my file, she told us what she thought of John Dewar and how he had handled me and the court cases. You could hear and see her anger. This was the first I knew that Margaret was so down on him.

After some time looking through the cupboard, Margaret got rather agitated. She kept saying that she'd kept my file, but now couldn't find it.

'I know I didn't destroy it,' she said. 'It was one of only a few that I kept. Where on earth is it?' She explained that she had kept it in a locked filing cabinet in Rotorua, and she was adamant she hadn't culled it in the move. It contained all her notes from our counselling sessions, as well as letters and even newspaper cuttings. She was upset that she couldn't find it, and wondered if it had been stolen.

Even though she couldn't find the file, she was still able to recall for Phil some of what happened back in the nineties. She said she had a diary that could be of some help, and promised to find it and see what it held. Most importantly to Phil, Margaret was more than happy to be interviewed, but he said he'd rather I wasn't there. Didn't bother me; it was such a beautiful day, I wandered on down to the beach and found a comfortable spot on the sand. This gave me the opportunity to reflect on the last couple of weeks, and also get my head around what the public — and, I guess, the police — reaction was going to be when this story came out.

After about half an hour, Margaret's husband Murray came to find me. Margaret and I were finally able to sit down with a coffee and go back in time. We both recalled certain issues that had occurred way back then, but Margaret's recall was a lot better than mine. I realised then how hard she'd tried to help me, but the main problem was that nothing she said was going to convince me Dewar was a bad person. I found myself apologising. Of course, Margaret wouldn't hear of this, because she knew what had been happening and, after all, we were about to right some — if not all — of the wrongs in my past.

We left Margaret and Murray, promising to keep in contact. On the way back to the Mount I asked Phil how the interview had gone. Really well, he said. What she'd had to say was going to add credibility to my story. He told me a bit of what Margaret had said, but not in any great depth. I guess the secretive habits of a top-notch journalist are hard to shake.

Sometimes Phil asked a lot. One day he came to me and asked if I would consider going face-to-face with John Dewar while wired up with a hidden microphone. The thought of confronting this man made me extremely nervous, but perhaps it would be an opportunity to get answers to some of the questions that had really started to eat away at me. So, on the agreed day, we drove to Hamilton and met the TVNZ cameraman and his partner. Phil had phoned the St John Ambulance headquarters, where Dewar worked, and found out that he was not in the office but was due to return to work at about 3pm. That gave us enough time to grab a bite to eat and get me all rigged up with the secret microphone. We had to use duct tape to stick the microphone box to my back just above my knicker line. A wire then ran up my back and over to the little microphone hooked onto my bra. Hopefully, Dewar wouldn't see any of this.

Phil explained to me that when Dewar drove into the car park of St John, I was to approach him. The cameraman and Phil hid in the bushes across the road from St John, while the cameraman's partner and I drove into the car park and waited. We did the old 'Testing, testing, can you hear me?' thing, and the response back from the bush was 'Loud and clear'.

As three o'clock approached, my nerves were really jangling. Hamilton had put on a scorching hot day, but I wasn't sure if the sweat pouring off me was from the heat or nerves. My main concern at this point was shorting out the little microphone box! It seemed like hours were dragging by, but it was really only a matter of about 15 minutes before we got the call: 'Here he is.'

My heart skipped several beats, and I suddenly felt very cold.

'Go!' said the cameraman's partner, as Dewar parked his car. 'Go now!'

I just froze.

'I really don't want to do this, mate,' I said.

She just glared at me, leaned across my lap, opened the door and damn near pushed me out. I figured it probably wasn't a good idea to argue with this lady, so I took a deep breath, puffed out my chest and walked over to where Dewar was getting out of his car.

As he walked towards the building, I called out his name feebly. It took several goes, then he turned around and looked at me strangely. Then it dawned on him who was calling his name, and he started to walk towards me. I smiled and stuck out my hand, but he moved straight in to hug me. I damn near died, as his hand was no more than a centimetre or two from the microphone rig. Phil had lectured me beforehand, telling me that if Dewar got suspicious about the questions and asked whether I was wired, I was to say yes, and then if I wanted to continue, I should keep questioning him.

But the big guy upstairs was obviously looking down on me that day. As I pulled away from Dewar's hug, I smiled and explained that a reporter had contacted me, asking a lot of questions about the court cases back in 1993/94. He responded that he couldn't understand why a reporter would want to bring all that up again, but I just said that it did bring to light a few unanswered questions for me and I hoped he would be able to answer some of these.

We spoke for around 20 minutes in the car park. Dewar hadn't really changed much: he did most of the talking, mainly about stuff that had no relevance to me or what I was wanting. Anyway, he did eventually say that I obviously hadn't dealt with those events properly and that if I wanted, I could contact him the next time I was in Hamilton and we could go for coffee and discuss what was still bugging me. He suggested that I go with him to his office so that he could give me his card. I had to make a quick decision and decided, bugger it. If it meant he kept talking, it was probably a good thing. I looked over to where the cameraman's partner was sitting in the car and figured she would click on to what was happening. I followed Dewar into the building and up a winding staircase to his office, hoping and praying the microphone would still be audible inside the building.

As we entered his office at the top of the stairs I stopped dead in my tracks and gasped. It was as though I'd gone back in time, as his office was damn near identical to the one at the Rotorua Police Station. It was full of police memorabilia and, to top it off, he still had the mounted baton sitting smack-bang in the middle of his desk. Hoping he hadn't noticed my reaction, I quickly sat in a chair opposite his desk. I tried to compose myself, but that bloody baton took away any train of thought I had. I really had to give myself a swift kick and try to tune in to what Dewar was blabbing on about.

I got him to admit that he knew the baton incident wasn't a consensual act, and that Shipton, Schollum and Rickards were 'party animals'. He never socialised with them, he reckoned. He was their boss and that was all. I was so stoked to hear all this that I couldn't wait to get out and make sure Phil had heard it too.

After rummaging around his desk Dewar finally handed me his card, with his home phone number written on the back. After a few parting pleasantries — I made damn sure there were no hugs this time — I left. As I descended the staircase, I looked down at my chest and said quietly: 'I hope like hell you got all that!'

I pretty much ran to the car, jumped in and gave a huge sigh of relief as the cameraman's partner started it up. Off we went to find the two bush bunnies! We met them in another area of the park, and it was like watching a dog receiving a bone. Phil couldn't wait to get his hands on the tape. He shut himself away in the car and listened and wrote, and listened and wrote some more, shook his head and made a couple of weird noises, shook his head again and then, after a while, emerged from the car grinning from ear to ear.

'Well done, Lou!' he said.

I said: 'Couldn't shut him up, and why would I want to?'

We sat and talked for a bit, and I explained how walking in was like walking into Dewar's office in the bad old days of Rotorua. Phil asked me several times if I thought Dewar had any inkling of what I was really up to. I said I didn't think he had a bloody clue, which in some ways was a bummer because if he had asked me if I was wired, I would have given him both barrels. How sweet it would have been to have had the opportunity!

After that Phil and I waved goodbye to the others and headed to Auckland for a meeting with the lawyer. Then we drove back to Rotorua. I got home at around nine o'clock, while Phil carried on to Taupo to stay with his in-laws. I tried to explain the events of the day to Ross, but after a while he said, 'Bugger off to bed, missus. You're making no sense. Try again in the morning.' With that, I had a hot shower, jumped into my jammies, and before my head hit the pillow I was out to it, stacking Zs.

Even though Phil had asked me not to tell anyone the story, over the past few months I'd been confiding in my friend and neighbour, Janine Palmer. I found talking everything over with her was a huge help — just having another person's perspective on things made making certain decisions easier, and it probably helped that she was a woman. Janine's the sort of person you can pour your heart out to and know it's going to go no further than her, the ashtray and the cups of coffee she so happily supplied for me. Janine suggested that with the story coming out that Saturday it would probably be better if we weren't home, just in case we started to receive some not-so-nice phone calls. She suggested we all congregate at her house. It was decided, too, that her cousin Michelle, who lived in Rotorua, would bring *The Dominion Post* out to us to read. The paper wasn't usually sold in Rotorua, but Phil had told me the editor had arranged for it to be sold through one of our bookshops.

At 8.30 in the morning of Saturday 31 January 2004, Michelle parked her car outside McLeod's Bookshop and waited for the doors to open. At exactly nine, the doors opened and the shop assistant brought out a billboard that had my face and a huge headline on it: 'POLICE PACK-RAPED ME'. Even Michelle couldn't believe what she was seeing, but she knew she was on a mission. She pulled herself together, walked into the shop and picked up half a dozen copies of *The Dominion Post*. The shop assistant looked at her, then down at the paper and then back at Michelle, and asked her if she knew the woman in the paper. Michelle told him she did. The shop assistant then told her that they didn't normally sell this paper, but after reading it he could see why it was being sold in Rotorua.

Michelle gathered up the papers and headed out to Ngakuru, where we were all waiting patiently. Mum and Dad turned up too, so it was a real gathering at Janine and Gary's house. Finally we heard the sound of Michelle's tyres on the gravel as she drove in. After a moment she brought the papers out to where we were all sitting in the garden. I was really nervous about seeing the story, to the point where after looking at the headline and my picture on the front page I just couldn't read it. I looked at it, lit a smoke and walked away. As I paced about, I could hear everyone who was reading making all sorts of comments, but the one that kept coming up was: 'Oh, my God!'

After an hour or so I decided it was time to get hard. I walked over and picked up the paper, but I was so transfixed with the headline and the photos of Rickards, Shipton and Schollum that all I could think about was whether the men I'd accused of doing all this awful stuff had read the paper yet. I figured someone would have contacted them — the telephone lines would be running red hot. I finally shifted my gaze to the start of the story, drew a very long breath and started to read.

Phil

THE STORY NAMING RICKARDS, SHIPTON, Schollum, Dewar and Clayton broke on Saturday morning, with Louise's face under an 'Exclusive' banner and the words 'POLICE PACK-RAPED ME'. It was plastered on billboards around New Zealand, as other Fairfax papers were given the story too. Pages one and two of *The Dominion Post* were blanketed with stories from our investigation. A beautifully crafted editorial, entitled 'Abuse of power and trust in macho force', ran inside. When we spoke later that day Louise told me the final paragraph had brought her to tears.

The television story was being polished to run that night. Harry and I had a morning meeting with TVNZ's lawyer, Willy Akel, and Harry, to the best of his ability, eased me though my apprehension at voicing the story. Meanwhile, my mind was working overtime trying to figure out a way to break the story of Carolyn Butcher's baton. Eventually I approached Bill Ralston, and suggested he might be able to use his high profile to talk her around to an on-camera interview.

Bill rang Carolyn Butcher and said he'd hired this green television reporter who was breaking this really important story. Couldn't she give the guy a break and do a short interview? She relented, and I raced out to her house with a cameraman. I took along a wooden police baton that Jim Crawford had given me months earlier. In what we journalists like to call a bizarre twist, this turned out to have been given to him by Sam Brown, who had busted it while belting a criminal. Jim had fixed it, prophetically declaring it might be useful one day.

During the interview with Carolyn Butcher, I passed the baton to her and asked if that was the kind she'd been told by a police officer had been used for deviant sex. We got some good pictures out of that stunt. You could see the revulsion on her face as she was handling it and describing what her baton had supposedly been used for.

I was on a plane heading home when the story was screened but saw a taped version when I got back to a house full of family. TVNZ had creamed TV3 with the story. The combination of the sensational revelations coming out in a major daily newspaper and on TV was a double whammy. It speaks volumes for the courage of my bosses, Pankhurst and Ralston. They'd stuck their necks out when many editors would have refused to run the story for fear of being sued.

But if you're talking about courage, of course, it all boiled down to the amazing bravery of Louise's decision to come forward so publicly. The sheer guts of the woman struck a chord with people right around the country, and sources in the Tauranga police told me the lights on the switchboard lit up like a Christmas tree that night as others complained about Shipton and various other police officers.

The days that followed were historic for the New Zealand Police. On Monday, Rickards went on leave from his new job as Auckland's top policeman. Commissioner Rob Robinson and Prime Minister Helen Clark promised independent investigations. As the story rolled on relentlessly, gathering momentum and new revelations by the day, the Prime Minister ordered a Commission of Inquiry — the most powerful instrument available to the government — into Louise's allegations. The same day, Robinson reopened a criminal investigation into the allegations, and Rickards was formally suspended from duty.

I was interviewing a former police officer when I was tipped off that the Commission of Inquiry was to be announced. I rang Louise to let her know. She was completely overcome, and poured out thanks to those who'd spoken in support of her, including Rex Miller, Carolyn Butcher and Margaret Craig.

While I was pleased at how swiftly and seriously the authorities were responding to the story, it worried me that there could be major problems with parallel inquiries underway. I told my bosses that I couldn't see how the commission could hear Louise's story if police were mounting a criminal investigation at the same time. Telling her story in the forum of a commission would be prejudicial to any trial of the three men, should it come to that.

Phone calls, many anonymous, flooded in with new leads. Many people named police officers they believed might have been the fourth man at Rutland Street. We never found him. I also got a call from a serving senior Rotorua policeman who I'll not name. It showed the essential decency and humanity of the vast majority of New Zealand police officers. He asked me to pass on to Louise this message: 'Can you tell her we feel for her and bloody good on her. We want her to know we support her.'

I also got a call from another police source who said that Dewar had left his last job, as boss of the police communications centre, under a cloud.

He was being investigated in regard to travel expense claims. To avoid the embarrassment of having an inspector of police charged, his superiors told Dewar he could 'perf' — extract his taxpayer-subsidised superannuation from the Police Early Retirement Fund — and leave the force. He had little option but to take the money and run, I was told.

I also got a call (followed later by a written apology) from the general manager of the country's district courts, apologising for the delays I'd experienced in getting access to documents I should have seen far earlier. The caller said court staff had finally found the missing transcripts from the third Brown trial.

We also got threatening letters from lawyers acting for the three men, and Dewar said publicly that he would sue for defamation. His lawyer later said this: 'John Dewar did his duty.'

Louise

READING THE FIRST PARAGRAPH OF Phil's story made me realise all over again that I was about to turn the lives of many people upside down, and that I was accusing the next Commissioner of Police of rape. As I read, I was picking that today's edition of *The Dominion Post* wasn't going down too well in the Rickards household this morning.

As I read on, I admired the way Phil had put the story together. He just put all the facts, the discrepancies and the lies out there in front of the public and let them decide for themselves where the truth might lie. It was interesting to read Commissioner Rob Robinson promising to 'study the published material' and to 'thoroughly look at' anything that called the integrity of the police force into question. I had no faith in any police inquiry, because what guarantee was there that they wouldn't like what was uncovered and wouldn't try to sweep it under the carpet, just as Dewar did? The story was accompanied by a call I had made through *The Dominion Post* for a proper independent inquiry into the way the system worked (or didn't work) 'to ensure that as a victim of police abuses I can finally be treated fairly and decently'. I wanted the Prime Minister to set up a Commission of Inquiry.

The other piece in that morning's *The Dominion Post* that struck me was the editorial, by Joanne Black. Reading it, I really felt I was being believed, and it was reassuring to know that someone else viewed what had happened to me as an abuse of the powers of the police. I found the last paragraph particularly moving:

> Light must at last fall in places where it has for so long been shut out. Those who conspire to protect themselves and each other from their own misdeeds should know that one day, however long it may take, they could be uncovered. We believe Mrs Nicholas. She does not see

herself as an heroic battler in the mould of Karen Silkwood or Erin Brockovich tackling the Establishment, though at times her journey may feel as never-ending. Rather, she is a woman who refuses to be broken by what happened to her. *The Dominion Post* shares her belief that people who are powerful should not assume there is one law for them, and one for everybody else.

Whatever doubts I still had about what I'd done just disappeared. I now knew I had taken a huge step towards finding justice, and hoped that people would understand the reasons for the journey I was about to embark on.

As the afternoon rolled on towards evening and the six o'clock news, the nerves started up again. Just before six, I noticed how quiet Jess had become. I pulled her to one side and asked her if she was all right. She told me that she wasn't going to watch the news, as she didn't think she'd be able to handle it. I told her she needed to do what she felt was best for herself, and that if she thought watching the news was going to be too much for her then I totally understood. I told her she had to remember that I was always there for her if she needed to talk about anything. I gave her a huge hug and she thanked me for understanding and wandered off to feed her horses. As I watched her go, I felt tears welling up.

A couple of minutes before the news started, I whipped outside for a nervous smoke with Janine. I told her I wasn't 100 per cent sure how the story was going to come across and that I was really nervous about the reaction of the public. Janine just shrugged.

'At the end of the day, mate, it doesn't matter what the public thinks,' she said. 'If you know you've done the right thing for yourself, and I believe you have, then you've got no worries at all.'

I realised she was dead right. I thanked her for her words of wisdom, stubbed out my smoke, and said: 'Well, let's do it!'

It was a real shock hearing the presenter of *One News* say my name. Then there were photos of me, and Phil appeared and told the full story, with pictures of me outside the Murupara Police Station and Rutland Street. Ross made a few wisecracks about how I looked, what I was wearing, and how I spoke. That lightened the mood of the room slightly, but by the end of the news item we were all in tears, Ross included. It was some time after it ended before anyone dared to speak. I received a glowing response from everyone on how well I had done. I'd come across as someone who'd obviously gone through so much, but was prepared to take this stand and show the public that I was no longer a victim of these men, I had become a survivor.

Ross and I decided that it would probably be best if I stayed at Janine's that night, because if there were any nasty phone calls or visits then I wouldn't get too upset or uptight. The next day, when Ross came back, I asked him if there had been any phone calls at home. There were two messages left on the answerphone, he said, and these were both from the mother of the lady who now lived in the house in Rutland Street. Ross found the first call really quite nasty: she was obviously upset that the house had been splashed all over the television. I felt really bad, and didn't blame her for being upset. In her second message, she apologised for being nasty, even if she basically reiterated her concerns. There was nothing we could do about it apart from feel for her. Other than that, all had been quiet.

Phil phoned to say that he was driving through to Ngakuru, as he'd found an ex-policewoman who thought the baton that was used on me by those guys at Rutland Street was hers. He'd interviewed her, and he wanted to film my reaction to this new development and to the previous night's news bulletin. I was happy to do the filming, and a bit later Phil and the crew turned up. My first reaction to this latest twist had been delight that this woman, Carolyn, had come forward, but when it was put to me in front of the camera, I actually broke down. It meant an awful lot to me, because it was another reason for people to believe me about the baton. Even though she didn't name names, it went a long way towards proving I was telling the truth. I thanked this woman publicly, stating that it must have taken a lot of guts to come forward.

Filming the piece about Carolyn Butcher's baton had its moments. Janine and Gary kept a few chooks in their yard, and they'd decided the deck right outside the lounge where we had the camera set up was the place to be. They made a hell of a noise scratching and clucking outside the windows. Being the man of the house, Gary decided it was his job to disperse the chooks. He'd never really had anything to do with them before, and it was hilarious watching him trying to entice them to the other end of the section with chook food. You could see him getting wild, and we wondered what he would do with them if they didn't heed his commands! Eventually he managed to round them up and move them out and filming was able to continue. As we watched the news that night, Janine was cracking us all up, as the filming had been done in her lounge. She pointed out her couch, her coffee table and so on in the background, and told us how very important she felt that her 'stuff', which was being beamed into the homes of hundreds of thousands of people, was helping in the fight for justice!

The other thing that blew us away on that evening's news was Prime Minister Helen Clark fronting the media outside her home on a Sunday, saying that she was going to give me what I wanted: she'd ordered an independent inquiry into the allegations I'd made. Well, Phil had told me the story would open up a can of worms, but I wasn't really prepared for the stir it was causing.

Ross and I were keeping an extremely close eye on the girls and how they were handling everything. Jess was our main concern, as she was still ever so quiet and not showing much interest in what was going on. The Sunday night after the story broke, she came to me and asked if she could stay home from school, as she was worried that if people knew I was her mother, they would tease her. I sat her down and explained that I didn't think that would happen, as she was in a school with over a thousand girls and it was only her close friends who knew she was the daughter of the woman on the news. I told her I'd ring the school and explain what was happening, and that if there was any trouble, they were to contact me. I could tell she wasn't that happy about it, but she eventually said she'd go.

'But,' she warned, 'if it turns to custard, Mum, I'm coming straight home.'

Monday was chaos, and it wasn't until last thing that afternoon that I remembered my promise to phone the school. God, I felt sick. I felt I'd let Jess down terribly. Because the school day was about to end, I thought I'd leave it till she got home to find out how her day had gone. Jess jumped off the school bus, and as she wandered up the driveway I was desperately trying to read her body language. As she entered the kitchen, I smiled at her and asked how her day had gone.

'Oh, my God, Mum,' she said, 'I couldn't believe it! As soon as I walked through the school gates, I had girls coming up to me and telling me that they reckoned you were so brave to come forward and do what you've done. And these were, like, girls I don't even really know! And then I was called into the school counsellor's office, and she told me that my teachers had had a meeting this morning and that they said that if I had any trouble with girls being nasty to me I was to report it straight away.'

I apologised for not ringing the school, but Jess told me not to worry about it. It was 'all good, 'cause nobody was nasty'.

While I was looking for signs as to how the story was affecting my family, I couldn't help worrying about the effect it was having on those men's families, too. When the rural delivery man dropped off a *Herald* for us on the Monday morning, I was a bit taken aback to read that Clint Rickards was taking three weeks' unscheduled annual leave from his new job as Auckland Central's Police Commander.

On 4 February, I learned that not only was there going to be a Commission of Inquiry into Police Conduct, but Rickards had been stood down because the police had decided to reopen the criminal investigation into my allegations of pack-rape by policemen in 1986. Things felt like they were happening way too fast, including the media storm that had been created. As it was, Ross was becoming an absolute expert at explaining to other media that we were unable to comment on certain aspects of what had developed over the last week. He always thanked them for the time and effort they'd taken in coming out, and told them we appreciated that they had a job to do, but it was just that we had to be careful about what we said from here on in.

The only reporter who really got up Ross's nose was Rachel Grunwell from the *Sunday Star-Times*. He politely explained to her that we couldn't comment but she became quite pushy — to the point where, when Ross tried to close the door on her, she put her foot in the way. Well, polite hadn't worked, so he let her have it with both barrels. Suffice to say she backed off quite quickly. What would I do without him?

I told Ross that I didn't want the police doing any of the investigation, because they could just cover it all up again. He told me to just hang fire and see what developed. Phil was of the same opinion.

Another revelation that hit the headlines and TV news that same week was the so-called 'deathbed confession' that Trevor Clayton gave my brother Pete. I only learnt of it when Phil first spoke to Pete. Trevor passed away in 2003, soon after he was diagnosed with cancer. In his final days, he asked to see Pete. When Pete arrived, he could see straight away that Trevor didn't have long to go. They had a few laughs and spoke about old times, but then, all of a sudden, Trevor got quite emotional. He asked for forgiveness — from me, from Pete and from my parents — for what he called issues that were connected to me. Pete reckoned Trevor basically wanted to come clean about what had happened to me. Trevor told him he'd been 'gagged' and was told to 'shut up' about what had happened. He told Pete that there definitely had been a cover-up. Pete said he found it hard to listen to all this about what had happened to his sister, but he did it for the sake of a friend who wanted to clear his conscience.

Before Pete went ahead with the interview with Phil, he phoned Debbie Upston, Trevor's partner of many years, to ask her if it would be all right for him to talk about the last time he and Trevor had spoken. Debbie told Pete she was fine with this, but she later changed her mind and insisted that Trevor never 'came clean with his conscience'. Instead, she said, Pete was lying: there had been no confession by Trevor. We were all taken aback by Debbie's sudden turnaround — Pete was gutted — but none of us were that surprised by it either. We all figured one or all of the Rutland Street three had got to her.

I had no qualms about forgiving Trevor. To me, he was a tortured soul and didn't deserve the pain and suffering he was going through prior to his death. He'd had more than enough of that when he was alive and well.

It wasn't long after the story first broke that I started to receive cards and letters of support from complete strangers. I was humbled that people would take the time out of their busy day to write and say 'thank you for coming

Louise

forward', or 'I've had bad experiences with the police, but haven't the courage to do what you have done, thank you' and so on and so forth. The only blot was receiving two nasty letters, one each from Tauranga and Whangarei. I figured that the Tauranga one might have been from a member of the Shipton family, but because there was no name or return address, I couldn't say for sure. As for the Whangarei one, I had no idea who would have sent it. I was upset to start off with, especially when they referred to my daughters as 'having a slut for a mother'. But as Ross pointed out, and he was dead right, we had received hundreds of cards and letters from people who supported what I was doing, so to receive only two nasty ones was pretty good really. I did hand them over to the police, but nothing that I know of ever came of it. I decided that everybody was entitled to an opinion on what I had done, and I had to accept that there were some who didn't agree with it. It just annoyed me that these two 'gutless wonders' didn't have the balls to say all those nasty things to my face or give me the opportunity to respond by return mail. Instead, they hid behind a piece of paper. Sticks and stones, you idiots!

Then came the day I'd been dreading. I received a phone call from the police. I was told that because of the seriousness of the allegations I had made, they were going to investigate. They asked if I would help with their inquiries.

Ross and I had discussed all this earlier, and had decided that if they wanted to talk to me, then I would be as open, honest and helpful as I could be. A time was made for a couple of detectives, Steve McGregor and Shona Low, to visit Ross and me to explain how they were going to go about reopening the investigation. A few nights later, we had Steve and Shona sitting at our dining-room table.

Steve explained that a team of detectives was being put together to start the interviewing and the processing of statements. Heading the investigation was Superintendent Nick Perry from the South Island. He, in turn, would be answering to Deputy Commissioner Steve Long. At this stage there would be around 13 police staff — mainly from the South Island, but a few from Auckland and Wellington — working on the inquiry. They would be based in Wellington until it was all over. Steve reiterated that they were well aware of my concerns over reopening things, but assured me that it would be an extremely thorough operation. He said that if at any time I had concerns about anything or anyone involved, I was to let him know immediately.

I was then asked officially if I would be available to make statements, starting with what had happened back in Murupara with Brown and moving on to cover everything that had happened afterward, including episodes such as the Murupara Four, Corlett Street, Rutland Street, Dewar and the 1993/94 court cases. Steve said Shona would take these statements, and that she was happy to come to my home and do it while the girls were at school, if that suited me.

Before I could answer, Ross suddenly blurted out: 'You didn't show us your ID when you came in. How do we know you're the cops and not from the other side?'

Well, the look on their faces was priceless! I knew Ross was taking the mickey out of them, and I kind of played along by looking sternly at them both. They jumped up, apologising profusely and at the same time performing the Pakeha haka, slapping their various pockets trying to find their wallets. I shot a scornful look at Ross for being so mean. All he did was laugh. As for Steve and Shona, well, I'm not sure they saw the funny side of it right away. After they left Ross said he wasn't sure who was more nervous, us or them. I told him that if his little antics with their ID didn't break the ice, I'm not sure what would.

A few days later, the statement-taking process began. We would spend all day going back over absolutely everything, but this time Shona was making sure that every detail, regardless of how trivial, sordid or upsetting it was, was covered. There were times when I would be recalling the most awful things and I would get emotional doing it, and that's when I found having a woman detective helpful. She would insist we stopped for a coffee break, talked through what I was having to recall, and ensured I was OK to carry on — always insisting that if it got too much, then we would stop and carry on another day. At no time did Shona ever try to put words into my mouth. There were times when I was trying to find the right word or wanting to say something in a certain way and she would help me out, but she never typed a word or a sentence that hadn't come from me.

For the next six weeks, Shona and I covered pretty much the last 20-odd years of my life. There was one day when I met her in town and she took me around to identify some Rotorua properties. Most I knew, like Rutland and Corlett streets, but there were two other properties that I didn't really know. One I had definitely never been to, but the other was a house in Kusabs Road that seemed familiar to me, even if I wasn't sure why I knew it. Shona asked me if I had ever been there, and I told her that I could have been there at some stage but wasn't really sure. She then told me that apparently I had in an early 1990s statement said that I had been to that house when I was around 15 or 16 years old and had sex with Schollum. I had said I was drunk and that there was a party going on there.

I sat there looking at Shona thinking, when the hell did I say that? I explained to her that I didn't remember ever being there, but because of my age, I must have been either living with the Browns or back in Murupara. I was quite sure

Jane Brown wouldn't have allowed me to go to a party at Schollum's house, and if I was living in Murupara there was no way in hell my parents would allow me back into Rotorua to attend a party. It was really, really confusing for me. Why on earth would I have said that in a statement? I asked Shona if I could think about all this and get back to her if I could recall anything.

The first thing I did when I got home was try to find the statement that contained this bullshit. Well, it turns out it wasn't bullshit after all. I found the statement. It was taken by Dewar on 4 February 1994. After reading it, I sat there with my mouth open, wondering why on earth I had said what I did. The statement in question concerned Schollum mainly, and besides the claim about having consensual sex with him at Kusabs Road, it mentioned what he had done to me while I was swimming in our pool at Murupara, and what he had done when I was on holiday with him and his family at Ohope. It also described what had happened with Trevor Clayton when I was babysitting and he came home early.

What on earth was I doing? Why would I make a statement like that when I knew damn well that none of that Kusabs house stuff had happened? I felt physically ill, and thought that the cops — and, no doubt, others — would consider me a liar. Everything else in that statement was the truth. It *couldn't* have happened: it just didn't fit into the timing, living as I was either with the Browns or at home in Murupara. I really had no answer.

I explained my confusion to Mum and Dad. Dad remembered the house; he said Schollum had lived there. When Dad lost his job with Armourguard he had bumped into Schollum one day and the policeman had asked him if he would like to take up mowing the lawns at Kusabs Street, as they were huge and he didn't have the time to do it himself. He offered to pay, of course. As soon as Dad told me this, I knew that that had been when I was at the house: I went there with Dad, not when I was 15 or 16, but when I was around 17 or 18 years old. It all fell into place. But still. Why did I tell Dewar a different story? All I could guess was that it was a cock-and-bull story like the one about being raped by Maoris on horseback I'd thrown in when talking about Brown with Mrs Radford. That was the best explanation I could give Shona about Kusabs Street. Shona said that if the information ever ended up in court, the defence would attack me with it. I just told her that I would tell the jury exactly what I had told her: there was nothing more I could do.

Later Dad told me that Schollum never did pay him for mowing those lawns. He did them once, then never went back. You could see it still pissed Dad off big-time.

Phil

IN EARLY FEBRUARY, JUST DAYS after Louise's story had broken in the national media, John Dewar was caught out by the *New Zealand Herald*. He'd supplied documents to the newspaper and TV3 to show he had done a good job investigating the pack-rape and baton allegations. Dewar implied the Police Complaints Authority documents proved he'd done a full inquiry into the allegations. But investigative journalist Phil Taylor discovered they did nothing of the sort. They were documents relating to another inquiry Dewar had done. Phil Taylor contacted Dewar to question him but 'the line went dead'.

Also at this time, I received the first couple of what were to be many, many tip-offs about other women who'd come across Shipton, Schollum, Rickards or Dewar.

The first woman lived in a remote rural area of the North Island. It took a couple of phone calls before she'd agree to meet. I drove to her house and we sat outside, and she told me the only reason she was talking to me was because she believed Louise Nicholas. She had good reason to. She broke down several times while telling me her story. As a 15-year-old schoolgirl she had wanted to be a policewoman and her school had arranged work experience with the Rotorua police. Bob Schollum was one of two officers who took her out a few times in the squad car. Just after she turned 16, Schollum told her one weekend to come to a house in Rutland Street, the same house in which Louise said she'd been baton raped. Schollum said he couldn't pick her up from her father's house that day.

Excited at the thought of getting first-hand experience in the area where she wanted to make her career, she described how she'd jumped on her bike and pedalled furiously to Rutland Street. When she got there, she was introduced to Brad Shipton. The two policemen took turns taking photos of her, first with Shipton, then with Schollum, each with a big grin, each with an arm around her. An excuse was made as to why they couldn't go out on patrol and, as they chatted, Schollum seduced her. She'd never had sex before. He led her to a bedroom, and while they were having sex the door opened. Shipton stood watching. Alarmed, she asked what was happening and was told Shipton was going to join in.

'I told him no, and I told him I wanted to leave now.'

Schollum continued and Shipton kept watching. When the sex was over, she was frightened. She said her father knew where she was. They warned her not to say anything unless she wanted her family to get in trouble with the police. She got on her bike and fled, her dreams of becoming a police officer in tatters. She hadn't seen the Rutland Street house since that day until she saw a woman she'd never met — Louise Nicholas — standing in front of it on the TV news.

Harry and I put her story together for *One News*, and it ran across most of the front page of *The Dominion Post*, with her photos of the two grinning cops in shorts at Rutland Street. The police launched an inquiry. In the end the case didn't make it to court, but her story was put to the Commission of Inquiry.

When that story broke, I asked a friend who'd expressed doubts about Louise how he'd feel if that was his 16-year-old daughter on school-organised work experience with policemen nearly twice her age. The look on his face was all the answer I needed.

A few days later, I went to meet a Rotorua woman with an equally explosive story. She'd seen John Dewar making this public statement: 'I would challenge anyone to come forward and tell me what relationship I have with those men. We don't socialise or go to each other's homes. We don't call each other up.' In the face of our reports that he'd been looking after his mates, Dewar had said he'd only ever had a professional relationship with Shipton and Rickards. He'd clearly forgotten that he'd told Louise in our hidden camera sting that they were friends of his. The woman I met told me she had met Shipton when he was investigating a family tragedy. Shipton befriended her and they later had sex. There was no crime involved, but on the face of it, it was another example of one of these men preying on a vulnerable woman. She said she was then manipulated into having group sex, albeit consensual, with Shipton and Rickards.

She hesitated. I told her I was not there to judge her, just to find out the facts. She said she really didn't want to come forward but felt she had to. With a little more prodding, she dropped the bomb. She said she was introduced to another of Brad Shipton's friends one night, a man whom Shipton described as his new boss. This man and Shipton later had group sex with her. It was John Dewar.

This was a huge scoop, because her allegation utterly destroyed Dewar's line that he'd never had anything but a professional relationship with Shipton and Rickards. But it wasn't all she had to say. She said there were times that Clint Rickards picked her up in a police car and drove her to a meeting place along the road between Rotorua and Tauranga, where Shipton was then stationed. Group sex took place in or on the car. One night, Rickards received an urgent call on his police radio. He told the woman she'd have to find her own way home, but relented when she protested at being left on her own on the side of the road at night. 'On the way back he told me to lie down in the back of the car so no one could see me,' she told me. She also said that one day she was asked to have a group sex session with a 16-year-old girl but refused.

Before we broke this woman's story, we took affidavits from her and from another woman whom she'd told about the incidents at the time.

This same woman also told me a lot more about Shipton and Rickards, but it was so personal and revolting she didn't want it aired in public. She has since told me she wants it revealed in this book.

This woman, who has name suppression, fell pregnant to Brad Shipton. She went to Auckland to have a termination, and the day after she arrived home she opened her door to a knock and found Rickards on her doorstep. He wanted full sexual intercourse. 'I never saw him in uniform, but I knew he was on duty because there were times I could hear the police radio going in the car he came in. I thought he'd come to see how I was because I'd told him I was pregnant to Brad and he even knew the date I was going to have the abortion. I can remember him just saying how randy he was. He repeated that several times. I had a pamphlet saying medically you shouldn't have sex for two weeks. I told him that and I just kept saying I couldn't.

'I was feeling really low, wondering if I'd done the right thing with the abortion. I'd hardly slept and was really emotional. I wouldn't cry in front of those guys but it was obvious to him what a low state I was in. He just kept on insisting he wanted full sex. I know it sounds silly now but I felt I had to give in to get rid of him. I performed oral sex on him and then he just left. Just like all the other times with him, Brad and even John Dewar, as soon as it was over they left. That was all they were there for.'

I remember sitting in her living room as this woman slowly and tearfully told me her nauseating story. I didn't want to believe it, but I did.

The Commission of Inquiry had started its first hearings but soon became bogged down because Police Complaints Authority files, of which the Miller report was an example, were covered by blanket secrecy. The government's response was to rush through a law change, opening thousands of files of complaints against police officers and witnesses' statements. This was problematic, because many witnesses who'd given evidence to the PCA in many of those files would have done so after receiving assurances that their evidence would be kept secret. Fortunately, however, the commission's terms of reference were something of a moveable feast, and the Commissioner, Dame Margaret Bazley, was able to find sensible ways around this difficulty.

At the same time the police were drawing the wagons into a circle. Police headquarters warned officers not to talk to any media about the Louise Nicholas case or about police culture — two of the very things the commission was investigating. The police force used lawyers behind the scenes to resist the commission's investigations, and even to seek its complete reconstitution.

At 1.45 in the morning of 29 March my home phone rang. I picked it up and there was silence at the other end. For the next four months, whenever Nicky or I picked up the phone in the early hours of the morning, we got the same response. I kept a note of the times and recorded the calls. I even started keeping the shotgun handy. Calls like that go with the territory for investigative journalists, but I didn't like the idea of someone trying to intimidate my wife. In July, I told Nick Perry, the head of the investigation, which had now been dubbed Operation Austin, about the calls. I don't know if Perry traced them but the calls stopped soon afterward.

Around the same time, the *Sunday Star-Times* ran a story that revealed that Louise's ex-flatmate, Sue Grant, had told Rex Miller that Louise had consensual sex with Shipton and Rickards. It was part of an effort on the paper's part to set itself up for an interview with Rickards, an interview it ultimately got. One of its senior journalists had a long association with a Mark Templeman, who was a private investigator defence lawyers had hired to dig into Louise's past. To give it its due, however, the paper did quote Miller as saying Grant wasn't a reliable witness. 'She was someone who didn't want to be interviewed,' Miller said, and he reiterated his view of Grant's flakiness on *One News* that night.

In early April, I was tipped off by a Bay of Plenty police source that Waikato Police Commander Kelvin Powell was going to be charged with raping a former police constable in Rotorua in the 1980s. I spoke to the complainant, and she told me she didn't come forward at the time because she'd been drinking heavily — it was the night of her 21st. She said she'd just begun her police career and thought that complaining would end it. She knew her chances of winning the case were not good, because she knew full well what it was like 'for rape complainants in the witness stand . . . especially ones who've been drinking'. Sure enough, the case went to court, and Powell was acquitted.

Meanwhile, Harry and I had been working with Cameron Bennett, an experienced TV anchorman, on a two-part documentary on Louise's story for the *Sunday* current-affairs programme. While I was credited as co-producer with Harry, I was completely out of my depth. In effect, my role was to do the research. It was great working alongside such an experienced crew, but when the story was being finalised my eyes were opened to the differences between print and television journalism. The golden rule of television is that viewers are bored by any detail that doesn't have a picture to illustrate it. Bored viewers change channels, and as TV reality show queen Julie Christie has put it, there's no point in making television if people don't watch it. So regardless of how important it is, even in current-affairs documentaries, there's less focus on providing information than there is on how pretty the supporting pictures look.

Our strong suit was information, some of which was pure dynamite. But as we didn't have pictures to go with it, some of our best material was left out. I was furious. Even Harry, who was an old hand at this game, was upset, because he too had grown very close to the story. Bennett was in a no-win situation — staff senior to him didn't want chunks of text appearing on the *Sunday* programme.

It was television's loss. Much of the material that would have been revealed for the first time on the show appears in this book.

Around the time the documentary went to air, a woman who had been living in Australia returned to New Zealand for a holiday. A friend of hers was telling her about the Rotorua woman who'd been baton-raped by three cops in the 1980s. Their names weren't mentioned, but the woman guessed immediately who two of them would be. Shipton and Schollum had done the same thing to her in a Mount Maunganui lifeguard hut one day in 1989. She contacted police to tell her story at last. She was able to supply the names of four of the five men who had pack-raped her. She didn't know the name of the fifth and, like the fourth man at Rutland Street, the Mount Maunganui fifth man has never been found. The men she named were Shipton, Schollum, high-profile Tauranga businessman Peter McNamara, and fireman Warren Hales.

The investigation secretly recorded phone conversations between some of the men as they talked about what had happened that day 15 years ago at the Mount. The tapes were not completely incriminating evidence, but they were extremely damaging for the defence case. The Crown chose to use them as a bargaining chip, and the accused were offered a choice between two tricky admissions: either they conceded they'd had group sex with the woman, or the jury got to hear them talking on tape. They opted to admit they'd had group sex with the complainant, but claimed, of course, that it was consensual. They said there were hugs and laughter as they did it on a dirty mattress in a lifeguard hut in the middle of the day.

I remember thinking when I heard this story that no jury was ever going to believe a self-assured 20-year-old woman would choose a small, shabby lifeguard hut as a place to have group sex in the middle of her working day. If group sex was really her thing, surely she'd choose a motel or a bedroom or somewhere a little more salubrious?

I didn't cover the trial, but I've met the complainant several times, and I can see how she would have made a very compelling witness. And she did. For all their years of police training and their extensive experience of giving evidence in court, Shipton and Schollum were no match for her. She spoke of the men treating her like a pack of dogs with a piece of meat. She spoke of having a police baton rammed into her, up to 20 times. She spoke of the men saying 'Ooh, yeah — get her', while watching it happen.

The four were found guilty of rape but, interestingly, not on the baton charges. It seemed the jury, while revolted by the pack-rape, didn't want to believe that police officers would use a baton like that.

All four were jailed, Shipton for eight and a half years and Schollum for eight. The judge called the pair corrupt police officers who had treated their victim like a piece of meat. Their partners stood by them and made harrowing, emotional appeals to the court on their behalf. But there were things they didn't know about their men. Shipton's wife, Sharon, spoke of the soft and gentle human being her husband was. She didn't know her mother had told Operation Austin police that she'd arrived at their home one day to find Shipton and some mates drinking with a live cat in the hot oven. Shipton's excuse? The cat had got wet and he was drying it out.

All four appealed their convictions and sentences, but only Hales was partially successful. A defence lawyer produced fresh evidence in the shape of two new witnesses who backed up Hales's testimony that he had met the complainant at a concert after the alleged rape and she'd been friendly to him. But the police obtained emails from these two new witnesses. One described the rape victim as a 'slapper'. The other witness asked the first to read his draft statement then prepare his own but 'with differences'. The Court of Appeal said it looked like 'a jack-up'. Nevertheless, Hales was granted a retrial. The two email witnesses were arrested and charged with attempting to pervert the course of justice. Their trial was due to start as this book was going to print.

In November 2006, just before his retrial, Hales and the Crown struck yet another deal. He pleaded guilty to abducting the victim in return for having the rape charge dropped. The Crown would doubtless have had in mind the fact that Hales was the lookout while the others were inside the hut performing the pack-rape. The victim said in a statement to police that when Hales came in, she said, 'You may as well, because the rest of you have all had a go.' She was sobbing at the time, and the words were in no way an invitation — not that Hales seemed to recognise the difference, because he proceeded to take his turn too. Juries can be fickle beasts, especially in rape trials. I suspect the deal was done because the Crown feared the complainant's remark might have resembled consent sufficiently to get Hales off the hook.

Louise

OVER THE NEXT SIX MONTHS there were a lot of new developments, not only with the Operation Austin investigation, but also with the Commission of Inquiry. Not long after my story came out, another woman came forward. Judith Garrett spoke publicly about being raped by a Kaitaia policeman back in 1988 at the Kaitaia Police Station. After this new revelation, Prime Minister Helen Clark confirmed that Ms Garrett's case would be taken into account when the terms of reference were drawn up for the Commission of Inquiry.

In April 2004 I was invited to Wellington to give a statement to the commission. I insisted that Ross come with me. I was told that it could take a couple of days to do this statement, so Ross and I were booked into a hotel in central Wellington. Just before we headed off to the commission's offices I received a phone call from a member of its staff to warn me there was a large contingent of media waiting at the main entrance of the building. Sure enough, when we arrived a crowd rushed towards us with cameras and microphones at the ready. I held on to Ross's hand tightly as we walked towards them, smiled and quietly made our way into the main foyer of the building without answering any of the questions they yelled at us. We were met by a staff member and taken to the 14th floor, where we were made really welcome. We were introduced to a number of the staff, including Rebecca Boyak, the commission organiser, then taken to a room where the statement would be taken. Ross excused himself and went off for a wander about town.

I can't remember the name of the lady who asked the questions, but she was a very warm, sympathetic person and I felt quite relaxed with her. Our sessions were audiotaped rather than written up, which made it easy to just talk. Basically all I did was tell the commission what had happened to me from Murupara right through to the court cases with Dewar.

After lunch, I started to talk about what had happened at Corlett and Rutland streets. I found myself getting rather emotional — and the commissioners were in tears too. I found myself wondering why I hadn't run or fought the men, and why I followed Schollum into the house. I guess I was wanting them to help find the answers for me, but of course that's not what they were there for. I'm not sure I'll ever have answers to those questions. We hadn't quite wrapped it all up by the end of the day, so it was decided that I would return the following day for another few hours.

When Ross picked me up he said that he'd found *The Dominion Post* building and called in to see the editor, Tim Pankhurst. When he'd asked at reception, the lady had said Mr Pankhurst was busy and could she take a message. Ross, the cheeky bugger, said yeah, just tell him Ross Nicholas is here, the husband of Louise Nicholas. Well, he said, she was on the phone that bloody fast, and in no time Tim's personal assistant was hurrying out of the elevator and telling Ross that Tim would like to see him. So Ross talked with Tim, who asked him to bring me back up to the office after I had finished with the commission. Off we wandered, back to *The Dominion Post*, where I finally got to meet the people who had been instrumental in helping Phil get the story out. We had a lovely time yakking about all sorts of things, and then Tim gave us a guided tour of the newsroom.

I was expecting a lot of noise, with people running around like busy little bees, but no. It was all very quiet, with the only sound the clicking of computer keyboards. Tim then showed us the board on the wall that shows how many papers are sold each day. He told us that they sold a huge number when the story went out, not only on the Saturday, but also as it kept unfolding over the following days. While we were there they took the opportunity to get some up-to-date photos, so we spent the next hour doing our best to look good for the camera.

I finished giving my statement to the commission the next morning, then Ross and I flew home. Soon after this, I was told by Op Austin personnel that a woman had contacted them stating that she had been raped by four men in a surf-lifesaving tower at Mount Maunganui in 1989. I wasn't given a lot of information, but I learned that Shipton and Schollum were involved. I wasn't even allowed to know who the woman was or where she was living at that stage. But I was grateful for the fact that she'd come forward, and I asked that Op Austin pass on a few words of thanks and encouragement.

Around July that year, Shipton, Schollum and two others were arrested and charged with this woman's brutal rape. This is when I found out exactly what she had said happened, and I can tell you now, I felt physically ill. It was almost a mirror image of what had happened to me. This poor woman was lured by one of the men to the lifeguard tower, thinking she was being taken to join one of the other men for a lunch date. She told the courts that there were five men waiting for her, although she'd only been able to identify four of them. In that tower, her worst nightmare took place. She was repeatedly raped by all five men and once they'd finished mauling her like a starving dog does a piece of meat, one of them took her back to her place of work. Like me, she was too scared to complain to the police and, like me, she had had to live with this nightmare ever since.

As all these events were unfolding, Ross and I were still trying our best to keep our home life as normal as we could. Each day he would go off to work to drive his milk tanker and I would do my morning and afternoon stints in the cowshed. I'd changed farms by now, and was milking for Trish and Mike Douthett, whose farm backed on to our lifestyle block. When the cows were down our end of the farm, I would get them in, saving Trish the long ride out to the back. Otherwise, it was a two-minute drive to work!

It should all have been working out really well, but unfortunately, with all that had been going on, my concentration levels were at an all-time low. You might think milking cows doesn't require much brainpower, but you've got to be onto it. One mistake could spell financial disaster — if I milked a cow that had been treated with penicillin, for example, and that milk went into the vat, the whole truckload would have to be dumped. I wasn't prepared to expose Trish and Mike to that risk, so I talked to Ross about my concerns, and our own financial situation. We decided it would be best for me to step aside for a while, until we knew the outcome of the investigation. We both realised it would be a struggle for us, but with sensible budgeting and cutting back on a few luxuries we felt we'd get through OK.

Someone suggested I look at asking ACC for financial help: after all, I was being forced to stop work because of what had happened to me. Margaret Craig put me in contact with a friend of hers who was a psychologist, as she felt I really needed to talk to someone about all that was happening, someone who was qualified to listen and who would help me with any emotional issues that arose. I found I could talk to Felicity Leach for hours, so comfortable did I feel with her. She was like Margaret Craig's twin, and that was the best thing for me. Trouble was, because Felicity wasn't ACC accredited, they wouldn't pay for my sessions and travelling costs. We didn't mind about that so much, because what we were really after was getting ACC to help me out financially now that I couldn't work.

ACC assigned me to a case manager by the name of Amelia. She was a lovely lady, and I got the impression she wanted to do everything she could to help. I was absolutely blown out when Amelia came back to us to say that in order for me to have ACC help, I would need to have a psychiatric assessment. Apparently ACC would fly me to Auckland, where I would meet with a psychiatrist who would basically examine me to see if I had a mental illness caused by the abuse. At first I thought this would be OK, but the more I thought about it, the angrier I got. If the doctor decided I didn't have a 'mental illness', then ACC wouldn't help me. On the other hand, if the doctor decided I did have a mental illness, I could see the fun the defence would have with *that* piece of information if we ever ended up in court.

Basically, I politely told them to shove that idea and that I would go it alone. I told Amelia that instead of blowing the $3000 ACC reckoned it would cost to have this report done, they should just give me the cash to put towards the housekeeping. And then, as if that wasn't enough, I was told that I was going to be assessed so that I could have someone come out to my home and clean my house and cook the family meals. I was so insulted. I was under a lot of pressure and stress, but I wasn't bloody well handicapped: we needed financial help, not a babysitter!

Felicity wasn't happy either, but despite a long, detailed letter she wrote seeking special consideration of my case, we were disappointed again. When I reread what Felicity had written, it dawned on me that ACC had no system whatsoever for dealing with sexual-abuse victims individually. Without a doubt ACC needs to buck up their ideas. It's perfectly possible to have been damaged by sexual abuse to the point where you can't function in a normal work environment without actually having a mental illness.

One day I was told that the Operation Austin team had executed search warrants on the homes of the three accused, Shipton, Schollum and Rickards. Nothing of any great significance was found at Rickards's residence as far as I was aware, but the team did find my brother's wedding video at Bob Schollum's home, and seized it as evidence. The biggest 'haul' of evidence came from Shipton's place. There they seized his old police notebooks, which held some really interesting and extremely disturbing notes. In one notebook, it was found that he had my details — the address of the Corlett Street flat, where I lived at the time, and my phone number. It got worse. Lynne Adamson — who had now taken over from Shona as the Operation Austin person dealing with me — phoned and asked me if I remembered anything about Meade Street in Rotorua. It rang bells, but I couldn't think why.

In the end I got so frustrated trying to put my finger on it that I phoned Mum at work and asked her to look up Meade Street in the Rotorua road atlas. As soon as she told me it was off the top of Fenton Street, just before Whakarewarewa, I knew immediately that that was where I had lived with my friend Tracy Malaquin when we were working at the K Market around 1984. I phoned Lynne back and let her know this. She told me that the address of the Meade Street flat was in Shipton's old police notebook too, along with a phone number and my name. My mouth dropped wide open. I told Lynne that I didn't even know Shipton then. Why on earth would he have my details in his notebook? Of course, Lynne couldn't answer that for me, but she did say my details kept cropping up in those notebooks. It was deeply disturbing, but I had to laugh at his pitiful attempts at putting my name in code. He spelt my name backwards, 'esiuoL'. Hell, he was clever — NOT! But it really did freak me out, big time. It was pretty obvious that he'd been told about me. I could guess who by.

Lynne threw another couple of phone numbers at me and asked if I recognised them, but I didn't, and I hadn't kept any old phone bills that would help identify them. Besides the notebooks, the other find Op Austin made was a Colt .45 calibre pistol concealed in Shipton's ceiling. He was eventually charged with illegally possessing a firearm without lawful and proper purpose, and was remanded on bail until a hearing date was set.

While all this was going on, Ross and I were keeping the girls informed about all that the investigation was doing. They were hearing and seeing things in the media and were always asking questions about it. We explained the goings-on as best we could, as sometimes even we weren't sure about the ins and outs of certain aspects of the investigation and what the media were reporting.

It was around this time that Jess came home one day and said she had to do a speech, which was one of her biggest pet hates at school. I asked her what topic she was going to speak on, and she said 'the person that I admire the most'.

'Oh?' I said. 'And who's that, sweet?'

'You, Mum,' she replied.

You could have knocked me down with a feather!

Jess joined the long list of people who'd sat opposite me at the dining-room table and asked me questions. When I read what she'd written about me, it had me in tears. I was so proud of her.

> Hello, my name is Jessica and my speech is on a person I admire. The person that I admire is my mum. Now you're probably thinking a boring speech on and on about a mum. Well for those who don't know my mum, she was pack-raped by policemen in her teenage years. But with all the bad things that have happened to her she has been able to do a lot of good for a lot of other women out there. She was thrown into the media spotlight several months ago because of what had happened to her, and even though I did not want people to know who she was, she stood tall and told me 'that she needed to do

this not only for herself but for hundreds of other women out there too'. I was scared to face school because of what I thought people were going to say. But I was really taken aback by how many people knew what was going on and were very supportive. As the months rolled by everything was becoming clearer for me.

The one thing that I have learnt from all this is never to be afraid if bad things have or are happening to you — tell someone. Mum explained to me that when this was going on she had pretty much three options:

a) she didn't want to fall pregnant

b) she didn't want her father to find out, so she went with option c

c) take her own life.

She told me it was a pretty difficult decision to make but the best thing to do was to commit suicide. Fortunately the tablets she attempted to take weren't strong enough to do any damage.

The one thing that I have noticed a lot was the word 'NO' arose a lot. With that we now know that if something is happening to you and you say 'NO' and that person carries on that's RAPE and that is as simple as I can say it. It doesn't matter how well you know the person or if you don't know him at all it is still RAPE, my mum learnt that in a hell of a hurry. Even though at the start Mum was scared to show her face on TV and come forward as she has done, it was actually really cool because we got to meet Cameron Bennett and he is really cool. But on the subject of media they wanted so much for Mum's story to come across so that heaps of other women would come forward as she had done. IT WORKED. Loads of women came forward and told their point of view of what had happened to them. At first there were so many phone calls and letters and other goodies in the mail. Most of it was asking Mum how they could get help. Mum couldn't believe how many women from all over New Zealand came forward.

I admire my Mum for what she has done but not only for herself and other women but for my family and their families and I think that helped a load of misunderstandings. Today she is getting back to her old habits and a slight slice of normality. Her case is one of the last to be dealt with and I hope that the men who have done this to her get the harsh punishment that they deserve. I love my Mum sincerely for what she has done and I would never let anyone hurt her emotionally again. She is scared on the inside and hiding it on the outside. This is something that she will not forget over night or forever it will stick with her for life.

This speech showed Jess had come a long way from when all this started, and I knew then she was going to be all right. I shouldn't have been surprised. After all, she comes from a long line of strong, independent women.

When Operation Austin first started their investigation, they told me they thought it would take around six months. Now it was Christmas, nearly a year on. They'd underestimated how many people there were out there with information. It's like Steve McGregor had said earlier in the investigation — you talk to one person, who then gives you a couple of names, and those people give you more names, and in the end you find you're talking to hundreds of people. It was also pretty clear they weren't leaving any stone unturned, even though I'd suspected in the beginning that they wouldn't like what they were finding out and might try to hide things. Ross and I were so grateful for all the effort they were putting in. Although most of them got to go home over the Christmas period, the majority of them were a long way from home and didn't get to see their loved ones for weeks on end.

The first inkling we had that 2005 was going to be another busy year was in February, when there was an article in the *Sunday Star-Times* with a headline stating: 'Flatmate describes consensual sex with rape-inquiry police'. It was an interview with Sue, my flatmate in Corlett Street. In it, she said she'd witnessed sex between me and two of the accused (Shipton and Rickards) and that she sometimes joined in. The article quoted the statement Sue had made to a private investigator by the name of Mark Templeman, who was working for the solicitors of the three men. Apparently they were able to track her down in Aussie before the Operation Austin team did. She told him that if she said no to sex with these guys, they would have been fine with it. She admitted that something might have happened to me that she was unaware of, but she couldn't 'recall any change in [my] demeanour, mood or attitude during this time'.

I was in a total state of shock when I read this article. Everything she said was utter bullshit. There was never a time where group sex took place with her as a participant. The question that kept going over and over in my head was, why, Sue? Why say all this, when it's just not true? I thought perhaps they'd got to her somehow. I also thought to myself, how much did they pay you, mate?

When I'd calmed down a bit, I could think of more charitable explanations. Sue was by no means shy around guys; in fact, she was the type that enjoyed the attention. But I couldn't help but wonder whether they had turned up at the flat when she was there on her own and bad things had happened to her just as they had happened to me, and she was too scared to say or do anything about it.

Whatever her reasons, she had made a statement that consisted of nothing but lies and bullshit and there was nothing I could do about it.

The biggest news of 2005 came on 16 March when Shipton, Schollum and Rickards were arrested. Rickards appeared in the Auckland District Court and was remanded on bail. Shipton and Schollum appeared in the Tauranga District Court where they, too, were remanded on bail. The Op Austin team had told me the day before that they were off to arrest these guys. It was truly amazing to hear that news, but to actually see and read all about it in the paper the next day was surreal. The article didn't say it, but I knew that they would face about 20 charges. The law of averages said we had a damn good chance of finding them guilty on at least some: perhaps justice was finally about to be done.

Still, we knew better than most that the arrests were just the start of it: we knew we still had a long way to go before we actually got into a courtroom. There was still a depositions hearing to go through, as well as pre-trial arguments. The Op Austin team was still working on finding witnesses, but they all said we had a really solid case to take into battle. A Crown Prosecutor from Christchurch, Brent Stanaway, would be overseeing the case. From what everyone told me, he was a highly respected prosecutor who fought hard but fair in the courtroom.

The first big disappointment of 2005 came when I learned that the Commission of Inquiry had been put on hold until Commissioner Bruce Robertson and Dame Margaret Bazley, who were heading the inquiry, could work out how to proceed while criminal investigations were going on. My concern, which became greater the more they discussed things, was that they would shut the inquiry down and not reopen it until after the court cases. This would be extremely unfair to those who had come forward to the commission. After all, it was a commission that we had called for from the outset, not a criminal investigation. I made a submission to them to that effect.

While I was waiting to hear their decision, the Operation Austin team was back in touch to say that they were going to be arresting Dewar and charging him with four counts of 'attempting to obstruct, prevent, pervert or defeat the course of justice'. These charges related to allegedly suppressing my rape and sexual assault allegations and complaints, allegedly manipulating me during the police review, and giving inadmissible hearsay evidence in the Brown trials.

The Op Austin team turned up at Dewar's home at 7.30 in the morning. He was arrested and taken to the Hamilton Police Station for processing. He was then taken to the Hamilton District Court, where he was remanded on bail. I was even more confident of the case against Dewar, because there was such a long paper trail showing what he'd been up to, covering up for his mates. All I hoped was that Dewar would be brought before the courts before the other three. Hearing how those events had unfolded would certainly help the public understand things a whole lot more.

It wasn't long after receiving this good news that I received a full-on kick in the guts from the Commission of Inquiry. The Attorney-General, Michael Cullen, had, in his wisdom, decided that Judith Garrett and I would no longer be a part of the Commission of Inquiry, as our cases were subject to criminal proceedings. As far as I was concerned this was a huge crock of crap. Both Judith and I vented our outrage to Dr Cullen by emailing his office and letting him know directly how angry we both were. I got a form letter back — the kind they send to fob off every mug who writes to or emails a politician, and boy, did I see red! Did they think I was so stupid I would think for a minute that they had 'read and considered my concerns'? Yeah, right!

Well, with my blood boiling, I decided Cullen was going to hear me, come hell or high water, so I phoned his office. The phone was answered by a bloke — I've got no idea what his name was — and being as polite as I could I asked to speak to Dr Cullen. He asked who was speaking. I told him it was Louise Nicholas and I wished to talk to Dr Cullen about his changes to the terms of reference for the Commission of Inquiry into Police Conduct and, in particular, how my case was being kicked out of the commission. This bloke told me to go back to the commission for answers to my concerns. I told him it was Cullen who had changed the rules, and it was Cullen I wanted to talk to about it. He again told me to go back to the commission. I then totally lost my cool and threw my toys out of the cot.

'Look, mate!' I practically yelled. 'I haven't busted my arse to see a Commission of Inquiry into the police set up to then be told I will have no part in it! I want answers, and I think I'm damn well entitled to them!'

He just told me again to go back to the commission.

I knew I wasn't going to get anywhere, so I hung up in his ear. When Judith and I were asked if we wanted to voice our discontent publicly by speaking out on the TV programme *Close Up* we both jumped at the chance, but I had to be careful not to mention anything concerning the investigations that were underway. Both Judith and I knew that it wouldn't change anything, but at least we were able to state publicly our disgust at being given the boot by Cullen.

I knew I had to leave it alone after that and concentrate on the investigations. To my surprise, about three weeks later I received an email from Dr Cullen explaining his reasons for the changes to the commission. If this email was meant to make things all good, I'm afraid it didn't happen. Regardless of what Cullen said — and his reasons were long and technical — I was still bitterly disappointed and really angry at being treated this way. But there was obviously nothing I could do about it, so I focused all my energies on my family and what was developing in the investigation.

Ross was still working as a tanker driver for Fonterra out at Reporoa, and he heard through the grapevine that there was a temporary vacancy coming up with the irrigation department on the Fonterra farm that was located behind the factory. The hours were pretty good and, with the investigation moving along, it seemed like a good opportunity to get back into the workforce and start helping out with the family finances once again. After an interview with Eric Earle and his wife Daphne, I was fairly confident I had a good chance of getting it. I did tell Eric and Daphne that I was involved in a police investigation, but Eric told me he knew all about it and that it wouldn't affect my chances. Shortly after, I got the call to say the job was mine and that I could start the following Monday.

It wasn't long before I got into the swing of things. I found the practical stuff, like shifting irrigators around the farm, pretty easy, but learning the paperwork and the computer was a bit of a challenge. But with the help of my workmates, Pike and Daph (the Earles' daughter — just don't call her Daphne!), I soon found my way around those as well. It was a great workplace, and we had a lot of fun with the farmhands, who played some mean tricks on us — the hot-wire they ran from the electric fence to the door, for example, or the times the buggers silage-wrapped the motorbikes, booby-trapped the bike shed, stole the keys out of the bikes, and so on. Our job — the work that we were employed to do — took priority most of the time!

Ross had been with Fonterra for about seven years by then, but he left just before I started. His new job was driving a truck for a Matamata-based business that had bought rights to mine for zeolite on one of the Ngakuru farms. Zeolite is a product that is crushed to make kitty litter and that stuff the police, fire crews and service station forecourt attendants use to soak up petrol or oil spills. Ross had had enough of the night-shift hours at Fonterra, and when he saw this job advertised he jumped at it. The truck was based at the quarry, which was only a five-minute drive down the road for him. Unless they were super-busy, he didn't need to work weekends, so after years and years he finally had time to get back into his trail-bike riding. It was like watching him returning to his youth; I was so happy for him. After all his hard work and the burden of looking after me through these topsy-turvy years, he really did deserve it.

Jess was still doing well with her riding, and we thought Kerriann was going to follow her into the world of horses. But once Ross got his motorbike, she decided she liked the look of that better. Ross managed to pick up a second-hand Honda XR100 for her, and it didn't take Kerri long to get really cocky on it. I guess that's the advantage of living rurally and having so much land to play on. Some friends of ours had children around the same age as ours, and they had an old car they'd named 'the paddock basher'. It would only really get up to 40 kilometres per hour. The girls learned to drive in that car, flogging it around the paddock. They learned to control a vehicle before they were legally allowed, and they had a lot of fun doing it.

I had settled into work really well, but it was hard to relax while the trial was going on in Wellington over the pack-rape in the Mount Maunganui lifesaving hut. One afternoon I received a phone call from Lynne Adamson telling me that the jury had retired to consider their verdict. Every time my mobile beeped after that my heart leapt into my mouth, but it wasn't until the next day that I received the call I had been so anxiously awaiting.

'Guilty!' Lynne said. She was damn near crying on the other end of the phone.

'What?' was all I could say.

'Guilty,' Lynne repeated. 'All four were found guilty!'

I couldn't believe what I was hearing, and I couldn't hold back the tears. I lost my voice for a bit, and when it came back all I could do was whisper. The jury had taken 12 hours to come to their decision, with two of the accused being acquitted of charges of sexual violation with an object. I couldn't understand why, but on reflection I reckon normal Joe Bloggs Citizen just can't get his head around cops doing such horrific things to women. But at the end of the day the bastards were going to pay for the hell they'd put that woman through. It seemed there was justice in the world after all, and it boded well for my case later in the year. The only downer for us was that the suppression orders were to remain, which meant that the public wouldn't know it was Shipton and Schollum who had been locked up for rape.

With all this going on, I became more and more paranoid about leaving the girls at home when both Ross and I were working. Even though they were old enough, it worried me that somebody who didn't like what I had done might try something stupid. It reached the point where I felt like every strange car that drove past was someone watching the place. Eventually I told Ross I couldn't live so far out any more, and I wanted to put the house on the market and buy in town. The girls would be safer there, with both our parents living in Rotorua. It was a hell of a decision to make, but one we both thought was best for us as a family. The house went on the market and within a few months had sold. I heard about a house for sale in a good part of town from a lady at Fonterra. It had everything we wanted — four bedrooms, large lounge, beautiful kitchen, large garaging and a rumpus room to boot. We settled on a price, waited for our house sale to go through, and before we knew it we were living in Rotorua.

My fears for my family's safety left me as soon as we moved in. The only bummer was having our neighbours living so close. Quite often we'd have to tell the girls to keep the noise down, and they'd say, 'But we are being quiet.'

'Yeah, country quiet!'

Ever since the story had broken, I had received a number of phone calls from other women. Some — there's no easy way to say this — were nutters, and both Ross and I had learned to pick them pretty early on. But there were plenty of others who were genuine, and who had suffered nasty things at the hands of other police officers — not only sexual assault, but also the further indignity of having the police fail to take their complaint seriously.

When Suzie contacted me I could tell straight away she was totally sincere in what she was saying. You could hear the anger, the hurt, the deep sorrow in her voice. When she had finished telling me about what had happened to her 21-month-old granddaughter I too had become very angry and sickened. But what rang alarm bells for me was the fact that when she went to the police about it, they deliberately swept it under the carpet — protecting their own, as usual. Because, you guessed it, he was a cop. Suzie had taken her complaint to the highest-ranking member of the Christchurch police, but to no avail. End result: this paedophile walks free among the women and children of Christchurch, and is still a policeman.

Suzie and I spoke for several hours on the phone the first night she rang, and I was in tears for a lot of that time, not just because of what he had done but with the failure of the police to act on her complaint. Suzie had decided to take her complaint to the Commission of Inquiry, and I told her that while I was unable to be of much help because of the investigation into my complaint, I was only a phone call away if she ever needed someone to talk to. I was there with her in spirit and backed her 150 per cent all the way.

Over the next few months we became very good friends and talked regularly. She kept me updated on what was happening at the commission — as far as anything was happening — and soon enough it was Suzie's turn to meet them and tell her story, which ended up taking several days. She was impressed with Dame Margaret Bazley, and thought she was definitely the right person for the job. She was confident that at the end of it Dame Margaret would bring out a thorough and robust report.

One day when I had a couple of days off adjacent to a weekend, I phoned

Suzie out of the blue and told her I was coming down to Christchurch. She was stoked, and sent me text messages each day before I left, counting down the sleeps till we met. I had no idea what she looked like, but when I got off the plane on a lovely hot Christchurch day and was walking through the terminal, I suddenly spotted a blonde woman looking at me with this beautiful smile on her face. I knew straight away it was her, and we hugged and cried like two very long-lost friends.

Suzie and I had got to know each other pretty well during our long telephone conversations, and now that we had met in person we found one of the things we definitely had in common was that we both enjoyed a nice tall, cool rum and Coke. That was the first thing I was offered when I got settled in, and from there it was just talk, talk, talk. Suzie and her partner made me feel so welcome: you'd think I'd known them all my life.

Suzie took me to meet her friend Angela George at her home the next day and, once again, it was like meeting a long-lost friend. Ange told me she had seen the TV news the night the story broke and had turned to her partner, Michael, and said to him: 'I'm going to meet that lady one day.' So it proved, and we became great friends. I had a lovely four days in Christchurch. There's no doubt time away does wonders for the old head.

I needed all the mental strength I could get, because as soon as I was back in Rotorua I was steeling myself for the sentencing of the four men who had pack-raped the woman at Mount Maunganui. Even though it had nothing to do with me, I still felt very much a part of it. The woman had read her own victim impact statement to the court, and I found that incredibly courageous — she had to stand up not only in front of those men, but in front of their families, and tell them to their faces how that horrific ordeal had affected her life in the years that followed. Good on her for doing it.

Justice Ronald Young sentenced Schollum to eight years for rape, four years for unlawful sexual connection and three years for unlawful detention. Shipton was sentenced to eight and a half years for two counts of rape, three years for unlawful sexual connection and three years for unlawful detention. Peter McNamara was sentenced to seven years for rape and three years for unlawful detention. Warren Hales was sentenced to five and a half years for rape and three years for unlawful detention. All of these sentences were to be served concurrently. This was a huge win for all concerned but, if possible, it was even more significant for every other victim and survivor of rape and sexual abuse out there. It gave them reason to hope that perhaps a tide was beginning to turn within our justice system, and that complainants' voices were beginning to be heard.

This also made me think that if we made it to court, we could hope for the same conscientious treatment by a jury as the Mount Maunganui woman had received. It was a much-needed boost as I learned that depositions for my case were soon to be heard in the Rotorua courthouse.

Shipton, Schollum and Rickards were all present at the depositions hearing before Judge Chris McGuire. It had been set down for two weeks, but most of the witnesses' statements were read out, which meant the witnesses themselves didn't need to appear. That included me. Unlike the debacle of the Brown depositions, where Dewar told me I had to appear, this time my 32-page statement was simply read to the court. It took two days rather than two weeks for the judge to conclude that there was a prima facie case to answer, and within a few weeks it was announced that the trial would be heard in the Auckland High Court, with a date yet to be announced. Pre-trial arguments would be heard in October, and were expected to take around four days.

So, once again, I had to play the waiting game, something we were all getting pretty used to. And this time, we knew we were hitting the home straight.

During the pre-trial arguments, 13 March 2006 was chosen as the date that we would head into the Auckland High Court to resume my battle for justice. I was told by Op Austin that Justice Tony Randerson had been appointed.

Not long into the new year, the time had come to start preparing for battle. Op Austin had started to rally the troops, preparing us all for court by going over our briefs of evidence and doing the general housekeeping stuff, such as organising accommodation. I spent a whole week being briefed in Wellington just before the trial started, as there was so much to go over. Normally, the law does not allow for someone's past to be brought up, but the defence had successfully argued that aspects of my past, particularly concerning the Brown matters, were fair game. This was a blow. Our other stumbling block was going to be Sue Grant and what she had said in her statements. The police were unable to convince her to come back from Australia to testify, so it was really up to me to try to convince the jury that her version of what had happened at Corlett Street was not a true account of events.

So, for the fifth time in my life, I was going to have to go back into court and relive all those bad memories. This time, I hoped it would be for all the right reasons, and justice was finally going to be served. The whole time I was in Wellington, I found that when I was alone at night the old noggin was working overtime. I kept wondering what it would be like to hear that one sweet word read out 20 times. My expectations were pretty high: I had no doubt whatsoever that all the lies these men had told were finally going to catch up with them, and they were now going to pay for all the hell they had put me through. It reached a point where I just had to get up one night and write my victim impact statement, which I fully expected to read at their sentencing. That's how sure I was of a guilty verdict being reached.

VICTIM IMPACT REPORT

First I would like to thank the court for the opportunity to read my victim impact report as this for me is the final curtain call in what has been a life of extremes for both myself and my family.

I today look upon the faces of the men that 20 years ago instilled such fear that to live day to day has been a monumental burden for me to bear. You were arrested and charged with a number of offences pertaining to the hell that you put me through but the charge of rape in my view should also carry with it a charge of burglary as you stole so much from me. You stole my dreams and ambitions that I had planned for my life. You took away my dream of taking a year off work and doing my big OE, to follow the footsteps of my grandparents who travelled the world and brought home with them many wonderful stories of what they had seen. I wanted to be able to bring home wonderful stories of what I would have seen of the world so that I could one day tell my children and maybe they, too, would want to follow in my footsteps and travel the same path. You also took away my ambition in life to climb the ladder of my chosen career. Instead I hid behind a desk and typewriter and prayed that five o'clock would hurry up so that I could go home and not have to deal with anything other than trying to keep myself sane. What you did to me back then I would liken to a disease. This disease had no name and at that time no cure, but the symptoms were very, very apparent. I have suffered from low self-esteem, I have suffered humiliation, suffered a strange sense of sadness, suffered a loss that I just can't explain, but more so I have suffered the emotion of anger. Anger that I didn't have the guts to stand up to you back then and wipe the look of satisfaction from your faces. But the worst symptom I have had to try to live and deal with on a daily basis has been fear. Every time I see a cop car or a blue uniform, it's like you're there taunting me and I relive the horrors of your actions, sometimes to a point where I have panic attacks, with my stomach churning so bad it takes all my time not to be physically ill. The only medication that helped to ease some of the pain came from a man, a man by the name of Ross, who without ever knowing it back then saved my life, a man who became my best friend, my soulmate, the man I ended up marrying 18 years ago, and whom I will love for eternity. Because of those awful memories I have etched in my head, it has only been in the last year or so (with much trepidation) that I am now able to look at unwrapping the safety net, the cotton wool from around my daughters. As they are now blossoming into beautiful young women, I have to re-educate myself as a mother and learn to stand back and let them grow but at the same time not allow the symptoms of this disease that has suffocated me spread to them and prevent them from spreading their wings and finding their own dreams and ambitions in life. Today the court will hand down your punishment, but I know in my heart that the sentence will not be as long as mine. Twenty years is a long time to be incarcerated in your own private prison cell, but that is where I have been, unable to move on from my fears, unable to live a normal life. I was told by a family member that once this whole nightmare has ended she was sure that I would learn to forgive and to forget. My response to her was that I will never, ever be able to forget what you did: I will only learn to live with it, so I will never be able to forgive, and that is now my choice and my right. You may have stripped the clothing from my body, burnt the very essence of my soul, stagnated my love of life, but you will never again take away the dignity I have fought so hard to regain over the last few years so that I can once again look at myself in the mirror and love the person looking back at me.

On 31 March 2006 I was finally handed the key to that prison cell and today I can now walk free. Today is also the day that a cure has been found for the disease that has lived within me for the last 20 years. For the last two years of my life it has only been the truth that I have spoken, so today I say to you: justice has finally been served.

Phil

IN MARCH 2005, 13 MONTHS after the story broke, I was tipped off that Rickards, Shipton and Schollum were about to be charged. It was a landmark day, a disgraceful day, for the New Zealand Police. The news led all the national newspapers and television bulletins. Rickards, with his trademark shaved head but now sporting a goatee beard, strode into the Auckland District Court with an entourage of media at his heels. Shipton and Schollum appeared at the Tauranga District Court. On arrival, Shipton jumped from a car and barged into TVNZ's cameraman, Zane Willis, almost knocking him over. After he'd regained his balance, Zane had a rapt look on his face: that was exactly the kind of shot he was after. Schollum, always the milder-mannered of the three, walked calmly in and out of court surrounded by supporters. All three were remanded on bail.

It took a year of legal wrangling before the case got to trial. Defence lawyers tried but failed to get the charges 'stayed' or struck out. Chief High Court Judge Tony Randerson had also decided to run two trials as one. Two or more complainants can have their cases heard in the course of one trial when there is 'similar fact evidence' involved in both complaints. In this instance, the 'similar fact' evidence was substantial. There were many, many similarities in Louise's allegations and those made by the another Rotorua woman whose case would be heard alongside hers. This complainant had been a 16-year-old girl when Shipton had a sexual relationship with her in the mid-1980s. He'd tried to persuade her to let Schollum join in. She'd refused, but on another occasion they didn't take no for an answer. She claimed that Shipton, Schollum and Rickards took her to a house, dragged her to a room, handcuffed her and violated her with a bottle. She thought it was a whisky bottle because, although she couldn't see it, that was what they'd been drinking just before the assault occurred.

This woman, who has name suppression, didn't go to the police when she saw Louise's story in the media. Operation Austin detectives found her when they tried a telephone number in one of Brad Shipton's old notebooks. The words 'milk bottle' were written next to it. Shipton, Schollum and Rickards were charged with handcuffing and indecently assaulting her with a bottle, but all details of the charges were suppressed.

In the pre-trial argument, the defence conceded there was no evidence of any collusion between Louise and the other complainant. Randerson described the similarities between the activity alleged by both complainants as 'striking'. Just as striking was the defence lawyers' claim that violating a woman with an object was not an uncommon practice in Rotorua at that time. Justice Randerson disagreed. 'A police baton and a bottle could not be described as ordinary sexual aids as counsel submitted,' he wrote when ruling the two cases could be heard together.

The defence appealed. The Court of Appeal affirmed there was no evidence of collusion between the complainants, and described 'the common features of the two incidents' as 'remarkable':

> Both complainants say they were forcefully violated by objects . . . the three accused are said to have been present on both occasions and to have been actively involved in the abuse. On both occasions the complainant was brought to the scene by one of the three to find the others present; an element of pre-planning is suggested. Both complainants say that Mr Schollum brought the abuse to an end by saying words to the effect of, 'She's had enough now.' The complainants were both teenagers living in Rotorua and, it would seem, vulnerable to the attentions of older uniformed police officers; two of the three were in their thirties. The incidents occurred within less than two years of each other when all three were serving police officers.

But then the Court of Appeal overturned Justice Randerson's decision to run the trials as one, saying there was a risk of prejudice to the accused. It would be unfair, their honours said, if a jury allowed the evidence given by the other complainant to influence its decision on the rape charges arising from the visits the accused had made to Louise's Corlett Street flat, when no baton was involved. Sure, the Court of Appeal acknowledged, the judge could direct the jury to keep the two matters separate in their minds when they were deliberating, but they preferred to avoid 'the potential for confusion'. The cases would be heard separately. Boiled down, the Court of Appeal overturned the decision because it was worried the jury might get confused.

It was a huge win for the defence, a huge blow for Operation Austin and the

Crown. All details of this strange decision were suppressed, including the fact that the three would face another trial after Louise's case had been heard.

What became known as 'the Louise Nicholas trial' began on 13 March 2006 at the High Court in Auckland before Chief High Court Judge Tony Randerson.

It was one of New Zealand's most high-profile and controversial trials ever, but I didn't cover it. When someone went to trial as a result of a story I'd written, *The Dominion Post*'s lawyer Peter McKnight had told me years ago, I had to stand aside for the trial, but by all means pick up the story after the final court proceedings had ended. I was, however, in Auckland for the last week of the trial, working alongside another hugely experienced TV producer, Janet Wilson, preparing stories on Louise's long battle for justice for TVNZ's *Close Up* programme. My wife Nicky, who'd become so engaged in the case after years of enduring me thrashing it over and over with her as a sounding board, was determined to be there for the summing-up and for the verdicts.

We heard that Rickards got the trial off to a controversial start by breaking police rules and wearing his police chief uniform on the first day. Shipton and Schollum wisely chose not to wear the uniform they'd been putting on each day since they were convicted of the Mount Maunganui pack-rape. The jury didn't know they were taken off to prison each night after the day's hearing.

When the jury retired, we waited in the hotel where Louise, her family and some close supporters were staying, straight across the road from the High Court. At night, Nicky and I would return to the hotel where I was being put up. If the verdict was 'Guilty', TVNZ wanted an exclusive TV interview — Louise had always promised *The Dominion Post* an interview as well. If it was 'Not guilty', the three still faced another trial in which Louise might have to give evidence, so there could be no interview.

The wait was hellishly long — 27 hours, in total. We crammed into the little hotel room, from which we could see the jury coming out to a small park behind the court for cigarette breaks. The mood in the room swung wildly. One minute family members were confident there'd be a conviction; the next, they'd be consumed by nerves because they were suddenly unsure. Louise's brother Rob, a policeman from the South Island, wisely cautioned the family not to get their hopes up too high. He'd seen enough rape trial verdicts to know how hard it is to get a conviction.

There were many deeply emotional moments, but a few to lighten things up too. Louise's daughter, Kerriann, had told us she wanted to be a judge when she grew up. By the time day three rolled around and the jury was still out, Louise's father Jim asked Kerriann if she still wanted to be a judge. She did. 'Well, by the time you are a judge, if this jury doesn't hurry up and make up its mind you might be judging this case,' Jim said.

Twice, while the jury was in the park for a cigarette break, I saw members talking to passers-by, a definite no-no. As the hours dragged on, the defence doubtless became increasingly apprehensive they'd lost. Had they seen those exchanges between jurors and the public, it's likely they would have demanded a retrial.

The waiting became unbearable, for the Nicholas family and their supporters and for the families of the accused and their supporters. Each night as the jury finished its deliberations, unable to make a decision, we saw the prison van drive from the bowels of the court taking Shipton and Schollum back to jail for the night. On day three, 30 March, Ross and Louise packed their daughters off to look around the Sky Tower.

In legal circles, there's a widely accepted theory that it's better for the Crown to have women on the jury of a rape case than men. The theory is that women are more likely to convict than men are. However, I have heard a counter-argument and it is this: in the absence of overwhelming forensic evidence, women jurors often put themselves in the shoes of the complainant and say things to themselves like: 'Would I have done that? Wouldn't I have screamed or gone straight to the police?' and so on.

Nicky had been watching the jurors in the park. On the morning of the third day of deliberations, she said to me quietly: 'They're going to find them not guilty.'

Cynically, I asked how she knew.

She replied that the jury foreman, a woman, was laughing and swinging her arms casually. The other women jurors also looked relaxed. But we could see two male jurors with their heads down, pacing around.

'I know if I hadn't made up my mind, as a woman, I just couldn't laugh and feel relaxed,' she said. 'And if I was going to find them guilty, I just couldn't feel relaxed because I'd be feeling for them and their families, knowing they were going to jail. Those women have made their minds up and it's not guilty. It's the two men holding out.'

The end came quickly. Just before three in the afternoon, one of the Operation Austin team arrived to say the jury was back.

People rushed around trying to get dressed up. Jim changed out of his slippers and gave me a small smile. He'd been on a jury himself and convicted the accused. Jim, more than anyone, had been steadfast in his belief they had to be found guilty. 'They've gotta go,' he said.

I stayed behind watching from the hotel balcony for the family to return. My mobile phone was going ballistic. I watched the court from several stories up. Waiting. Then I saw photographers and cameramen running to cover the exits. A group appeared. The media rushed. First I could see it in the body language. Louise and Ross were moving quickly. Then, as they got closer, I could see their faces as they walked, then almost ran, hand in hand across the road, with Operation Austin detectives trying to get them to the sanctuary of their hotel. And I knew.

Ever since that day, I've wondered whether Nicky wasn't dead right about what was going on in the jury room.

Louise

I SPENT THE WEEKEND BEFORE the trial was due to begin with my family, then on the Sunday afternoon I headed to Auckland where Lynne met me and took me to the Copthorne Hotel, directly opposite the High Court. My room had a perfect view of the courthouse, and I was able to see who was coming and going from the hotel. I was thankful that my room had a balcony, as I was able to sit out there and enjoy the odd cigarette without 'contaminating' my room.

Lynne explained to me how things would work on the Monday before I was called. The jury would be selected and the Crown would open and give an outline of their case. The defence would follow, and since there were three lawyers to do this, their opening statement could take a while. Then I would be called as first witness. No one could say how long I would be in the box, but Lynne guessed at least three days, maybe longer. It was imperative I didn't associate with any other witnesses who were going to be staying in the Copthorne. It was decided I would have a policewoman as a minder, not only to keep me from bumping into other witnesses, but also to prevent me being hassled by the media — or anyone else for that matter — and to provide an escort to and from the courthouse. The policewoman assigned to me, Vanessa, was such a warm and friendly lady, in all honesty I would never have picked her as a copper.

As a rape complainant, I was entitled to have a support person in court with me when I gave my evidence. Many months beforehand I had asked my good friend Janine if she'd be my support person, but unfortunately, due to her family and work commitments, she couldn't do it. I then asked Suzie if she would, but we both decided that her plate was full with the Commission of Inquiry. Suzie suggested that I ask Ange, which I did. Ange said she would be honoured to be there in support.

We laughed and joked about what a support person was allowed and not allowed to do. I told her that the Op Austin team would fill her in, but that she would need to have a huge amount of self-control while she was sitting behind me. If things were said that pissed her off, or if the defence got nasty, she wasn't allowed, under any circumstances, to get up and bash anyone. The sole purpose of a support person is just that: to support the complainant without communicating with them. For a victim having to go through all the pressures of being in court, to know you have someone sitting right there behind you really does ease the tension, because when the victim gives her evidence before a closed court she has no friends or even anyone she knows (apart from the police and the prosecutor) to look to. And it was really neat that the support person was Ange. At least I had someone who, even though she wasn't family, was about as close to it as you could get. Her presence helped calm the nerves, big-time.

It's no reflection on the hotel, but I didn't sleep that well that Sunday night. My dreams were haunted by that single word, 'Guilty'.

Monday morning rolled around, and after a nibble at my breakfast and a few more cigarettes and cups of coffee than normal, I showered and readied myself for the day of reckoning. I was amazed at how calm I was feeling, but also how focused. I kept realising all over again that today was the first step I was taking to finally put the demons of the past behind me. Mind you, that calm only lasted until I heard a knock on the door and opened it to find Lynne bouncing in, full of smiles and confidence. I figured it was a bit of an act to put me at ease about what the day could bring.

The jury selection was going on as we spoke, and after that the Crown was due to open. This was a good time to go over some of my brief, but I think this was just another ploy to keep my mind off the time. Lynne received a phone call halfway through the morning to say that the lawyers were in chambers with the judge squabbling over some legal points, and that even though the jury had been selected and was ready to go, the judge had ordered the court to close for the day. Just another day of anguished waiting for me, but it was made a whole lot easier by Ange and her sense of humour.

The following day it was all on again. I was escorted to the courthouse in the morning by Ange, Lynne and Vanessa. As we came around the corner of the building and headed towards the side entrance, there to greet us was a small contingent of media. Cameras flashed, and then we were heading up the staircase towards Courtroom 12. Ange and I were taken to a small room where we were out of the public eye and where, if we wanted, we could make a cuppa. It had been arranged that Ange and I could have a quick look inside the courtroom before anyone else got in there, to give us an idea of what it looked like and where everybody would be seated.

The room was huge and rather daunting, even for an old hand like me, used as I was to the smaller rooms at the Rotorua courthouse. At each desk where the defence, crown, judge and jurors would be seated were computer screens. Steve from Op Austin explained that instead of relying on booklets of documents and evidence, everyone involved in a big trial can now have it all brought up on the computer screen whenever it is required. It saves a heap of time and effort, especially for the jurors, who apparently tend to flick through the booklets instead of concentrating on the page that has been requested.

Steve showed us where I would be and where Ange would be sitting. The only downfall of the layout was that I would have to walk right past the three accused and their lawyers, but Steve told me I should just ignore them and concentrate on where I was walking, as there were lots of cables I would have to step over. After our little tour we headed back to the anteroom and waited for the action to begin. While we were waiting, we had a quick visit from the head of the Op Austin team, Superintendent Nick Perry. He looked really relaxed, and just smiled and said to me, 'You'll be fine.' I smiled back at him and thought to myself, 'Yeah, right. Try telling that to the bloody bats flapping around in my guts!'

Then the door opened, and a short man was standing there looking awfully officious. With his hands clasped together he asked us to follow him to the courtroom, where he would show us where to sit. Ange and I looked at each other, took deep breaths, and did as we'd been asked. The little man led us to Courtroom 12, where the door was opened for us by a very smart-looking gentleman in a police uniform. He gave us a big smile as he held the door open, which I thought was rather nice of him. As we entered the court I could hear the judge talking, and I thought to myself, that shouldn't be happening. But, as ordered, we continued to follow the little man to where we were to be seated. As I arrived and positioned myself in the witness box, the court registrar, a very pugnacious-looking Maori lady, walked up to me and asked what I was doing here. I explained that the little man had told us to follow him. She then proceeded to burl him out and asked us to go back and wait to be called again, as the judge hadn't finished talking to the court. Ange and I felt like big idiots walking in past those guys then having to turn around and walk out again. The faces of the Op Austin team were a picture: they couldn't work out what the hell had happened. From that time on, we nicknamed the little man 'the court jester'.

We settled ourselves back into the little room again. We didn't have that long to wait before the court jester returned, not quite so officious this time, more like a naughty little schoolboy. This time, he apologised to us and quietly asked us to follow him into the courtroom. Once again, we received a lovely smile from the policeman at the door, and into the courtroom we went, all over again. I seated myself in the witness box, felt Ange's reassuring presence behind me, took another deep breath and waited for the court jester to ask me if I would be prepared to take the Bible in my right hand. I answered yes, and after I had sworn on the Bible to tell the truth I reseated myself and quickly scanned the room.

'Bring it on,' I thought.

Brent Stanaway, tall and rugged-looking, more like a country-and-western singer in a gown than a lawyer, opened by engaging me in a leisurely question-and-answer session about my years growing up: where I went to school, the jobs I'd held over the years, where I lived . . . and then we came to it. How had I met the accused?

This is when I knew I had to be really strong and not allow the emotions to take over. I held a hanky in my hand, not that I had any intention of using it to wipe away tears — I wasn't going to let myself fall down emotionally in front of those men — but because it gave me something to do with my hands. I figured if the going got tough, I could vent my frustrations on it and tear it to bits.

As I answered each of Brent's questions, I made sure I directed my answers to the jurors. After all, it was they who wanted to hear what I had to say, and it was they who were going to make their decision based on what they heard and saw. It also gave me the opportunity to look at each juror and see if I could gauge their thoughts. There were seven women and five men on the panel, with the youngest looking, a European woman, picked to be the foreperson. An interesting array of people had been chosen, from an elderly gentleman to middle-aged men to a couple of younger-looking blokes. As for the women, there were a couple of middle-aged Samoan or Maori ladies, with the rest being European. As for gauging their thoughts . . . nah, that was never going to be easy, so I just concentrated on Brent and his questions. I knew it wasn't going to be long before he would lead me into the nasty stuff, where I was going to have to tell these people exactly what had happened at Corlett Street and Rutland Street.

Throughout this material, my hanky was getting tied up in all sorts of knots, but it was just sheer determination on my part to make sure the jurors heard exactly what had happened. I wasn't going to gloss over any of it. It was while I was describing what had happened at Rutland Street that I found the courtroom had turned into a bedroom, and I was back there reliving the horrors of that day. I don't remember the jurors, I don't remember the judge, I don't remember Brent from this passage: I just remember that awful time back in that bedroom. I allowed myself to go through the whole hideous experience again, something I had promised myself I would never have to do again, but I did. It was an absolutely amazing thing, to be able to go back and relive that day as I did. By the time I had told the jury the words Schollum had spoken as he dropped me off — 'Sorry, Lou' — I was a crying wreck. It was like I'd snapped out of a really bad dream and had woken to find all these strangers staring at me. I was so embarrassed I just let my head fall into my hands and sobbed.

The judge then called for a recess so that I could collect myself. All I wanted to do was disappear from that courtroom and never return. That wasn't possible. After about fifteen minutes, we carried on. Then it was the turn of the defence. John Haigh QC, acting for Rickards, was the first to stand and make himself known.

I had decided not to look at any of the lawyers when they asked me questions, because in doing so I would see those three men. In the box where I was sitting, there was a screw in the board in front of me. I decided to focus my attention on that while I was being asked questions, and then I would answer to the jury. It worked. I was a lot more aware of the questions being asked, which gave me time to think about them before I lifted my head, looked squarely at the jury and answered to the best of my recall. I was also determined not to get angry with the defence — I was going to be the better person. But I tell you now, it was bloody hard. That hanky of mine got a fair old workout.

Haigh started off nice enough, but it wasn't long before he got into the full swing of being a defence lawyer. Throughout his rampage he never relented in accusing me of lying and of being a consensual party to the group sex. He brought up Sue Grant's statements, suggesting I was a willing participant with her and these guys. My one and only answer to him concerning all that was: 'That's Sue's recall of events, not mine. At no stage was she there when these guys called.' This really frustrated Haigh, to the point where he raised his voice and swung his spectacles even faster. I wasn't going to give in to this man, and it didn't matter how he shouted, waved his hands or put the question to me: I answered in the same way. I couldn't answer any other way. It was the simple truth, and I couldn't speculate as to why Sue would say we were willing to do these things with these men.

Haigh then tried to insinuate that I was deliberately trying to destroy Rickards, and that I was enjoying all the media attention the case had brought. I just looked at the jury and explained to them that when Phil Kitchin first approached me, I didn't even know Rickards was Assistant Police Commissioner. And as for the media, I never asked for an investigation, I asked for a Commission of Inquiry, and while I didn't like the media attention that had come my way, I had to accept it was part and parcel of coming forward with my story.

Then it was the turn of Schollum's lawyer Paul Mabey QC to smash me around the courtroom like a tennis ball. He questioned me about what I had told my school counsellor concerning the Maoris on horseback. He questioned me about Kusabs Street, and then he accused me of getting flirty with Schollum at my brother's wedding. That's when I got angry and broke my rule of not looking at the defence. I gave him the nastiest stare I could muster and told him, 'I definitely did not do that, thank you!'

He then asked me if I remembered lifting my skirt and showing Schollum my suspender belt. I once again glared at him, and said, 'Is it on the video? Have you seen the wedding video?'

'Yes,' he answered.

'No,' I said. 'I did not.'

Shipton's lawyer, Bill Nabney, was the only one to show the nicer side of being a defence lawyer, to the point where I found I could look at him while I answered his questions. He really didn't go into anything too much, except to come out with a cockamamie bullshit story about my being at a party and getting a ride home with Shipton and Schollum and having consensual group sex in the car. It was the only time I'd felt like laughing since I entered that courtroom. I just informed Mr Nabney that his client must have me confused with someone else. I had never had sex in a car in my life.

Then it was all over. I couldn't believe the vultures were going to leave me in peace. Brent Stanaway asked me to verify a few things, which I did, and then the judge thanked me and excused me. I couldn't believe that I had only been on the stand for two days, when we were all expecting it to take most of the week. The relief was overwhelming.

Looking back on those two days, I can say now that the most frustrating thing for me was being under oath to refrain from talking about what was going on in the courtroom, even to Ange. I couldn't speak of my frustrations or ask the many questions I had until I was excused by the judge. As much as I wanted to be in court for the rest of the trial, it was decided it wouldn't look good. I was bitterly disappointed, but totally understood, so I ended up relying on Dad to tell me everything that was going on. Mum and Dad had driven up to Auckland on the Wednesday, and Ross had flown in, as they had all been told they would be called after me. As it was, Mum didn't give evidence as, for whatever reason, the Crown decided not to call her. As for Ross, my heart was breaking for him the whole time he was over at the court, because I knew it was going to be really hard on him in that courtroom, as the emotions of those days will always be raw memories for him. He did break down when asked about the muslin dress he'd bought for me at Whangamata, but composed himself enough to continue and, from what Dad told me, answered questions from the defence really well. He made me so proud: it took a lot of guts for him to do what he has done. He returned to Rotorua that night.

I managed to have time out from the trial when my workmate, Daph, her sister Pam and their mate Rachel decided to spend a few days with me. Daph was itching to go to Sky City, so we decided we'd head there for tea. Mum, Dad,

Daph and I got a taxi that night and headed for the Sky Tower.

As soon as we stepped inside you could almost see the drool running out of Daph's mouth, as she loved the pokies and tables. As for me, well, I didn't have a clue what to do when it came to gambling. I'd decided to take only $80 with me, which would pay for my tea and drinks, and I would play the machines with whatever was left over. Dad sat at the bar, and Mum asked if she could have $20 to go and play some of the machines. Dad obligingly handed her the green note, but when she arrived back five minutes later asking for more, he snapped his wallet shut and told her to sit down and stay there. I followed Daph around like a bad smell, watching and learning. I then found a machine that had heaps of pretty lights on it and decided to give it a go. I popped my $20 in (it damn near killed me, seeing that machine swallow up that amount of money!) but I told myself I had to get hard and remember I was there to have a bit of fun. Anyway, Daph showed me what to do and, once I got the hang of it, she wandered off to find the roulette table. So I sat there pressing this button, not really knowing what I was doing, but the machine looked and sounded pretty so I just carried on pressing the button. Eventually Daph came back and said to me: 'Louey, do you know what you're doing?'

'No, not really,' I replied.

She told me I was winning and should quit now before I lost it all again. I squinted at her and asked how she knew I was winning. She sighed and rolled her eyes.

'Look at all those credits you've got!'

'Oh. OK,' I replied, and asked her how I got my money out. She pressed a couple of buttons for me and this bell went off. Next minute, a man turned up with a receipt book and informed me that I had won $280. I was absolutely flabbergasted, and so shocked that the two ladies sitting at the machines next to me totally cracked up laughing. I damn near ran to the money people to collect my winnings, which I put straight into my wallet and left there. We had had such a cool night, but I was knackered. We headed for the hotel.

The next day was Saturday, and the girls and I left Mum and Dad at the hotel and headed to the Otara markets for a look. From there we went to some massive shopping mall to have lunch. I was sitting there having a coffee and talking to Suzie on the phone when I noticed Daph talking to a couple of ladies. After I got off the phone, I asked Daph who she'd been talking to. 'Louey,' she said, 'I nearly scored five bucks off those two sheilas.'

'Yeah? How come?' I asked.

She told me she'd noticed them staring at me, so she went up to them and told them if they paid her five bucks, she'd get my autograph for them. I just looked at her with my mouth open and said, 'You didn't.'

'Yeah, mate. I did. Bugger them. There's no need for them to be staring at you.'

Daph and the girls headed home after the weekend, and I returned to trial mode. The Crown called a number of witnesses, including a woman who had also been brutally pack-raped by Shipton, Schollum and Rickards. Her case was almost a mirror image of mine; the main difference was that they used a bottle on her, not a baton. She had kept quiet all these years, not wanting to relive the whole nightmare, but had finally decided to break her silence. The jury weren't allowed to know that the same three accused who stood before them in my case were also going to face charges over what they had done to this witness. We really felt that, thanks to this woman's courage in fronting up, we would convince the jury of what animals these men were. I was so grateful to her. Then the Crown called another woman who admitted she too had had sexual encounters with Shipton and Schollum where a baton was used, but she'd been a consensual participant. This showed the guys were in the habit of using batons and objects on their victims, even though they had publicly stated that they would never do such a thing. The Crown also called ex-cops, who told the court what they had heard about the Rutland Street incident.

When the Crown had finished calling their witnesses, it was the turn of the defence. Rickards went into the box and did nothing but call me a liar the whole way through Brent's questions. I expected nothing less of him, but at least he wasn't trying to impress anyone by wearing his uniform, as he had on the first day of the trial. That was a stupid thing for him to do, and he got hauled over the coals by the police hierarchy for it. Rickards's only witness was an ex-All Black, Steve McDowell, and all he could offer was character evidence. Were we meant to be impressed that he was once a good rugby player? If that was the idea, the reports we had suggested it didn't work. Still, I guess desperate times call for desperate measures!

Schollum didn't testify, but had two witnesses. One was a work colleague of mine from the BNZ days, who told the court she'd come out to my house at Collier Road to see my horse back in 1985/86. She said while she was there, Schollum had turned up. This never happened. The only time she ever came out to Collier Road was one Guy Fawkes night, when there were quite a few from the bank there as well as Ross's relations and our friends. Her husband is a cop, and a good mate of Schollum's, and I wondered if they had cooked this story up.

His other witness was the matron of honour from my brother's wedding, who said she saw me flirting with Schollum. I'd said in court that didn't happen. It *couldn't* happen, as I had my hands full keeping track of the ratbag flower girls, my daughter Jess and her cousin, both of whom were only four years old at the time. I was far too busy stopping them swigging out of the bridal party's bottles and cans of booze to flirt with anyone, even if I'd wanted to. It's a real pity the Crown has no idea who the defence is going to call. Their stories could easily have been shown to be false. But that's how our justice system works.

As for Shipton, he didn't take the stand or call any witnesses. It was no surprise at all that Shipton and Schollum didn't testify, because they'd both made that mistake in the Mount Maunganui trial. Once bitten, twice shy!

The Crown then gave their closing statement to the court, followed by the three defence counsel. The judge then summed up the case for the jury and they retired on the Wednesday to start their deliberations. I have to say, we were pretty confident. During the course of the trial it had become obvious to us all that the 'other side' was nervous about how it was proceeding. One afternoon, when we were all down in the restaurant having lunch, Dad noticed a well-dressed chap sitting at the bar watching us. He made a comment to my brother Rob about him, and Rob said that he had noticed him walk in and plug his cellphone into one of the wall sockets by the reception area. Both Dad and Rob kept a close eye on him, but that didn't stop him watching us with great interest.

Was he just a nosy member of the public — someone staying at the hotel who recognised me, perhaps — or was he a 'spy' for the other side? This idea made all of us laugh, except Rob. The suspicious cop side of him was coming out. After a while, this bloke got up from his chair at the bar, grabbed his cellphone and wandered out of the Copthorne. Rob didn't hesitate, and followed him out. About 20 minutes later, Rob came back and reported that, sure enough, this guy had headed straight back to the courthouse and into the other side's camp. So all we could guess was that he was trying to catch us out discussing the trial or doing something that he could give to the defence to call a halt to proceedings.

As the jury deliberated, we had time to reflect on the past two and a half weeks. It was a useful time, actually, and we should have looked at it as some sort of debrief. But with my family and our friends having such a warped sense of humour, we found ourselves laughing a lot of the time. There had been some funny little incidents scattered throughout the whole stressful experience. Dad told us about the witness who said she 'enjoyed' her time with Shipton, Schollum and the baton. Everybody in the courtroom was just sitting there with their mouths wide open. A visitor from overseas sat in the public gallery of the courtroom wearing a pair of Lycra bike shorts. Some silly woman tried to tell members of the jury what she thought of the trial and ended up spending the weekend in jail because of it. And Rickards turning up in his uniform — God, what was that man thinking? Saying good morning and good night to the boys as they arrived and left in the prison van each day. They were all just silly things that helped keep things light for us.

But day one of deliberations turned into day two, and our nerves really started to show. Because we couldn't go anywhere, the sixth floor of the Copthorne was overrun by my family and friends who were there to support us. At one stage, I had just finished a call to Jess, who was off shopping for a dress for the school ball, when Steve from Op Austin phoned and asked me to get off the balcony. The defence was doing a war dance, as they thought the jury could see me out there when they came down to the park for their break. It wasn't me they were seeing out on the balcony, it was most likely Ange or Phil's wife, Nicky, both of whom had the same hair colour and cut as me. The defence apparently felt a glimpse of me might influence the jury.

Why on earth, I asked Steve, if we're talking about influencing the jury, doesn't someone move the family and friends of the three accused along, as we'd been told they were hanging around having prayer meetings and singalongs within earshot of the jury room? Steve told me they'd approached Rickards's lawyer John Haigh, and he had said he'd ask them to move. Yeah, right. From then on, when Op Austin knew the jury were coming out, I would get the phone call to remove myself from the balcony. I got one call from Nick Perry, who said he was sending up a balaclava for me to wear and that I should get under the bed and hide as the jury were on their way out.

On the third day of deliberations, Ross and I suggested to the girls that they should go and have a look at the Sky Tower. We sent them off with the video camera and some money and told them to keep together and be safe. Jess told me to text her if the jury came back. I promised her I would, and off they went. It was just before three o'clock on Friday 30 March when Lynne walked into Room 615 and announced that the jury had reached their verdicts.

My mind was back in Murupara. My eyes were on that small rip in the courtroom carpet. The forewoman had finished when I was jolted back to reality.

'Come on, Louise. Move.'

It was Lynne, telling me to get to my feet and leave the courtroom. I looked at her, and said: 'But I haven't heard the guilty verdicts yet.'

Lynne looked at me strangely and said, 'It's over. We've got to go.'

I looked at Ross, and he just grabbed my hand and pulled me up out of my chair. All I remember as we were leaving the courtroom was people yelling and cheering, and someone yelling out: 'We love you, Brad!'

'Have we lost?' I asked Ross as he half-led, half-dragged me out of the courtroom. He didn't need to answer, as the look on his face said it all. I was having trouble comprehending anything. I was obviously in a state of shock, as I was finding it hard to breathe, let alone think and take it all in. It was so hard to keep moving: all I wanted to do was pause and let my mind catch up with everything that was going on. Between them, Lynne and Ross kept me moving.

As we descended the staircase at the Auckland High Court for the last time, we caught up to a lady who was heading down too. She turned to me when we caught her up, looked at me and said: 'I'm so sorry.' She was in tears, so I stopped, put my arm around her and told her it would be all right. I didn't get a chance to say anything else, as Ross started to drag me off again, with Lynne pushing me from behind. When we reached the side entrance of the building, the media swarm was unbelievable. We had trouble getting through them, and all I remember is flashes and microphones and people all talking at once. I was too stunned to acknowledge any of them and just kept walking in a straight line. Just before we turned to walk across the park, I could see that one of the cameramen was going to trip over a pole that was stuck in the middle of the pathway. My instinct was to grab him, but he fell before I could do or say anything. I felt terrible walking past him, but I had no choice, as Ross had me firmly by the hand and just kept me going.

When we reached the road to cross over to the Copthorne, the media scrum had grown and we had trouble getting across, not only because of the traffic, but because of the frenzied media pack. All I could hear were people asking me how I felt about the verdicts. At that point I really wanted to scream at them, 'How the hell do you think I feel?' but I knew just to keep my mouth shut and concentrate on getting across the road. In the end Margaret Craig's husband Murray walked out into the middle of the road and stopped the traffic. Ross ran me across, and as we entered the Copthorne I noticed the hotel staff were there ready to stop the media coming in. I was so relieved to see my brother Robert holding the door to the elevator open for us. I hit the back of the elevator and burst into tears. It finally hit me then that they didn't believe me.

The silence on the ride up to the sixth floor was so eerie. Phil was waiting for us in the room, and I just fell into his arms and cried, telling him over and over that they didn't believe me. As I pulled away from Phil, wiping away the tears, I saw the devastated looks on the faces of my family and friends. I looked at each face, and I could see so much sorrow, so much anger, so much bewilderment. But the one face that completely shattered my heart was my father's. I will never forget, for as long as I live, how he sat in the chair and wept. I walked up to him and hugged him with all the love I could put into a hug. There were no words: they weren't needed. I looked my dad in the face and smiled. What more could we do? Then Phil appeared with a beer for him.

After a time, while everyone just mourned, the questions started flying around the room. So much anger — and fair enough too — but we all knew there was no way we could go back and change things. We had to accept what had happened and move on. I knew that was going to be more easily said than done, but we were a tough bunch, and I knew we would manage it. I walked out into the corridor to find Ross, and asked him if he'd contacted the girls. He'd phoned them and told them to come back to the hotel.

After a while someone called out to say the girls were coming into the hotel. I said to Ross, we'll have to tell them before they get to the room. We heard the elevator open and we started to walk towards them. Then I started to panic, because as soon as I saw them I could see they were crying. I was thinking something had happened to them, but they just ran up to me and hugged me hard. Jess said: 'We know, Mum', and it was then that I really broke down. Ross, the girls and I hugged, finding comfort in each other.

I looked up and my heart started to break all over again. There in front of me were some of the team from Op Austin, all with tears running down their cheeks. It hit me that this was just as hard on them as it was on us. The thousands of hours and hard work that they'd put into the investigation, the amount of time they'd spent away from their families — yeah, this was just as devastating for them. Phil then walked out of the room with some beers in his hands and passed them to the coppers.

That was when I said, 'Hell, this has to stop. All this sadness — let's remember, we did the best we could, and we've got to remember that they haven't won the war, just this battle. There's still the other woman's case. Come on. Let's celebrate the fact it's over, and as far as I'm concerned, it's all onwards and upwards from here. Where the hell's my rum and Coke?'

It was killing me to see all the sadness, and I just needed everyone to be OK.

The drive home from Auckland was really subdued. All we heard on the radio was the news of how the men had been acquitted. It all seemed so one-sided. I phoned Nick Perry and asked him if it would be all right for us to make a statement thanking all our family and friends and members of the public for the love and support we'd received over the last few weeks. Nick thought that was a great idea. I phoned Phil and asked him who I could ring to organise this. Phil just said, leave it with me, mate. I'll sort it for you. And within an hour of that phone call, we heard our statement come over the radio.

Phil

THE DOOR TO THE ROOM opened and there were Louise and Ross. Louise reached out to me wordlessly. I hugged her, and she started crying — not uncontrollably, just quietly. But the anguish in her voice was harrowing, as she just kept repeating, 'They didn't believe me. They didn't believe me.'

Eventually I let her go. I hadn't felt able to say anything, apart from 'I know.'

Ross, with tears in his eyes, asked if he could borrow my mobile phone. I heard him call his daughters and say, 'Come straight back to the hotel. Don't walk past the court. Just come straight back.'

The moments that followed in the hotel corridor where Louise's family and supporters had reserved several rooms were heart-wrenching. I've seen police officers trying to comfort the families of murder victims when juries have returned not guilty verdicts, but I've never seen the likes of what I saw that afternoon. After all, these were police officers who'd worked tremendously long hours on an investigation into their own people, away from their families and without even the whole-hearted support of their colleagues to count on. They tried to hold themselves together, but I saw tears on the cheeks of one granite-faced detective who looked as though he'd stepped straight out of a movie role as a hard-arsed New York cop. A female detective was crying openly. Another detective told me: 'You've got to tell this story one day. You have to. It's got to come out.'

Nicky hugged me. I could feel the fury in her body, and hear the absolute despair for Louise in her voice. Feeling completely ineffectual, I opened a few bottles of beer to hand around. Jim was sitting in a chair, his head bowed, his eyes going like faucets. 'I just can't bloody believe it. Twenty charges. Twenty bloody charges,' he said. Barbara was sitting too, stunned. She didn't say anything that I heard for a long, long time.

Then the girls arrived. They were hustled to the end of the corridor, to Louise and Ross. The girls were crying, but crumpled into the arms of their parents. The family went into a protective huddle. The girls kept saying, 'I'm sorry, Mum. I'm so sorry. I'm sorry.'

Trying to reassure them, Louise and Ross said it would all be all right. Then, typically, Louise said something like: 'Onwards and upwards. It's onwards and upwards from here.'

The rooms filled with family members and supporters. About five minutes later I saw Louise and Ross's youngest daughter, McKaela, sitting alone at the end of the hall, her back slumped against the wall. I thought to myself, she just wants to be on her own for a little. When I looked again several minutes later, McKaela was still there, head down, terribly alone. I wandered down and asked, 'Are you all right, sweetie?' She looked up. There was no sound, no sobbing, just tears pouring from her eyes. I choked, and said, 'Come on, let's go find Grandma. She'll want to talk to you.'

I put a call in to TVNZ to say there would be no interview with Louise Nicholas. They did a great job that night, running an interview with Dr Jan Jordan, a university lecturer who'd studied rape victims. The programme was one of the very few media reports that took an obvious angle against the three acquitted men, two of whom we again saw going back to prison from the windows of the hotel.

Whole front pages of newspapers were devoted to the decision the next day. Most focused on the tears of relief from the acquitted men and their families. Rickards was given star treatment, saying he'd been through two and a half years of torture. Shipton's brothers vented their anger for the cameras. Craig Shipton, a senior manager at ACC, said his faith in God had been restored. 'These are good men,' he said. 'The world needs more of these men and we should all be proud of them.' Greg Shipton said the prosecution had been 'about stopping the first Maori Commissioner of Police'.

Bill Ralston was on holiday in the South Island, and he called me after the television news broadcasts. He wasn't happy. 'The public don't know it, but we and the rest of the media bloody well know it,' he fumed. 'Two of them are fucking convicted pack-rapists. They've all still got another trial to go. Knowing what we know, the media shouldn't be giving Shipton's and Schollum's families an unchallenged platform.'

Tim Pankhurst rang, and I described to him the scenes in the hotel. He went quiet, then said: 'Phil, you must write all this down . . . Write it down.'

Later that night — and it was a long, emotional night for everyone — I was having a drink with Louise on the hotel balcony. I told her I was terribly sorry. I told her I wished I'd never pursued the story, because she'd just ended up getting screwed again. She wouldn't have a bar of it.

'All good, all good,' she said. 'I wouldn't change a thing.'

The next day Nicky and I went home. The fury in Nicky was out. She let all and sundry know her thoughts on the verdicts. It wasn't anything to do with the three accused; she actually felt upset for their families. Like many other people, right around New Zealand — and they didn't yet know the half of it — her trust in the New Zealand justice system had been damaged. As she fulminated about the inequities in the way evidence had been handled in the trial — with potentially vital testimony ruled out — I found myself trying to protect my job as a journalist. I told her to tone it down before she let slip something that she should never have known about the trial but had learnt from me. But like hundreds of thousands around the country, our social gatherings were dominated by talk of the trial and speculation over what the jury didn't know. It was hard to rein Nicky in.

A few days later, I got a call from a high-profile lawyer asking after Louise. I said she would get through it, the way she'd got through it all before. The lawyer said: 'She's an absolute saint, that woman. Far-reaching changes will come out of all this, in the police, in the justice system, all because of her courage.' In the flatness I felt in the wake of the verdicts, I wasn't so sure.

Injustice, it seemed, was everywhere. Nicky said she'd seen one of the Shipton clan get in the face of Superintendent Nick Perry, the head of Operation Austin, in the courtroom immediately after the verdicts. Perry was sitting with his head in one of his hands when the man leaned in and almost spat at him, 'You piece of shit.'

The outcome of the trial is what it is. It can't be changed. But there were some highly unusual things about this trial.

One of the easier ways to understand the intricacies of the trial is to split the 20 charges into two street names: Rutland Street and Corlett Street. The baton rape allegedly occurred at Rutland Street. The other allegations — of visits to Louise's flat by Rickards and Shipton for non-consensual group sex — centred on her Corlett Street flat.

Having covered many criminal trials I was certain, and so, I suspect, were the police, that the jury was unlikely to return guilty verdicts for the Corlett Street charges. So let's look at those. Crown Prosecutor Brent Stanaway faced a conundrum. It was a big ask to get a jury to believe a woman in full possession of her faculties was repeatedly raped in her flat but didn't officially complain — even if the jury believed Louise did complain to former cop Trevor Clayton but nothing happened. Stanaway could have called a sexual-abuse expert to tell the jury that if they believed Louise had been raped by Sam Brown at an early age and her complaints had fallen on deaf ears, her behaviour at Corlett Street was absolutely understandable — almost normal, in fact, for a sexual-abuse victim. The problem was that if he did call an expert witness, the defence lawyers would call three sexual-abuse experts to say it wasn't necessarily so. Expert witnesses can be a mixed blessing, and Stanaway opted not to go there. But with no expert witness to back Louise, she was going to have to say Brown raped her in one breath, then in the next admit that Brown was found not guilty. Stanaway's decision was rational, but it had a cost.

The way the system is geared to protect the defendant in a criminal trial from the introduction of potentially prejudicial material meant that there were a number of damning facts that the jury couldn't be told. They couldn't know that two of the accused were already in jail for pack-raping a Mount Maunganui woman, in circumstances that bore no little similarity to the Rutland Street incident. They weren't allowed to know that all three accused had yet to be tried for kidnapping, handcuffing and indecently assaulting another Rotorua teenager with a bottle. They didn't know that ten months before the trial started, John Dewar had been charged with four counts of attempting to pervert, obstruct or defeat the course of justice in relation to the way he had handled Louise's complaints about Sam Brown, for which he was subsequently convicted. Of course, if they'd known how justice had been deliberately derailed in the Brown matter, the jury might have taken a very different view of Louise's credibility on that score. As it was, confronted by the facts of Louise's allegations and Brown's acquittal, the jury were left with the firm impression that she was wont to make wild allegations of sexual assault.

The second question, perhaps the most important question of all, revolves around written statements made by Louise's Corlett Street flatmate, Sue Grant, being used at trial. By the time Louise gave evidence, Grant had told three different stories. She later told a fourth. At one point she agreed to come back to New Zealand to give evidence for the Crown, but then almost immediately changed her mind. She was promised name suppression if she came to give evidence. At the time of writing, *The Dominion Post* was challenging that privilege considering she refused to come to court.

In their pre-trial theatrics, the defence lawyers argued that if the Crown couldn't get Sue Grant to come and give evidence in person, her statements should be admitted as evidence or they would apply to have the case thrown out completely. I say theatrics, because in my view it's unlikely the defence wanted Sue Grant anywhere near the witness box. I'd suggest their private investigator, Mark Templeman, would have left them in no doubt about how she would come across. Under questioning, she'd have been made to look utterly unbelievable, purely on the basis of the several different stories she'd told. The defence knew the police couldn't get Sue Grant to come over to give evidence, so the best slant I could put on it was that they were able to play legal games: they could say how critical her statements were to the accused receiving a fair trial, all the while keeping their fingers crossed that she wouldn't change her mind again and come to make those statements in person. The Crown also knew how contradictory her statements were. If the statements were going to be admitted as 'evidence', the Crown wanted every statement she'd made read in its entirely to the jury. That way all the different stories would be heard.

It's almost unheard of for written evidence to be presented in a criminal trial, unless it's done with the agreement of the Crown and the defence and that's usually when the evidence is uncontested. Nothing is more certain than that Grant's evidence would have been hotly contested, and the Crown and the defence were at loggerheads over how much of her statements should be admitted. It was like a game of poker. The Crown risked a potential legal challenge that could have seen the whole case thrown out. The Crown blinked. A deal was done and a censored version — selected portions of the statements — was read to the jury. The expurgated version did contain some of the inconsistencies with which Grant's statements had been riddled, but not all of them. And what I believe were crucial remarks she'd made were left out altogether.

In her last statement, for example, she said she didn't want the policemen coming around to the Corlett Street flat for sex but felt she couldn't say no. That's almost exactly what Louise had told the jury, but the jury never got to hear Sue Grant saying it. Instead, the censored statements the jury heard were hugely damaging to Louise's credibility. In many criminal trials there's a turning point in the minds of the jury — a point where they decide who they believe. It's reasonable to speculate that Grant's selectively presented statements must have left 'a reasonable doubt' in the minds of the jury. And did they transfer their doubts about Corlett Street to help make up their minds about Rutland Street? The media in New Zealand are not allowed to approach jurors after a trial — although jurors are allowed to approach the media — so we may never know if the flatmate's so-called 'evidence' was the turning point in the Louise Nicholas trial.

Louise was judged just as harshly in the court of public opinion after the trial as she ever was in the Auckland High Court, and 'the flatmate's evidence' was held up as a smoking gun for those saying the men were innocent. Talkback callers dined out on it for days. Louise was labelled a slut and a liar by people who knew nothing of her sexual history. In fact, till she met Ross, I've yet to see a shred of evidence Louise Nicholas had sex with anyone but police officers.

Sex, she said, she did not want. Most of the public — and, I'd suggest, all of those talkback callers — are still ignorant of the fact that Grant didn't even come to court to give evidence, and that what the jury heard and what the media reported was a cut-and-paste job of her various statements.

And as for her credibility as a witness, quite apart from what she said, I asked Rex Miller after the trial what he thought. He was unequivocal.

'When she signed the statement, I immediately faxed it to Bruce Raffin and told him it was all bullshit. She was lying. When I spoke to her, I don't know what it was but I had a gut feeling someone had spoken to her before me . . . someone had got at her.' Miller told me back in 1995 Shipton had almost insisted he go to Australia to talk to the flatmate.

To lay to rest any doubts we had, one way or the other, about Grant's real position, I'd asked Bill Ralston to approve Louise, me and a *Close Up* team flying to Brisbane to try for an interview with her. So on 29 May, two months after the trial, Louise knocked on the door of Sue Grant's suburban Brisbane house. Producer Janet Wilson and I believed she'd slam the door on us if we called on her with cameras and microphones, so to ensure we had an absolutely accurate record we wired Louise up and waited down the road. We didn't ever broadcast the discussion between Louise and Grant, because we never got pictures of her. She declined our requests for an interview and went to ground the day after we secretly taped her. It took another six weeks before she answered Louise's telephone calls and said she didn't want to have anything more to do with what had happened to her. But what she told Louise was astonishing, and here's what the jury might have got to hear if she'd given evidence in person.

The Operation Austin detectives she spoke to, she told Louise, helped her remember a lot more. 'What I could remember was more of a case of, at that age, we didn't realise [saying] no was a viable option . . . I couldn't remember . . . It was like three times I remember them there. It's not like I was a fly on the wall . . . I said [to the Operation Austin officers] hypnotise me, because I can't remember it . . . Maybe I have completely blocked it out.' She said Shipton and co were slimy bastards who used their 'power and uniforms to intimidate' her. 'I probably could have stopped them but I didn't know better . . . to me, it was more my stupidity at letting shit happen than anything else . . . I don't know how to describe anything. I mean it was gross and creepy and nasty . . . I don't know, it's buried so deep.'

Then Grant made a critical admission. 'If anyone said to me, "Can you swear on what you said?" I'd say no . . . I've said so many times, this [what she'd said in the statements she'd made] is only what I can vaguely remember . . . It beats me how that can be used as evidence because I could not swear on it being true.'

It couldn't help Louise now, but in that meeting Sue Grant admitted her statements were so flaky, so unreliable, that they should never have been allowed in the High Court. Her evidence was critical both in the criminal case and in the court of public opinion, and she has all but recanted it.

Even if I didn't believe the jury would find Shipton, Schollum and Rickards guilty on the Corlett Street charges, I was not alone in thinking there was a good chance they would return guilty verdicts on the Rutland Street charges. In his directions to the jury, the judge was at pains to get them to separate the charges. The issue in the Corlett Street charges was consent. The accused admitted having group sex with Louise: she said it was rape, they said it was consensual. But Rutland Street was different. The jury only had to decide if the baton rape had happened. If they believed, beyond reasonable doubt, that it had happened, it was rape. Consent didn't come into it, because whereas Louise was claiming it was non-consensual, the accused all denied it had even happened.

To support Louise's contention that the incident happened, the Crown called extraordinary evidence about the men's serial use of police batons in sex — evidence the media wasn't allowed to report at the time. They'd denied ever using batons for sex and, in fact, when Shipton was interviewed by one police officer, he said the idea he'd use a baton on any woman was 'just bizarre'.

Two policemen were called who testified that Shipton had described using a baton in group sex sessions. Another police officer told the jury he and Schollum had consensual group sex with a young woman they met in a bar. At someone's suggestion a police baton was used by the witness and Schollum. They inserted it into the woman's vagina.

A woman took the stand. She said she had a consensual threesome with Shipton and Schollum around 1984 and, again with her consent, they used a police baton on her. Then the Rotorua woman who had allegedly been violated with a bottle gave evidence. Her testimony was constrained, because the jury weren't allowed to know that the three accused had yet to stand trial for kidnapping and indecently assaulting this witness.

So much for what the jury did hear. They never got the chance to consider another piece of evidence, one that has not been revealed until now. A few weeks before the trial started, police tracked down another former detective, John Flannery, who made a statement to police saying he'd been in Rotorua around the time of the alleged baton rape of Louise and had gone to the Rutland Street police house to see Brad Shipton. Another man was there too, a Maori, but Flannery didn't know his name. While he was in the house, Flannery said Shipton told him they'd used a baton on a girl in the bedroom. The other man, whom Flannery didn't know and whose name he could not remember, told Shipton to shut his mouth and keep it shut.

So why did this witness not come to court to give that evidence? Unlike Sue

Grant, he'd agreed to testify, but the defence argued the evidence had come to light too late. As they wouldn't be able to investigate it properly, it was unfair. Justice Randerson agreed. It seems unbelievable. They say justice delayed is justice denied, but here's a glaring example of where the opposite can be true. For the sake of putting the trial back a few weeks, a crucial piece of evidence was denied the Crown. Who knows what effect it would have had on the outcome?

In short, when they retired to consider their verdicts and focused on the Rutland Street charges, the jury had merely to decide who was telling the truth. The accused all denied using batons for sex, yet here were several witnesses, including ex-police officers, who told a different story. Brad Shipton had described the suggestion that he would use a baton for sex as bizarre. Yet here were witnesses to say they'd heard him bragging about doing just that, or who claimed they were actually present when he was doing it.

The jury in the Mount Maunganui case could believe cops were capable of pack-rape, but they didn't want to believe policemen — including Shipton — would use their batons for deviant sex on women. Nor did this jury want to believe that.

Louise

AFTER THE TRIAL, THERE was a huge groundswell of anger against the verdicts, the police, and against the three accused in particular. Some people knew that Shipton and Schollum were in jail for the Mount Maunganui rape, and they passed out fliers to the public letting them know this and asking why this information was not produced during the trial. This was a breach of suppression orders, and unfortunately these people were charged and fined for doing this, but it would have been hard to find anyone who would condemn them for taking this stand and showing the powers-that-be that people weren't prepared to sit back and just accept such a travesty of justice. I was blown away, too, when I learnt there was going to be a march down Queen Street in Auckland on 30 April in support of me. I was invited to attend, and I was going to go come hell or high water, but then the brakes came on, not only from Op Austin, but also from Phil. Both thought it would probably be more of a media circus than a public stand in support of me. It took a lot of talking, but eventually I saw their reasoning. Op Austin felt it could jeopardise the next trial, of the other Rotorua woman, as at that stage it seemed likely I would be called as a witness. So it was decided that I would write a letter of thanks to those who were going to attend the march, and get Dr Kim McGregor from Rape Crisis (now called Rape Prevention Education) to read it out for me. The speech read like this:

> When I heard about today's march taking place, I was hellbent on being here with you all so that I could personally thank you for the support you have shown me. Unfortunately, due to circumstances beyond my control, I am unable to be here in body but I am with you in spirit. I have asked Kim to read out a few words on my behalf.
>
> For the last 25 years of my life I have lived day to day as that was the safest way for me to be. But now, because of people like

yourselves who have given up your day to be here and because of people throughout New Zealand who took time out of their busy day to send me the most beautiful cards and letters of support, I can now remove my safety net, hold my head high and with my husband Ross and our three daughters finally look ahead to a bigger, brighter and safer future.

To the women who organised the march, I thank you from the bottom of my heart. I will treasure you all and this day always.

Lastly, please let's not forget that Rape Awareness Week starts tomorrow. We all need to show our support to the Rape Crisis and Sexual Abuse Centres who have the most amazing people working for them, who go beyond the call of duty to provide so many women, men and children with the help, guidance and the safety net that all victims/survivors seek so that they, too, can look ahead to a bigger, brighter and safer future.

With love and forever thankful

Louise

I wasn't there, but I could feel the electric atmosphere through the TV. I just sat there and cried as I watched these people support me. It is a day, a time in my life, that I'll never forget.

I figured that everything would calm down after a few days, but hell, was I wrong. Over the next few months our mailbox was inundated with cards and letters from complete strangers outraged at the verdicts and offering their love and support to me and my family. As each bundle of letters was brought home, I would read out loud every single one of them to the family. More tears were shed as I did this, as it was overwhelming to read out the wonderful words that people had written — complete strangers from all over New Zealand. The girls and I had a great time putting together a letter that we could send back to those who had provided return addresses, to thank them from the bottom of our hearts for their kindness.

A lot of the letters and cards we received came from people who had gone through bad experiences themselves. It was as though the stand I'd taken — the fact that I'd come forward and taken on not only these men, but also the justice system — seemed to help a lot of other victims and survivors deal with their own demons. For example, I received a letter from a lady who was 86 years old. She told me that she had been raped at the age of 16, and it was only since I had come forward that she'd been able to finally tell her family about what had happened to her. She said that I'd given her the strength to come to terms with what had happened, and that in turn had encouraged her family to talk to their children about keeping themselves safe.

This was when I suddenly saw the reason I was put on this earth. I said to Ross that I now knew what path I needed to follow, and that I'd been to hell and back for a reason. My fight for personal justice had now become a fight for all who found themselves in my situation, and I was now more determined than ever to see that changes are made within our legal and justice systems so that victims and survivors of rape and sexual abuse are given fair and just treatment if they decide to lay complaints.

It was soon after the Queen Street march that I got to know a woman by the name of Jane Smith (not her real name — this name is used because of a supression order). She phoned me one day and told me she knew Shipton. He'd failed to investigate a complaint she'd made against a relative, who had abused her and other children. She also revealed that her mother, who has since passed away, actually lived with Schollum for a while in the Rutland Street house. Many of the details of what she told me about Shipton were quite revolting, and have chilling parallels with what happened to me.

And like so many others who came forward to the Commission of Inquiry, Jane got nowhere complaining to the police. Tragically, in her case the police investigated for 18 months before deciding they didn't have enough evidence to prosecute anyone over her allegations — just long enough, as it turned out, to have her case ditched from the commission. Jane had been to every day of my trial, and she was the woman I had passed going down the stairs at the Auckland High Court after receiving the verdicts. Jane and I have since become very close friends.

One day out of the blue I received a phone call from Phil, asking if I would be interested in paying a visit to my old flatmate, Sue. It would mean a trip to Brisbane, but the chance to ask her face-to-face the questions that had confused me for so long was one I couldn't pass up.

I knocked on the door of Sue's Brisbane home and her husband answered. I asked if Sue was home and he said yes and called her. She got halfway to the door when it obviously dawned on her who was standing there. She stopped dead in her tracks, stared at me for a minute, then rushed forward and gave me the biggest hug ever. She was genuinely happy to see me. I hoped she would be genuinely happy to talk too, because I was wired with a microphone so that our conversation could be taped.

For an hour or so we talked about old times, our friends and what they are all up to now. We talked about the trial and all I had been through on account of her evidence, and it was then that she said she couldn't come back and testify as she didn't think she could swear on the Bible that she would tell the truth. She was unsure of her recall, and she also spoke about the statements taken by Rex Miller, Mark Templeman (who was hired by the defence) and Op Austin. She spoke about her absolute disgust for the three accused.

I was hoping and praying that the tape was working, as she was saying exactly what I needed to hear. When I left her house I walked back to the car, got in and sat for a minute. There was something at work deep down in Sue's life that wasn't right and wouldn't let her tell the truth, and I wondered what it was. What had those bastards done to her?

Phil

INEVITABLY, THE SO-CALLED LOUISE Nicholas trial had its sequels and consequences.

The verdicts reverberated around the country. There were protest marches, vigils, angry letters and comments on blog sites. Word began to filter out that there was suppressed evidence that had outrageous implications about the justice of the outcome. Nine days after the trial ended, blogger David Farrar discovered that 82 per cent of the previous day's top 100 search terms used in Google in New Zealand had been entered by people trying to find out what the suppressed evidence was. Some knew, and openly flouted the law by breaching suppression orders hiding the fact that Shipton and Schollum were convicted rapists. It's highly unlikely those breaching the suppression orders knew that the main reason they'd been imposed in the first place was because the same three men had yet to face another trial — the one involving the 16-year-old they had allegedly violated with a bottle.

The court orders were starting to look silly in the face of the public outcry, and I suggested to Bill Ralston that the media should be challenging them. He agreed, and spoke to other news organisations. Lawyers acting for several media outlets successfully challenged the orders. The story — that the same three men were facing yet another rape trial — led newspapers and television bulletins, and prompted another public uproar. But it was to be nearly another year before the next trial began.

Meanwhile, still more women were coming forward to tell me their stories, many of which featured sexual assault by police officers, the failure of the police to investigate and, more often than not, some of the same names. One woman told me how she'd been the target of unwanted sexual attention — and finally indecent assault — by Sam Brown. Around the same time, Brown spoke anonymously to the *Sunday Star-Times*. He said Louise Nicholas lived in a fantasy world, and that she'd ruined his life. He said his marriage had collapsed after Louise's story broke in 2004. He had been working as a nurse, but said he was now a North Island farmer. He said he planned to start a new life overseas.

One woman I spoke to was at school with Louise in Murupara. We met in a motel — not far from where Sam Brown lived. I explained what I knew of the Sam Brown case, the latest trial and what John Dewar had been up to. She handed me a piece of paper. She said she'd never told anyone the whole story and the statement was the full story. It's a story that's never been revealed till now.

Aged 14, she was staying with her best friend on a farm in Galatea on New Year's Eve. Her older brothers were holding a party in the shed beside the house, and Trevor Clayton and Sam Brown turned up. Brown was introduced to the two 14-year-old girls as a 19-year-old mechanic. They learned he was in fact a 29-year-old policeman. Clayton was drunk and didn't stay long but the school girls were like a magnet to Brown.

'Things got a bit stupid after a few drinks, and I guess my friend and I were flattered with the attention — it wasn't like we were dressed to impress — both in jeans and a T-shirt, no make up. He took turns kissing both of us for a while and we all laughed about it.'

Then, as she went to the house to use the toilet, Brown came out of the dark.

'He moved me against the house at the back. He started kissing me again and got his hand up my shirt and bra. It felt like I was being smothered. I managed to push past him and said I needed the toilet.'

Nearly 10 years later she told John Dewar that story. Operation Austin had told her subsequently, however, that Dewar recorded only a fraction of what she had told him. He made no apparent attempt to pursue her allegations.

So that was all she told various people about Sam Brown till I met her and she handed me a statement — a statement she later made to police.

In it she described going back to the party after Brown's first attempts to have sex with her. She said she and her friend were plied with more drinks by Brown, who later asked her to go for a walk.

'I honestly don't know why I did. We walked past the water tank. Then he stopped and grabbed me, starting kissing, groping and feeling between my legs. He put my hand on his penis. I think I was sort of frozen — didn't know how to get out of the situation but thinking I had caused it. He got my jeans down and had his hand down my knickers. I managed to pull my jeans back up, but he got them down again, along with my knickers, and got us on the ground. He started rubbing himself on me and trying to push into me and this is where I really got freaked. I told him I couldn't. We then heard voices coming closer and he got off me. I got my pants on and took off to the house. My friend told me later that they had come looking for me.'

After speaking to me, this woman spoke to Detective Senior Sergeant Steve McGregor from Operation Austin, but after seeing what happened to Louise Nicholas and the other woman who alleged she was violated with a bottle by Shipton, Schollum and Rickards, she chose not to take it further.

"In this country, it appears you are damned if you do make a stand on issues like this but almost equally damned if you don't. Either way the humiliation still lingers.'

I also spoke to another woman who'd made yet another complaint against Brad Shipton. She'd publicly accused him — in the newspapers and on television — of forcing her to give him oral sex. The Crown said there was not enough evidence to prosecute. This woman was Jane Smith (not her real name), a Tauranga woman who'd seen our *Sunday* programme and shuddered because she knew she was not Shipton's only prey. Jane didn't know Louise Nicholas but went to the entire 'Louise Nicholas trial'. She wanted to exorcise her demons through what she hoped would be justice for Louise. She wanted Shipton exposed.

In a strange twist of fate, a member of the public came up to Jane during the trial. She told Jane, who already knew, that Shipton and Schollum were already in jail. Jane could have keep quiet and hoped that if a random member of the public was spreading the word the jury might hear it. But she did the right thing and told police. If she hadn't there was a risk the trial could have been aborted.

Justice Randerson immediately closed the court to everyone but the accused and the lawyers. Jane Smith came in to identify the woman breaking suppression orders. The three accused watched Jane. When it dawned on Shipton who he was looking at, he began dry retching.

Jane's story and its links to Louise Nicholas were mind-boggling. Jane was sexually abused by a relative from the age of six. In the early '80s, aged about 14, she ran away for a weekend because her relative was coming to stay. Jane wanted to tell her mother why but was frightened she would not be believed. Her mother, believing she'd become sexually active, took her to Tauranga Police Station for an internal medical examination with the official police doctor, Ronald Lloyd Morgan. Dr Morgan confirmed Jane was sexually active. He did not know it was from abuse. Dr Morgan was a police doctor for about 20 years, frequently examining sexual-abuse victims and rape victims. Jane later discovered Dr Morgan was jailed in 1992 for holding the hand of an underage girl while his step-son, Tauranga businessman Motu Hata, had sex with her.

When Jane was 14, her mother separated from her stepfather, and moved to Rotorua. About a year later Jane told her stepfather about the relative's abuse.

He told Jane's mother who, as Jane feared, didn't believe her. She sided with the relative. Jane didn't know it then but later discovered her mother lived in the Rutland Street house that Shipton and Schollum lived in — the house she saw Louise standing in front of on the *Sunday* television programme.

Soon after Jane broke her silence, Brad Shipton arrived to talk to Jane about her allegations. She said Shipton took her to a park and interviewed her in a car. She says his questioning was lewd and vulgar and he put his hand on her knee. She said Shipton asked her how far she could put her finger up her vagina because she'd need to tell a court if it went up as far as her relative's penis. 'I was petrified I was going to have to tell the court that.' Then Shipton's investigation died, all went quiet.

Four years passed before Jane heard back from police and it came in the form of a court summons delivered by Bob Schollum in the late 1980s. She learned that her abuser had been charged with abusing three other children. Jane's fears he would abuse other children once she was gone had come true. Shipton took Jane to Palmerston North to give evidence at the trial. Her abuser confessed and was jailed. Jane's mother had meanwhile died and around July 1994 Jane said Shipton arrived at her workplace and told her to come to a nearby café. Jane said Shipton pointed to another man sitting in the café and warned her the man was a cop. Jane said Shipton told her: 'Some bitch is talking shit about me in Rotorua.' He said he or his mate in the café would know if Jane spoke to anyone about 'this bitch'. This bizarre meeting was taking place when Louise Nicholas's allegations against Shipton, Rickards and Schollum at Rutland Street had come out in the second Brown trial. But back then Jane didn't know anything about Louise Nicholas or the woman Shipton said was 'talking shit' about him. Years later it dawned on her that Shipton was worried Jane's mother might have told her about the goings on at Rutland Street.

Then a year later, out of the blue at 1am on the morning of July 1, Jane got a phone call from Shipton. Jane had never been friends with nor had sex with Shipton, but he said he was coming to her house, a house he'd never been to. Jane said no, don't come. She told him she'd just got out of hospital. Shipton said he was coming and hung up. When he got there a few minutes later he allegedly said he had a colleague, 'Gerbo', in the car. He wanted to bring him up. Jane again said no. Shipton told Jane he was there for full sex. She said no. She told him she'd just had a gynaecological procedure. She said he didn't care and wanted full sex. She said he eventually forced her to give him oral sex and left.

Within a week, she said Shipton was back on her doorstep, this time with other men. Jane recognised one of them because he was involved in rugby with her stepfather. When she said she knew him, the men quickly left. Jane told me she has 'no doubt that they were there to do to me what was done to Louise Nicholas'.

Terrified, she moved house several times. Shipton found her. Finally she realised she couldn't hide anymore. In 1996 she went to the Papamoa Police Station and spoke to Constable Phil Appelman. In a statement to Operation Austin, Phil Appelman confirmed Jane was 'shit-scared' when she started telling him about Shipton hassling her for sex. Appelman said something 'like a radio call' then distracted him. He asked Jane to wait in the station foyer. Jane said, while waiting, that another policeman appeared. This cop told her he knew what she was talking about and told her to get the hell out of the police station. She fled. She said soon after trying to complain to the Papamoa police, Shipton arrived and threatened her. When she moved again and shut up, the visits finally ended.

So Jane went to 'Louise's trial' hoping it would help. It didn't and afterwards she saw Craig Shipton, a senior ACC manager, on television making negative comments about historic rape complaints. Craig Shipton was the man who'd described his brother, Schollum and Rickards as good men, men the world needed more of.

Jane emailed ACC's general enquiry website, saying she would like to know if the comments were being made in his capacity working for ACC — an organisation that deals with thousands of sex-abuse victims. She signed her email J. Smith.

She was shocked to receive an email in return, not from ACC, but a threatening email from Craig Shipton, who even knew who she was.

Craig Shipton wrote: 'J. Smith (Jane), I do still work at ACC and as you are fully aware my views are my views, not that of ACC. I will warn you, however, that if there are any further attempts at undermining my position within ACC through this type of needless questioning to my employer, I will take legal action against you for harassment. I trust you will not be foolish enough to test my sincerity in this matter.'

Jane also received a copy of police notes of a conversation an Operation Austin detective had with former Detective Sergeant Warren Gerbich. Police spoke to Gerbich because they suspected he might be the 'Gerbo' Shipton allegedly tried unsuccessfully to bring along with him when Jane was allegedly violated. In March 2004, Gerbich told police he worked with Shipton and still had contact with him through his gym and pub. But Gerbich told the detective he 'didn't really socialise with those guys'.

In March 2007, Gerbich's former wife, Debbie, showed *Sunday News* a sex video made in 2001. The video showed Shipton and Gerbich and another man having consensual group sex with Debbie Gerbich. Debbie Gerbich told the paper Shipton once bit her during a group sex session. She said in other group sex sessions — she did not say who with — a police baton and handcuffs had been used by serving police officers. She said it was consensual, but now believed she'd been made to perform like a circus seal. Debbie Gerbich said one of the reasons she spoke to *Sunday News* was because of the disbelief by many of Louise Nicholas's baton allegations.

The story did not name Debbie Gerbich but caused a sensation when it was published days before the Commission of Inquiry findings were due. A Sunday newspaper war erupted as reporters tried to find out just who was making such serious allegations about serving cops. A *Herald on Sunday* reporter, Stephen Cook, was caught out sending what the paper later admitted were 'inappropriate' emails to Debbie Gerbich. She didn't talk to the competing newspapers, but sadly for Debbie Gerbich, she'd been paid for her story. She'd made incredibly serious allegations but did not want to be named.

I spoke to Debbie Gerbich and her partner Bill McNeilly two nights after the *Sunday News* story broke. I asked to meet and said it was only a matter of time before other reporters found them and named them because of the seriousness of her allegations. They wouldn't agree to meet nor do an interview. Though I argued against it, *Close Up* chose not to identify Debbie Gerbich. But the Sunday newspapers did. Police investigated, but because the sex was consensual dropped the inquiry.

Three months later, Debbie Gerbich's life ended. She was found dead in a car. Bill McNeilly later spoke exclusively to *Close Up*, blaming her death on newspapers outing her. The *Herald on Sunday* apologised. It was all a tragic mess.

Meanwhile, Jane Smith refused to give up. In 2007 she believed she was close to discovering a key potential witness. At the time of writing, Operation Austin, had reopened their investigation into her case. Jane said, ever since she went public, people have asked her why she didn't complain at the time. The fact is she did. Just like Louise Nicholas did.

In February 2007, Rickards, Schollum and Shipton found themselves facing another trial in the High Court at Auckland, this time before Justice Judith Potter.

The complainant was the woman Shipton had had a sexual relationship with in Rotorua in the mid-eighties, when she was 16. She accused Shipton, Schollum and Rickards of taking her to a house, dragging her to a room, handcuffing her and violating her with a bottle.

This woman, who has name suppression, did not go to the police when she saw the Louise Nicholas story in the media. As commented earlier, the only reason detectives found her was that they discovered an old telephone number and the nickname 'milk bottle' in Shipton's police notebook. The jury never heard this detail, because it was suppressed in another almost unbelievable pre-trial ruling. The Crown argued that it was the words 'milk bottle' that led detectives to the complainant in the first place, and that it was circumstantial evidence that Shipton was involved in a bottle incident. But Bill Nabney, Shipton's lawyer, successfully argued that because the notebook was dated 1986 and the alleged violation took place in 1984, the link was too remote in time. Justice Randerson agreed: he ruled it was a 'speculative' link and would seriously prejudice Shipton's right to a fair trial. The notebook was ruled inadmissible.

This ruling was a massive blow to the Crown case, just as the pre-trial rulings had been to Louise's chances of success. Police believed the notebook was their smoking gun. But there was more to come. I'd also learned that Claire Newcombe, a friend of the complainant's, had been prevented from giving important evidence as well. Claire had told police she was there the day the complainant was picked up by a police car in Rotorua. About a week later, Claire said, the complainant told her she'd been sexually assaulted by her policeman boyfriend. The law usually allows such evidence to be heard as 'evidence of recent complaint'. But her evidence was ruled inadmissible too. Why? Because it was felt the complainant could have told her mother, but didn't, before she told her friend, Claire. I wondered just how many 16 year olds would really want to tell their mother they'd been violated by a bottle by serving police officers.

The trial result was the same as Louise's: 'Not guilty'. But before it ended, there were some dramatic moments. Shipton's wife Sharon was caught out telling lies in the witness stand. She was accused of trying to coach her cousin on what to tell the police if they contacted her about an alibi she had tried to create for Shipton. The cousin was rushed from Australia to the High Court at Auckland to rebut Sharon Shipton's alibi story. Caught out under cross-examination by prosecutor Brent Stanaway, Sharon Shipton became hysterical. She sobbed. She swore on her 'daughter's life, as God strikes me down, I never said such a thing'. She said she felt like she was in a 'mad movie'.

After the result, the complainant, staggering from the jury's verdicts, was half-dragged, half-supported away from the court by police officers. The jury left the courtroom, and some of them mingled socially with members of the ecstatic Shipton clan.

That morning, a couple of hours before the verdicts in this trial, I was at TVNZ trying to arrange reaction stories and getting Jane Smith's story ready for *Close Up*. Six weeks earlier, Bill Ralston had resigned from TVNZ when he foresaw the scale of job cuts the organisation had planned for news and current affairs staff. So he wasn't in his old office when I was tricked into going there.

I walked in and was told by the acting head of news and current affairs and a human resources staffer I'd never met that TVNZ planned to axe my job. It seemed a crass time to tell me, considering the investment I'd put into the story I was about to bring to air, and the whole police scandal. As they finished, they made a point of saying the decision had nothing to do with the verdicts expected that day.

I knew it had everything to do with the verdicts. They'd made up their minds to get rid of me because investigative journalism is expensive journalism. But they wanted to tell me I was 'outski' that morning instead of later in the day, when the meeting had originally been scheduled, because they were second-guessing the imminent verdicts.

They knew if the verdicts were 'Guilty', they'd cop bad press if news filtered out they'd dumped the journalist whose story had started and continued it all, whereas if they told me I was being made redundant before the verdicts, they could put a public relations spin on their decision . . . something along the lines of 'how it was unfortunately made before the verdicts, but wasn't a final decision blah blah'.

Having been told I was getting the heave, I didn't particularly want to be in the TVNZ newsroom when the verdicts came out, so I paced up and down an alleyway waiting for Nicky to phone me. She was glued to the television and had the radio going so she could hear the verdicts and relay them to me. The dramatic destruction of Shipton's alibi had evened up the odds of a conviction in a historic sex offence trial — trials that seldom seem to succeed unless they involve male complainants. So I didn't really want to guess which way this one would go. I'd told Nicky about TVNZ's decision to make me redundant a couple of hours beforehand. She was spitting tacks and desperately hurt for me.

It can't have been easy for her, then, to put the call in to me. When I answered, she simply said: 'I'm sorry. It's "Not guilty".'

I didn't really know how I felt. You never wish for people to go to jail, but nor do you want people to get away with things, particularly the kind of things that have scarred others for life.

Much as I felt like telling them to stick it, I went back to work. I did the background story, and we got a great *Close Up* programme out that night with reporters Robyn Janes and Michael Holland capturing extraordinary reactions from Clint Rickards and Sharon Shipton outside the court. We had an exclusive TV interview with Louise, and we followed it the next night with Jane Smith's story.

If there had been anger before, the court of public opinion ran white-hot this time when those who didn't know about Shipton and Schollum's pack-rape conviction discovered they were already in jail. The *New Zealand Herald* ran a huge headline — 'Not Guilty Yesterday, But GUILTY' — above pictures of Shipton and Schollum. *The Dominion Post* headline said: 'Sex case bombshell. All acquitted but two already in jail for rape.' Pages of newsprint were devoted to the shocking details of the Mount Maunganui pack-rape.

Rickards, now free from an agonising three-year wait, fuelled the fire of public anger with his outburst outside the court. In one breath, Rickards told the media he wanted his job as Auckland District Commander back. In the next, he attacked the Operation Austin investigation as a 'shambles'. Then, eyes blazing and standing alongside his lawyer, John Haigh, he defended his mates and attacked their convictions. 'Brad Shipton is a good friend,' he said. 'Bob Schollum is a good friend. They are still good friends of mine and always will be . . . They shouldn't be where they are.' Louise Nicholas and the complainant who had just lost were liars, and they had been proven to be liars, Rickards said.

As I drove home two days later, my cellphone rang. Operation Austin boss Nick Perry's name flashed up on the screen.

'Is that Mr Shambles?' I asked. He was confused at first, then he chuckled.

We chatted until I ran out of coverage. I could hear the intense disappointment in Perry's voice. He'd headed one of the most extensive and expensive New Zealand police inquiries ever. He and his team must have felt at times as though they were crawling through a sewer. They'd won one pack-rape case, lost two and still had the John Dewar case over the Sam Brown trials to go. Along the way, their inquiries had also led to the conviction of another former Rotorua police officer who had mixed with Shipton and Schollum. His name is Peter Dunlop, and he was convicted of indecently assaulting a 14-year-old babysitter.

As the controversy over the latest verdicts rolled on, the woman who had alleged Brown indecently assaulted her as a 14-year-old schoolgirl at the party found these comments about Jane Smith's *Close Up* story. The comments were posted on New Zealand's most popular website, TradeMe.

> That slag that was on TV was really an ugly bitch She wont get her day in court as who's going to believe her that some one wants to shag her, God she's ugly just about cracked the screen and her breath . . .
> **sb00000** (this number has been changed because of a suppression order) **9:12 am**

The person posting the comments said he was a serving police officer, Sam, from the same place Sam Brown was known to be living. Later, when other people posted on the site saying they could not believe a serving police officer would make such remarks, 'Sam' admitted he was an ex-cop.

Then someone else posted comments in support of Louise Nicholas and got this response from Sam:

> X do you still have those hairy arm pits and wear jandals with the long flowery dress. I am seeing brad and bob next week I jack you up an evening with them. Tell me what sort a scene you would be looking for. Sure I know you want the Policeman type uniform included. **sb00000 9:17 am**

Then this:

> X just another one of those louise nicholas type slut swingers of the 70s she still got a hangup and was never satisfied. Stop playing with yourself X and get a life. **sb00000 8:45 am**

The woman I'd spoken to posted a message saying: 'I know who you are Sam.' Sam stopped posting.

All police officers have an official police registration number. It's on their police uniform. Sam Brown, the former police officer accused by Louise Nicholas of raping her when she was 13 and the man now accused of indecently assaulting another 14-year-old Murupara schoolgirl, had a certain police number. To post on TradeMe you need a five-digit number. 'Sam', the ex cop, used his initials then plonked a zero in front of this police number. This book can reveal that while he was hiding behind name suppression Brown was going very public with what he thought of anyone who dared criticise convicted pack-rapists.

On 3 April 2007, three years after it was launched, Dame Margaret Bazley released the findings of her Commission of Inquiry into police culture.

Police Commissioner Rob Robinson had resigned long before the findings came out, so it fell to new Commissioner Howard Broad to front the media.

The newspaper headlines the next day summed up Dame Margaret's huge report. 'SORRY. Boss disgusted by police behaviour' was splashed across *The Dominion Post*. 'Police chief: I'm truly sorry' led the *Herald*.

Dame Margaret said she had found evidence of disgraceful conduct and 'a wall of silence' from officers protecting their mates or colleagues. She had found 313 complaints of sexual assault against 222 police officers from 1979 to 2005. She had discovered appalling cases of police exploiting vulnerable people, including an intellectually disabled woman, for sex. Almost as bad as the crimes themselves, she found police officers had actively protected alleged perpetrators. I imagined Rex Miller having a chuckle when he read that.

Dame Margaret made 60 recommendations as she detailed case after case of sickening behaviour by, it must be said, a small percentage of the total number of New Zealand police officers who served in the time-frame her inquiry covered. Prime Minister Helen Clark and Police Minister Annette King said every single recommendation would be implemented. They said police would be monitored by the Auditor-General to make sure the necessary changes were made.

The Prime Minister praised the courage of Louise Nicholas and Judith Garrett, the two women whose stories had led her to set up the commission.

Like Louise, Judith had also lost her case. What had they achieved? Vindication of sorts, I suppose, from the Commission of Inquiry. A law change, and promises to look at more law changes on how rape or sexual-abuse victims are treated. An apology from the head of the New Zealand Police. An apology of sorts from the Prime Minister. Sweeping changes to how police deal with sexual assault cases, including a code of conduct for police that will include at least one new rule that Louise must have thought ironic, given her circumstances in the 1980s. Serving police are now not allowed to have sex with people they hold a position of authority over, or where there's a power imbalance. Shipton and Schollum are in jail and Rickards still faces police disciplinary charges. He may never wear a policeman's uniform again — a victory of sorts for Louise Nicholas.

But perhaps Louise's greatest achievement has not yet been set in stone. The government has promised major changes to how authorities deal with sex-abuse and rape victims. Having seen the 'Louise Nicholas trial', there are doubtless rape complainants who have shied away from complaining to police, fearing to embark on the same traumatic and fruitless road that she trod over the course of more than a decade. But she has the profound satisfaction of knowing that her decision to show her face when making her allegations has given courage to many others to complain.

After the release of the Inquiry's findings it all went pretty much silent until July 2007, when John Buchanan Dewar, former head of the Rotorua CIB, former Detective Inspector, former head of the Rotorua Armed Offenders Squad, was asked to plead to four charges of obstructing or perverting the course of justice. Dewar told the court he was not guilty.

Louise

WITH EACH OF THE DISAPPOINTMENTS I'd suffered in my quest for justice, I had thought that this would be the last hurdle I'd have to jump, and life would be smooth from then on. But it just doesn't seem to be able to work out that way for me.

I found the rest of the year following the trial extremely frustrating, as there was so much I wanted to do but I couldn't until both the next trial of Rickards, Schollum and Shipton and the Dewar trial were over. I was told that I would no longer be required as a witness for the former, as the Crown thought the defence could possibly turn it into a circus just as they had by bringing up my past in my own trial. In some ways I was relieved that I didn't have to go through that ordeal again, but I also felt really bad that I couldn't be there to support the woman who had supported me back in March at my trial. I did promise her, and myself, that I would be in Auckland to hear the verdicts, however. I knew it wouldn't look good to be sitting in court throughout the trial, but by God, come hell or high water I was going to be there to see these guys go down once and for all.

With the help of Kim McGregor of Rape Crisis and human rights lawyer Joy Liddicoat I did manage to draw up a submission to the select committee considering a 'new evidence' Bill that was introduced in 2006. My submission was based on what I felt were deep flaws in some of the laws associated with victims who received raw deals when facing a court of law. Whether or not this would carry any weight was hard to say, but I walked out of that room at the Beehive really impressed not only with what I felt we had achieved, but even more so with the committee members, who really appeared to be listening. I felt that even if nothing more came of this submission, the fact that we'd opened a few eyes and ears would be enough.

In early October 2006 I was feeling more washed out than usual. I couldn't work out why I was feeling this way, as there was no extra pressure at work and nothing out of the ordinary was stressing me out. Then it just hit me: I was pregnant. I headed to the supermarket and bought a pregnancy test. Mum was packing on the checkout I went through, but she picked up the blue box and popped it into the grocery bag without so much as a second glance. I smiled to myself and thought, if only you knew what you just packed there, Ma! When I got home I hesitantly did the test, then I left it sitting on the bathroom counter and walked away. An hour later I wandered back into the bathroom and saw the two blue lines I was dreading.

My heart dropped, and I just stood there and cried. So many thoughts were running through my head. How the hell do I tell Ross? I can't be pregnant: I'm too old! Do I keep it? What if it's born sick? Hell, I was a mess for most of that morning. In the end, I decided to ring Ross and tell him over the phone, as I figured that would give him time to digest the news before he got home and hopefully the shock (which I knew it would be, just as it had been for me) would have subsided a bit. When he answered his mobile, I just said to him: 'Hey, mate. How's it going?'

'Yeah, nah, all good,' he answered. 'What's up?'

'Umm . . . Well, hon, I've got a doctor's appointment this afternoon . . .'

He wanted to know why, of course, so then I told him. There was a long pause, then his first reaction was to wonder how the hell that had happened. We decided to talk about it when he got home from work.

The doctor confirmed our situation. At home, Ross asked me the dreaded question: 'Are you going to keep it?' I growled at him and said that this was not a decision for me alone, and having an abortion was something I would struggle to do. Because of my age and to be safe, I went off to see a specialist, who confirmed that I was about six weeks gone. That afternoon Jess, who had left school and was working on a dairy farm, phoned and said that she was going to call in. This was as good a time as any to tell the girls, so that night I asked them to come into the bedroom as I had something to tell them. Before I had a chance to say anything, that bloody Jess said to me: 'You're pregnant.'

I laughed, and said to her, 'Can you let me finish?

'You *are* pregnant!' she said.

In the end I just had to say yes, I am. They were so excited, I was relieved. And from that day on I knew this baby was going to be a special little addition to our family.

One day while I was at work, I received a phone call from Lynne, from Operation Austin, who told me that a date had been set for the Dewar trial. It was to be 28

May 2007. I laughed and asked whether the judge could bring it forward. Poor old Lynne: I don't think she knew what to say or do when I told her my news. I couldn't stop laughing, because I could just picture the look on her face! She promised they'd do a bit of reorganising.

The other bit of news that she had for me — once the shock of *my* news had abated — was that Dewar's lawyer had successfully argued that I could take the stand at a depositions hearing. I was no longer a witness in the next rape trial, and since I was no longer in any stressful situation, they felt that I could appear. The judge agreed. The hearing, originally scheduled to take place in Hamilton, went ahead in Rotorua. It was set down for two days, but we were out of there within a day. I was glad I had taken the stand, as it gave me an idea of how Dewar's camp was going to run its end of the trial. There was a case to answer: the trial would go ahead in Hamilton in July 2007. Sweet, I thought. Bring it on!

With the next rape trial looming, it was decided that my friends Ange, Jane, Dad and I would head to Auckland and support the complainant — not that I would be in court, but the other three could be. So on 19 February we set off for Auckland and settled back into the Copthorne Hotel. Jane decided she wouldn't go to court, as the Shipton family knew her and she didn't want any aggro. She stayed with me while Dad and Ange headed off every day.

Each day they would return and fill Jane and me in on the day's events. Dad took great delight in giving me a blow-by-blow account of what an absolute idiot Sharon Shipton made of herself trying to prove her husband's alibi, while all she managed to do was get snapped out with her lies.

Then we found ourselves playing the waiting game again, when the jury headed out to start their deliberations. Op Austin said that they would text or phone us when the jury were coming back, but I don't know what happened: we never received that call. Instead, just as I went to turn on the 12 o'clock TV news my mobile went off. There was a text from a reporter I knew from Rotorua telling us the jury were back, and at the same time we could see it was breaking news on TV One. We weren't really ready for it, but Dad did manage to swap his slippers for his good shoes. Unfortunately he still had his old track pants on, but hey, it wasn't a fashion parade, now was it?

Margaret and Murray Craig had made the trip up too, so we felt we'd mustered good support for the complainant. It turned out it was just what she needed. Despite me being four-plus months pregnant we still ran to the courthouse, pausing only to catch our breaths before we rounded the corner to confront the waiting media. This was the first time I had actually walked through the front doors of the courthouse. I had a gaggle of reporters wanting to ask me questions, but I managed to ignore them. Jane and I followed Dad and Ange to the courtroom, and I wished I'd had a camera to capture the looks on the faces of the Shipton, Schollum and Rickards families when we turned up. The pointing and whispering was a beautiful thing to see: they were obviously pissed off that we were there, and God it felt good!

As we hung back waiting for the doors of the courtroom to open I turned around to see the complainant coming towards us flanked by some of the Op Austin team. They took her straight into a side room to wait. Soon the doors opened, and everyone piled into the courtroom, media included. The public gallery was like a tin of sardines with so many people squashed in, but it wasn't long before the judge, jury and accused filed in. This was when I started to shake. Looking at those guys again brought back my day of hell. Margaret grabbed my hand and squeezed it: it wasn't enough to stop the shaking, but it felt good to have someone close by.

The foreperson rose and started to read the verdicts out. The horror of 30 March 2006 came back to haunt me, for all I could hear once again was 'not guilty, not guilty, not guilty, not guilty, not guilty, not guilty'. And then it was all over. Once again, the cheering and elated chants from the family were too much, and we hightailed it out of that courtroom as quickly as we could. As we headed out, I had a microphone shoved in my face and someone asked me what I thought of the verdicts. What could I say but 'the justice system sucks big-time'.

Back at the hotel we were once again in a total state of shock. Dad told me to ring Mum and let her know, which I was doing when I heard Dad say, 'Oh, hell. Here's a go.' I looked out over the balcony and there was Karen Schollum yelling up at us: 'I hope you're satisfied now!'

I yelled back, 'At least I can go home to my husband!'

I never stopped to see or hear her reaction to that, because next minute Jane damn near pushed me out of the way to see what was happening. When she spotted Sharon Shipton going on about something as well, Jane yelled out to her, 'Where's Brad?'

When I'd calmed down a bit, I turned to Jane and said, 'You do realise we just broke some suppression orders there?'

'Probably,' she said, and we both started giggling. As it happened, within half an hour of the announcement of the verdicts, the judge lifted the suppression orders, including the one covering the fact that Shipton and Schollum were in jail for the rape of the Mount Maunganui woman. The public of New Zealand were not happy at all with that revelation!

Once again, the debate started up over whether or not our justice system was fair for victims of rape and sexual abuse, and everyone seemed to want me to comment. Because of the Dewar trial, I had to be very careful about putting my two cents' worth in, but I spoke of my huge disappointment at the verdicts and said I hoped like hell this wouldn't put women off coming forward if bad things were happening or had happened to them. All we could really hope for now was Dame Margaret Bazley's Commission of Inquiry report into police conduct, which was due out at the end of March. We were really relying on that to be the light at the end of a very dark and dismal tunnel.

As promised, by the end of March, Dame Margaret had released her findings and, by all accounts, they were extremely damning of the police. Her recommendations were many and hard-hitting, and the one that stood out for me was the criticism that the police had no code of conduct in place. That absolutely floored me, and a lot of other people as well.

Just before the report was released, Phil asked me if I would go on *Close Up* and give my opinion. I agreed, and he also organised Judith Garrett to join me, which I felt was appropriate. We had both been chucked out of the commission, so we saw this as a good opportunity to put our thoughts about the report out into the public arena. We were asked that night if we felt vindicated by what Dame Margaret had recommended. In some ways, yes, it showed that even though the juries in both Judith's and my trials did not get it right, the report pointed to huge problems within the police, and uncovering these was something we had both been fighting for. So even though it wasn't going to change the verdicts, it was going to change how the police performed. It's a pity, though, that there wasn't a Commission of Inquiry set up to review the justice system: from my experience, it's just as badly in need of the same kind of scrutiny and the same kind of action. Wishful thinking? You just never know what the future could bring!

The rollercoaster rolled on. Both my parents gave me health scares: first Mum suffered what they initially thought was a heart attack. We learned that it was an angina attack — just in time for Dad to keel over as we were getting out of a hotel lift. I was sure he'd had a stroke, and all the first-aid training I'd received at work flew right out the window. I was yelling and screaming for someone to help, and was spitting tacks when help did arrive, never mind that it took a matter of minutes. Dad was kept in hospital for a while for tests, and after they'd ruled out major problems they decided it probably had something to do with diabetes. Maybe she was disappointed that Dad had stolen the limelight, because Mum then proceeded to break her arm by falling off the stool she was standing on to fetch the overnight bag she needed to bring along when she visited Dad in hospital!

A few months later Ross, the girls and I were blessed with the safe arrival of Luke James Nicholas, born 1 June 2007, weighing in at 8 lb 6 oz (ouch!). I was told right through the pregnancy that he was going to be a wee fella and that I wouldn't have much trouble 'spitting him out'. He proved not only the doctor and the midwife wrong but the scans as well, as he was neither so wee nor easy to spit out!

Luke is living proof that you can never tell how things will turn out. As if I needed to be told that. I was fully aware of it as the day of my showdown with John Dewar drew ever nearer.

Phil

I DIDN'T GO TO THE trial of John Dewar, but part-way through it I got a text from Louise. Apparently Anna Jackson, the policewoman she'd spoken to in the Rotorua Police Station before Dewar shifted her off the case, was about to give evidence. 'Anna looks very smart in her uniform,' the text read.

It brought back memories of the first time I spoke to Louise Nicholas. She'd physically shuddered as she told me the sight of a police uniform still scared her — even when she saw her brother, Robert, wearing it. I knew when I received that text that the policemen and women from Operation Austin had turned her attitude to the police force full circle.

I later told the story to one of those officers, and he told me a story of his own. He said he'd seen and heard all kinds of awful things during his career as a cop, but one that would stick in his mind forever was what he'd been told by the woman who, as a schoolgirl on work experience, had been fooled into having sex with Schollum while Shipton watched. She remarked that she'd told her children if they ever got lost or were in trouble, never go to a police officer. The cop telling me the story said it was the most shameful thing for a police officer to hear.

Midway through the trial I got a phone call from Louise. She had devastating family news about the death of her younger brother Kevin, and I wondered how much more Louise and her family could take.

The day before the jury retired, I drove to Hamilton to see how the trial had gone. Pretty well, I gathered.

The Crown called witnesses who testified that the way Dewar took over and ran the Brown trials broke all sorts of police rules. Margaret Craig, Louise's counsellor, spoke of her alarm at the way Dewar was dealing with a rape complainant — how he had even sat in on one of the counselling sessions. Then the Crown called journalists, who said Dewar tried to dupe them. After the story broke, Dewar gave them documents showing, he claimed, that the police had praised him in 1995 for the way he'd investigated Louise's complaint against Shipton, Schollum and Rickards. He had blanked out names in the documents, but the journalists easily determined the praise was for a different inquiry altogether.

Dewar's public claim that he had only a professional relationship with the three men was clinically shredded by Operation Austin. They found a senior policeman who said Dewar had told him about Shipton giving him a gift of a woman with whom he had sex. Then a crucial Crown witness testified. She was the woman who'd told me three years earlier that she'd had group sex with Shipton and Dewar. The covert camera sting we'd done with Louise and Dewar was also shown so the jury could hear Dewar saying he certainly knew the use of the baton was not consensual. They also heard Louise saying she'd heard that Dewar was mates with Shipton, Schollum and Rickards, to which Dewar replied: 'They were and still are.'

Dewar ran a high-stakes defence. His lawyer resorted to suggesting to the jury that Louise Nicholas was a sad and pathetic woman. Apart from Dewar himself, the defence didn't call any witnesses. In a nutshell, Dewar tried to convince the jury that the Crown witnesses were wrong — mistaken or lying — but he wasn't.

Then it was déjà vu: crammed in a hotel room, waiting for a jury verdict with Louise, her supporters and her family. Only this time, there were more faces. The witness who testified she'd had sex with Shipton and Dewar was there with her daughter. The Mount Maunganui pack-rape victim was there and Jane Smith was there. Jane kept them all sane with black humour. As the jury deliberated, there was a serial rapist on the loose in Hamilton, and when the clock showed we'd been waiting for fully eight hours, Jane piped up. She said the police had the perfect bait to catch the Hamilton rapist right there in that hotel room: 'We'll go out and space ourselves every kilometre along Hamilton's main street and he'll stop for one of us for sure.' Everyone laughed. 'But not you, Louise. The bastard will take one look at you and run a mile saying, "Get the media away! Get the media away!"'

When we'd been waiting nine hours, I wondered if the jury was going to return 'Not guilty' verdicts after all. The trial was serving as a sort of a distraction for the Nicholas family's grief, but how devastating would 'Not guilty' verdicts be for Louise's parents?

Then Louise's cellphone rang and everyone froze. Suddenly the room emptied as everybody returned to the courtroom and I was again alone in a hotel room, waiting. I didn't like it, so I wandered out into the street. Within a few minutes my cellphone beeped. It was a text from Nicky. The screen flashed up just one word: 'GUILTY'.

I phoned the chief reporter at The Dominion Post and said I'd get a reaction story to them in about 15 minutes' time, then I waited for everyone to return. Again, the body language said it all, but this time I read a totally different story in the smiles of the Operation Austin detectives, and in Ross's grin and eager handshake. He told me Nick Perry had even hugged him outside the court, although Perry later told me it was the other way around. Jim Crawford's tears were tears of happiness. I could see Nicky and my sister-in-law Pippa had been crying. As they poured through the front doors of the hotel I couldn't see Louise. I asked: 'Where's the girl?'

Louise's tiny frame materialised from the group. She hugged me for a long time, and this time she whispered just two words: 'Thank you.'

Once I'd got a couple of quotes from Louise, we had a few drinks and watched the late television news. There was powerful footage of Louise and Ross outside the court, with Louise praising Operation Austin for restoring her faith in the New Zealand police force. Rex Miller and his wife Jill were welcomed in and Miller bowled a bottle of red in about 15 minutes flat. The daughter of the woman whose crucial evidence helped sink Dewar was there and she told Nicky how moved she was to see her mother, a brave woman, hold her head up proudly for the first time in a long while.

The next day I sat down with Nick Perry, and it looked like the Op Austin team had partied fairly seriously. Perry had led an unprecedented police inquiry resulting in five trials, of which the Crown had won three. At least one more trial, of two men accused of attempting to pervert the course of justice in the Mount Maunganui pack-rape case, was still to be held. Perry told me how hugely damaging the scandal had been for the police — both their reputation and their morale — and how he'd told his troops from the outset that police credibility was based on integrity and professionalism, the two qualities that above all would dictate how they would run their investigation. He spoke of how heartened he was to hear Louise on national television the night before, her voice shaking with emotion as she called his team 'decent police officers who have toiled away from their families for more than three years. They have done their duty.'

Perry told me his detectives extensively investigated Sam Brown — the man with whom it all began for Louise — but could not charge him again with the same offence. 'But I am satisfied with the evidence we did have to hand that certainly the allegations we had with him sexually interfering with [Louise] while she was living with him were quite valid . . . We uncovered evidence to establish a prima facie case. It backed her up and certainly supported her.'

Perry spoke of how Operation Austin had been staggered to find that the use of police batons for deviant sex was not confined to the almost unbelievable allegation Louise had made on the front page of *The Dominion Post* three and a half years earlier.

'We had this rogue element, this predatory element operating in the Rotorua area at that time, and I am quite satisfied there are other victims of that. We spoke to complainants, victims who tacitly acknowledged that the rumours we were following up on were true, but they just weren't prepared to go down that track. They were married, had families.'

I told Perry about how Louise had sobbed the words, 'They didn't believe me, they didn't believe me', after the jury's verdict in her case against Shipton, Schollum and Rickards a year earlier.

'Do you believe her?' I asked.

'Oh yes, oh yes,' he said.

Louise

NO SOONER HAD I adjusted to being a new mum all over again than here we were, back in trial mode again. Steve McGregor from Op Austin phoned regularly to go over my statements again, to help me focus. I found myself going over everything as I fed Luke in the early hours of the morning. This was a really peaceful time for me.

A few days out from the trial, I spent a day with Steve going over my brief of evidence. Towards the end of that meeting, Steve asked if I was at all nervous about giving evidence again. I told him I wasn't nervous about that, but I was apprehensive about having to face Dewar's lawyer, Paul Mabey QC, again. Steve tried to put my mind at rest by pointing out this shouldn't be a 'nasty' trial, where the central issue was my credibility: it was to be more of a 'paper trail' trial. There were bound to be a few curve balls thrown at me, but nothing on the scale of what I'd dealt with before. So after he'd shouted me a coffee and sandwich — for the first time in three and a half years, I might add — I returned home to the family that afternoon feeling OK with all that the following week was going to throw at me. Mum, Dad, Luke and I headed over to Hamilton on the Monday, booked into a hotel, and waited. Ross and I had decided that he wouldn't need to come over until the jury was due to come back with their verdicts. He'd just started a new job, and it was unfair on his new boss for him to take time off.

Jury selection and judicial housekeeping occupied most of Tuesday morning, and then, for the last time, I walked into a courtroom, took the Bible, swore the oath, seated myself and waited for the questions to start. As I glanced around the courtroom, I saw for the first time Dewar's family and supporters, but any unease I felt was soothed when I spotted my dad and my good friend Jane sitting there with smiles of encouragement on their faces.

Much of what I was forced to admit about my relationship with John Dewar was embarrassing for me. I had spent so much time telling everyone how wonderful Dewar was, how he had helped me through the Brown trials, and how I had tried to help him when the Miller inquiry was trying to get him chucked out of the police. Well, that was how I saw it back then, and I couldn't deny it. The reality, which I'd seen much later, was that he was protecting his mates and his own skin, and he used me to do it. The point I had to drive home continuously was that I had, right from the outset, told Dewar that bad things had been done to me at Rutland and Corlett Streets by Shipton, Schollum and Rickards. It was pretty clear that his defence would be to say I'd never told him.

It always seems so easy to answer questions with the prosecutor asking them, but I had learned from my many experiences in the box that the battle of wills doesn't really start until defence counsel starts up. I wasn't disappointed. Mabey didn't hold back, firing such shots as that I had never told Dewar about Rutland Street, that I had told 'untruths' in the Brown trials, and how I told 'untruths' to the Miller inquiry. It was no more than I'd expected from him, and even though I knew this would be his tack I still found myself getting angry, not only with his questions and statements but with his theatrics. I knew he was only doing his job, but really, did he have to be so damn nasty?

The end of the day arrived, and I was both mentally and emotionally washed out. Another day dawned, bringing another bunch of curly questions from Mabey. Throughout, I kept telling myself to stay calm and just answer as best I could. And then it was over. My life had been thrashed out in two depositions hearings and five trials over the years, so I was determined to walk out of that courtroom for the last time with my head held high.

Because of the commitments of some of the witnesses — John McDonald and Les Atkins, who were judges these days — and the fact that Mabey got sick, the trial really only limped along over the rest of the week. We headed back to Rotorua for what we hoped would be a relaxing weekend. On the Sunday, McKaela and I headed into town to buy a mobile for Luke's cot. We were trying to put it together and had only been home about half an hour when I heard Ross yelling at me to come to the kitchen. I dropped what I was doing and headed for the kitchen, but as I rushed down the hall I saw my dad leaning awkwardly on the kitchen table. I looked at him and saw tears and heard him sobbing.

'What's wrong?' I asked.

Dad looked at me, then he said, 'Kevin's killed himself.'

I just stood there for a few seconds, then grabbed my dad and hugged him.

My poor mum and my poor dad had endured so much over the last 14 years. They had been my support through all that I had gone through, and now it was time to repay them as best I could. The next few days proved just how strong our family was.

The night before the funeral, we had a request from Kev's mates asking that he be taken to his friend Jason's house where they could farewell their mate 'Bucky' in their own way. Dad was a bit hesitant about this but, as my brothers and I pointed out, Kev had another family, another life, and we knew that this is what he would have wanted.

That night we learned so much about our brother. How he had an amazing voice, knew every word to every song. Played the guitar and drums like a pro. But more than that, we learned how he had this other family where the children knew him as Uncle Bucky. People from all over Rotorua came to Jason's 'shed' and paid their respects. When the hearse came to pick Kev up to take him back to the funeral home none of my family could hold back tears, for as he left a huge haka was performed, a Maori lady's wailing rang out into the night and a car smoked it up in front of the hearse. This was a time in our lives that we will never, ever forget.

We spent an afternoon sharing a few beers and stories with Kev's mates around at Mum and Dad's too: some of those stories contained way too much information! So much laughter entwined with so many tears. We all understood after that afternoon of sharing that we will never know his reasons for taking his own life, but that was OK. We knew we'd be able to move on from here.

Kev's funeral was held at 2pm on Wednesday 1 August 2007. My family and I walked into the chapel and were overwhelmed by the number of people already seated. Kevin's son Anthony sat between Mum and Dad, which was comforting for them. Kev never saw a lot of his son, as he had moved with his mother to Auckland, but the time he had with him was treasured. The service started with the band Kindred singing Kevin's favourite songs — seven guys, Jason, Bede, Dominic, Dean, Boss, John and Chris, on acoustic guitars, with Sonny and Whiskey on vocals. My eldest brother Pete delivered the eulogy, with Rob and I standing there with him. The boys and I could not believe our eyes when we stood to do the eulogy, as the chapel was full to capacity. I was asked by Kevin's girlfriend to read a poem that she'd found, and which she felt said a lot about Kevin and his life. Then Pete, Rob and I, with three of Kevin's friends, Jason, Lee and Kyron, carried Kev out to the waiting hearse.

As we walked out the door, the sea of people that met us was unbelievable. The car park was full of people who loved and respected Kev just as much as we did. We were told later that there were over 300 people there to farewell Kev. Ross was a bit worried, as we had decided that there would be refreshments at our house after the funeral. Luckily, the Brewers cricket team that Kev was involved with had organised a hangi. Once again, as the hearse drove away, the haka rang out and a lone Maori lady wailed in the distance.

My family and I said our final farewell to Kev at the crematorium. Before he left us, I laid my head on the casket and wished my brother a safe journey. The support and love we received from Kev's friends and other family was truly unbelievable. It was obvious to us that even though Kev didn't have much in the way of money or possessions, it turned out that he was the richest man around. He left behind a legacy of love, friendship and memories that will be celebrated and cherished forever.

It was amazing to find, at the end of that harrowing week, that life had gone on without us, even in the Hamilton District Court. The Operation Austin crew kept us informed of how the trial was progressing, and it was decided that Ange and I would head over to Hamilton on the Friday as the Crown was winding up its case. We walked into the courtroom, and I think by the look on the faces of a number of people sitting in the public gallery that nobody had expected to see us again. What they had failed to realise was that even at such a tragic time for my family, I needed to be there to see this trial to its end. My time to mourn the loss of my little brother would come.

We heard the last of the Crown witnesses give evidence. They were police officers, who explained to the jury how a detective inspector should conduct himself, and what protocols he or she should use in a situation when allegations as serious as those I had made against Brown, Schollum, Shipton and Rickards were involved. It was, to say the least, damning stuff. The Crown closed their case that afternoon.

Over the weekend, we heard via the media that Dewar was going to give evidence. We figured that would take up most of Monday, and then on the Tuesday the Crown and defence would do their summing up. So we decided that we would pack an overnight bag for Tuesday and stay in Hamilton.

Monday rolled around rather quickly, and by 9.50am we were seated in the courtroom once again. Sure enough, Dewar was called — he was apparently the defence's only witness. Everything that flowed out of his mouth was what I expected from him. He claimed I had never told him about Rutland Street, and that he never associated with Shipton, Schollum and Rickards except when work required it. His story sounded plausible, but Brent Stanaway had yet to have a crack at him. Mabey finished with his witness around lunchtime, so we wandered off for a quick feed before the fireworks began.

We returned to the court at around 2pm and seated ourselves in readiness for what we hoped would be a very interesting afternoon. We weren't disappointed. The first question put to Dewar seemed to take forever to answer. He took an hour and 20 minutes to get his point across when all that was required was a yes or no. The judge himself had a go at putting the question to Dewar, in the hope that he might get a simple yes or no. He eventually answered yes to the question.

In the course of his questioning, Brent touched on Dewar's reasons for sabotaging the two trials back in the 1990s, and why he hadn't done anything about the allegations that I had made during the depositions hearings and the second and third trials. Dewar's response was that he was protecting me: I was lying under oath, and he didn't want to have to charge me with perjury. As I sat in the public gallery listening to this I was absolutely gobsmacked.

The battle continued, with Dewar becoming more and more agitated at the questions being put to him. So riled did he get that he literally came flying out of the dock, jabbing his finger and raising his voice at Rex Miller. What sparked that off, I'm not sure, but it was definitely not a good look. It didn't look as though the jury was too impressed by it either. I'm amazed at how calm and dignified Brent stayed when Dewar became personal towards him.

When we showed up in court the next day for the summing up, we felt that our case was unbeatable. Brent covered all the bases, spending several hours with his summation and pointing out 10 key points for the jury to consider. After lunch, it was Mabey's turn, and I was surprised at how lukewarm the defence seemed. He more or less tried to reiterate to them that Dewar had done a good, thorough and robust job with my complaint, and although he admitted to having made some mistakes, that didn't make him a criminal.

Ross came back to Hamilton with us for the judge's summing up the next day, which was huge for me. The girls wanted to join us as well, but we wanted to protect them, at all costs, from the hell they would go through if the verdicts turned to custard for us again.

We approved of the judge's summing up, and after he'd directed the jury, he dismissed them to go about their duty to reach either guilty or not guilty verdicts. He recalled them to clarify one or two points, and the jury asked if they could view the secret camera footage that Phil had taken of me and Dewar in Hamilton. Then we all headed back to the hotel where we were booked for the night, and the familiar wait began. This was the fourth time in my life I'd had to play this game, and I still found myself trying to second-guess the verdicts, even though I knew it was pointless. I have to admit that after eight hours had passed I was beginning to think things were not looking good.

At 8.45pm I received a call from Lynne to say that the jury appeared to be close, and to come over to the court. We all scrambled around finding coats and handbags, and once again I had to go looking for Ross, but he was all ready to go this time. We walked quickly but calmly to the courthouse and entered, half-blinded by camera flashes. We headed up the stairs and into the waiting room outside the courtroom. There was no one around, so we figured they must all be inside. Ross and I stepped into the courtroom, which was packed, mainly with Dewar's family and friends. There were no available seats, but I was more than happy to stand at the back and wait. It was a short wait — only a matter of minutes — before the jury were ushered in by the clerk and quietly took their seats. The court registrar asked Madam Forewoman to stand, and asked her if they had reached their verdicts. She answered that they had, and so the registrar read the first charge and asked her whether the jury had found Dewar guilty or not guilty.

'GUILTY.'

I wasn't sure if I'd heard right, so I waited for the next charge to be read.

'GUILTY.'

Yes. Yes! I did hear right.

My body started to shake and my legs started to buckle.

The third charge was read.

'GUILTY.'

Dewar's wife, Louise, began to cry out, and the rest of Dewar's family and friends were gasping.

The fourth charge was read.

'GUILTY.'

Oh, my God, we did it!

The Dewar family were grabbing each other and trying to comfort one another, whereas my dad was trying not to jump out of his skin. The judge spoke to the jury, but I wasn't hearing anything at this stage. It was all I could do to breathe properly and stay upright. In the end I looked at both Ross and Dad and said, 'Let's move.' I knew I'd have to face a barrage of media, but I had written a short statement during the day that I hoped would keep them happy. When we reached the bottom of the staircase I produced my little speech, took a huge breath, and with Ross beside me walked out to the waiting media. I explained that I had a statement and that I wouldn't be answering any questions at this time. They appeared OK with that, and I was grateful to them.

With a huge lump in my throat I read my statement, which was really just thanking my family and friends and the team from Operation Austin. All I wanted to do was get back to the hotel before the Dewar family came out. I didn't want to see their pain, because in a lot of ways I knew what they were going through. I thought the pain that I and the other complainants had felt when 'Not guilty' verdicts were returned was probably much the same as what the Dewars were feeling right now. So yes, I felt for the Dewar family.

We returned to the hotel in good spirits. But the strange thing was, I wasn't in the mood to pop open any bubbles. It was taking a long time for the word 'guilty' to sink in, to get used to the idea of victory after so many disappointments. I was sure someone was going to come in and tell us that the jury had changed their minds or they'd made a mistake.

The human spirit can only be crushed so far. Either it stays crushed, or you claw your way up again. With the help of so many people throughout my life, I have always managed to fight my way back. From the age of 13, I had to undertake a journey full of mental, physical and emotional hurt, but it was also a journey where I eventually found love, safety and freedom. I know that if I hadn't found Ross I wouldn't be here today. And if it hadn't been for Philip Kitchin, my fight for justice would never have got off the ground, and my right to be heard would have been permanently denied. My journey would have continued without any glimpse of the closure that I have sought for so long.

The verdicts from the Dewar trial have helped my family, especially my parents, to find the peace that they so richly deserve. Mum and Dad have been through so much over the last three years but their own fighting spirit has never faltered. They stood beside me from day one, and endured just as much pain and heartache as I did. Now that it's finally over, they deserve all the happiness that life can offer them. Somehow, I will help make that happen.

I have to thank the best in-laws a person could ever have, Linton and Phyllis Nicholas. For the 20 years that I have been part of their family they have loved and supported me as one of their own. It was Lin's courageous questions that set me on the path that has led me to where I am today, on the other side of a two-decade-long legal battle. And when Lin and Phyllis told me at the end of it all that they were proud of what I had accomplished — well, that was the icing on the cake.

The team of Operation Austin, after three and a half years of tireless work, can finally stand up and take a bow. For any copper out there reading this book, regardless of rank, I suggest to you that you take a leaf out of Op Austin's book: this is how policing should be, fearless and honourable.

For all their efforts, I know there are still a few bad apples in the police basket. But I'm sure that, if nothing else, the whole series of trials, ending with a bent cop's conviction, will have proven that if you step out of line you will get caught, whether it's straight away or years down the track: the error of your ways will come back and bite you on the arse.

As I have said a lot throughout this book, there were plenty of times when I wanted to just walk away from it all. But then I would receive a card or a letter from a complete stranger thanking me for helping to fight the battle that so many victims and survivors are engaged in. I knew I had to keep going, as it was obvious that one voice was helping many voices to be heard. I know that for those survivors who read this book it will bring back memories of your own abuses: but please keep in mind that you have nothing whatsoever to be ashamed about. You must hold your head high and remember that you are not responsible for what has happened to you. The ownership of abuse falls only to the person who has hurt you.

Equally, those falsely accused of rape or sexual abuse are victims too. I wish those making false rape allegations know how damaging it is for those who have been abused and struggle to be heard. If we all pull together and use the strength we have, we will win the war not only against sexual abuse, but also against a judicial system that fails abuse victims and survivors. The support that has come from thousands of New Zealanders has been overwhelming, and there are no words that I can find to thank you all.

I feel now that my path in life has been set, and all I can say is that I hope like hell that in another ten years' time I don't have another scruffy-haired reporter come knocking on my door.

Epilogue

Dr Kim McGregor
Director of Rape Prevention Education

LOUISE NICHOLAS'S EPIC FIGHT FOR justice has made her a heroine among survivors of sexual violence. Her battle became *the* battle for countless survivors of rape and sexual abuse throughout the country, many of whom have never received justice for themselves.

Louise's courage and tenacity are unique. For completely understandable reasons, as many as half of all survivors of sexual violence never tell anyone about their experiences. Only about 10 in a hundred report their experiences to the police.

International research suggests that of those reported to the police, up to 80 per cent of complaints of sexual violence fail to make it past the police investigation stage, and less than six per cent of crimes of sexual violation reported to the police result in a conviction. Louise's case against police officers Clint Rickards, Brad Shipton and Bob Schollum was one of the 94 per cent of rape cases reported to the police that failed to achieve a conviction.

Rape survivors often describe their court experiences as 're-rape'. In rape trials it is common for rape survivors to feel that they are the ones on trial, not the accused. The accused has the right to silence. The Crown has to prove 'beyond reasonable doubt' that the crime happened. With most crimes of sexual violence there is likely to be doubt, because only rarely are there witnesses to the actual crime or to whether consent was truly or freely given. Often the battle is over credibility, where one side tries to destroy the credibility of the other. In the context of this adversarial system, the survivor often has to relive in public, and in graphic detail, humiliating and degrading acts perpetrated against them. The survivor's evidence is tested by a hostile defence lawyer whose job it is to attack her or his credibility. Throughout her struggle for justice, Louise took the stand on no less than seven occasions, where she was cross-examined for a total of 10 days, by six defence lawyers.

Epilogue

Throughout Louise's court case against Rickards, Shipton and Schollum the unfairness, cruelty and traumatising nature of our current adversarial system and inequitable suppression laws were lit up for all to see.

After Rickards, Shipton and Schollum were acquitted on all 20 counts of the sexual violation of Louise Nicholas, around the country women and men from all walks of life again took to the streets in outrage, especially when they discovered that Shipton and Schollum were already serving prison sentences for rape convictions. Some even risked being jailed for distributing this suppressed material. The wave of public outrage was of a kind that I have not seen in my 20 years of working with survivors of sexual violence. People were angry and vocal. Their rage focused on the failure of our court system to provide survivors of sexual violence with any form of justice or fair trial.

But Louise's fight was not over. Although it was not publicly known at the time, a prosecution was also being taken against senior policeman John Dewar, the officer to whom she initially reported the actions of Rickards, Shipton and Schollum. The guilty verdict in that case confirmed that Louise's right to justice had been thwarted for almost two decades.

Despite all obstacles thrown in her way, Louise has continued to fight to have her truth heard, and a great deal of good has been achieved through her ongoing battles. Because of the injustice seen to be perpetrated against her, the very loud and at times heated public protest on her behalf and the willingness of the government not only to listen but to be proactive, change seems possible. Louise's fight for justice has been a fight for *all* survivors of rape and sexual violation. Her fight was pivotal in Prime Minister Helen Clark establishing the Commission of Inquiry into Police Conduct and the resulting changes recommended by Dame Margaret Bazley. Over the next decade, changes designed to improve police procedures, attitudes, training and investigations of crimes of sexual violence will be implemented.

In April 2006 I stood before a huge crowd that had gathered at the end of a march through Auckland's Queen Street in support of Louise. Those of us who spoke at the march called on the government to set up a task force on sexual violence. Since the 1980s the enormous problem of sexual violence had fallen off the public and political agenda. As a result, today, around the country, specialist crisis counselling and medical services for survivors of sexual violence are extremely limited and often remain in existence solely due to the personal commitment of dedicated and often overstretched staff. There is very little government funding for sexual-violence prevention education. There is a lack of sex-offender treatment services, particularly for those who sexually offend against adults. There have been few effective improvements to police investigations of crimes of sexual violence or indeed to the effectiveness or responsiveness of the criminal justice system for survivors of these crimes. As this book goes to print, however, the country's first ministerial task force focusing on sexual violence has been set up and has begun to look at all of these issues.

We all have a great deal to thank Louise Nicholas for. Her heroic fight for justice has already achieved more for New Zealand/Aotearoa survivors of sexual violence and their loved ones than any other individual in the last 20 years. Her name is known in many households around the country and is often synonymous with injustice, but also with bravery. Louise's commitment to create positive change continues as she relentlessly advocates improving all services for survivors of sexual violence in whatever forum she can. She has also generously donated a portion of the royalties from this book to Rape Prevention Education in the hope of preventing further sexual violence.

Louise deserves a very high honour for her courage, tenacity and bravery. Many survivors have already bestowed this honour on her in spirit. Louise Nicholas is seen as an inspiration to survivors of sexual violence and those who support them.